DESIGNING EFFECTIVE INSTRUCTION

Second Edition

DESIGNING EFFECTIVE INSTRUCTION

Second Edition

JERROLD E. KEMP
Professor Emeritus
San Jose State University

GARY R. MORRISON
University of Memphis

STEVEN M. ROSS
University of Memphis

Merrill,
an imprint of Prentice Hall
Upper Saddle River, New Jersey   *Columbus, Ohio*

Library of Congress Cataloging-in-Publication Data

Kemp, Jerrold E.
    Designing effective instruction / Jerrold E. Kemp, Gary R.
Morrison, Steven M. Ross. -- 2nd ed.
        p.   cm.
    Includes bibliographical references and index.
    ISBN 0-13-262080-4
    1. Instructional systems--Design. 2. Curriculum planning.
I. Morrison, Gary R. II. Ross, Steven M., 1947-   . III. Title.
LB1028.38.K46   1998
371.33–dc21
                                                                97-7380
                                                                CIP

Cover photo: Caffee/Photosynthesis/International Stock
Editor: Debra A. Stollenwerk
Production Editor: Mary M. Irvin
Design Coordinator: Karrie M. Converse
Cover Designer: Russ Maselli
Production Manager: Patricia A. Tonneman
Electronic Text Management: Marilyn Wilson Phelps, Matthew Williams, Karen L. Bretz, Tracey B. Ward
Marketing Manager: Kevin Flanagan
Advertising/Marketing Coordinator: Julie Shough
Editorial/Production Supervision: Custom Editorial Productions, Inc.

This book was set in New Baskerville by Custom Editorial Productions, Inc., and was printed and bound by
R. R. Donnelley & Sons Company/Harrisonburg. The cover was printed by Phoenix Color Corp.

 © 1998, 1996 by Prentice-Hall, Inc.
Simon & Schuster/A Viacom Company
Upper Saddle River, New Jersey 07458

Printed in the United States of America

10   9   8   7   6   5   4   3   2

ISBN 0-13-262080-4

Prentice-Hall International (UK) Limited, *London*
Prentice-Hall of Australia Pty. Limited, *Sydney*
Prentice-Hall Canada Inc., *Toronto*
Prentice-Hall Hispanoamericana, S. A., *Mexico*
Prentice-Hall of India Private Limited, *New Delhi*
Prentice-Hall of Japan, Inc., *Tokyo*
Simon & Schuster Asia Pte. Ltd., *Singapore*
Editora Prentice-Hall do Brasil, Ltda., *Rio de Janeiro*

We would like to dedicate this book to our mentors.

I would like to express my appreciation in the memory of Dick Lewis, who was director of audiovisual services at San Jose State as my career started in instructional technology.

—Jerry Kemp

I would like to thank Denny Pett, my advisor and chairman at Indiana University, for providing the opportunities and challenges that made graduate school an important part of my career.

—Gary Morrison

I thank Frank Di Vesta, who was my advisor and chairman at Pennsylvania State University, for the training and mentoring that so well prepared me for writing, research, and teaching.

—Steven Ross

FOREWORD

For me, selecting a textbook for an introductory course in instructional design has always been an exercise in frustration. For years, I have been plagued with indecision on this matter, causing me to try nearly every text in the market and abandon them all, try using no text, and rethinking that, try using selected papers and getting buried, and even contemplating writing my own text. No textbook can possibly meet the variety of needs, purposes, and beliefs to which such a textbook can be subjected. Why? Instructional design practice is ill-structured, because instructional design problems are situated in and emergent from specific contexts (corporate, university, public school, international, etc.), so instructional design problems and constraints are not clear or well defined, as they are often portrayed in textbooks. And, for most instructional design problems, there are many alternative solutions, each one of which may work as well as any other. Those situations, while appearing to be very objective, and therefore susceptible to systematic control, often have unclear goals and unstated constraints and possess multiple solutions or no clear solutions at all, as well as multiple criteria for evaluating solutions. As a field, we have always sought a set of generalized rules or principles for describing, predicting, and solving most design problems, but, alas, we must admit that such principles do not exist, because there are very few empirically validated principles about how to teach across domains and contexts. So, without empirical proof, the designer is required to make judgments about the situation and prescribe solutions based on them. But judgment-making does not fit well into instructional design models that are illustrated by closed loops of boxes and arrows.

Selecting an introductory textbook is problematic because instructional design is a very complex, interrelated, and ill-structured knowledge domain. The knowledge required to solve instructional design problems must be synthesized from several content domains, such as learning psychology, evaluation, communications, and so on. It is difficult to adequately convey that interrelatedness and complexity at an introductory level. As evidenced by a variety of recent debates in our field, including threats of disassociation with the discipline of instructional design, there are very diverse beliefs about learning, instruction, and instructional design. So whose perspective do you represent in the textbook?

Selecting an introductory textbook is also problematic because instructional design is synergistic. As an activity, it is more complex than the sum of its component parts. But it is difficult to represent that synergy in a coherent model or collection of chapters.

So, writing an introductory textbook in instructional design entails a delicate balance of comprehensibility, complexity, flexibility, and predictability. Being informative without being overly prescriptive is difficult. Being understandable without oversimplifying the field is nearly impossible. I believe that in the second edition of *Designing Effective Instruction* Jerry Kemp, Gary Morrison, and Steve Ross have achieved that balance as well as anyone ever has.

The feature of this book that I admire the most is their lack of prescriptive sequences. There are activities, but they are not strictly ordered. Rather, they are thought of as interactive and iterative. I know that this is not a revelation, but it does diverge from a number of introductory textbooks. I like the **From Here to There** transfer scenarios included at the end of each chapter. Transfer is what instructional designers need to learn. I very much appreciated their detailed descriptions of needs assessment methods (the conceptual and procedural glue that binds together the many theories, models, and methods of instructional design). And they have provided the most comprehensive and comprehensible explanation of assessment and evaluation issues that I have read in an introductory design textbook. Finally, they are perhaps the first to address all of the important contextual methodologies, such as consultation and management skills and environmental analysis, that Marty Tessmer has been writing about for so long. The authors must be commended for addressing the weakest link in instructional design practice—implementation. So many instructional design projects (one could speculate a majority) have either failed or at least not fulfilled expectations because of poor implementation. Not only do instructional designers need to acquire knowledge and design skills, they also have to assimilate into the culture and practice of instructional design, so they will need these important perspectives as well. The examples in the book are plentiful (though you can never have too many) and grounded. Practice will have to be provided by the teacher/professor.

From my perspective, and probably from yours as well, there are ideas, skills, or methods that are missing or under-represented in this book, just as there are some that you may feel are over-represented. With the complexity, ill-structuredness, and diversity of opinions in our field, that is inevitable. We shall all, to some degree, have to complement, supplement, explain, and interpret (good heavens, do you mean *teach?*) the many good ideas included in the book. It provides an excellent foundation for further study. And, at least for next semester, I will have once again resolved my dilemma about selecting a textbook.

David H. Jonassen, Professor
Instructional Systems Program
Pennsylvania State University

PREFACE

Thinking back over our combined 75 plus years of experience in instructional design and evaluation, we have seen a field that has matured into a discipline and profession that is well respected and valued by our colleagues in higher education, K–12 teachers, and managers in the public and private sectors. Individuals who have worked on a design team, learned from a product developed by an instructional design team, or simply observed the benefits of using well-designed instructional materials see the benefits of instructional design and will request more instructional materials that are interesting, effective, and efficient. Similarly, students and graduates of instructional design programs have requested a practical approach to the instructional design process that they can apply in a variety of settings and that can grow with their experiences. Our purpose in writing this text was to present an instructional design model and related information that is practical, applicable to a number of situations, and can mature with the instructional designer.

THE CONCEPTUAL FRAMEWORK

The model presented in this book is eclectic in that it borrows ideas from many different disciplines and approaches to instructional design. We believe that there is never one perfect approach to solving an instructional problem. As a result, we have incorporated both behavioral and cognitive approaches into the model so that we can reap the benefits of each. For example, we present two approaches to developing instructional objectives. The first approach is based on the classic Mager-style objective, while the second is based on cognitive objectives. Any single project might include only one style or a mixture of the two. Similarly, our approach to designing instructional strategies uses two steps. First, we incorporate an initial presentation that typically uses behavioral principles. Second, we develop a generative strategy that is based on cognitive psychology principles.

An effective instructional design model is both flexible and adaptable. No two designers will approach a problem in the same manner and no two problems are exactly alike. The model in this book is circular rather than the traditional flowchart. Our experience has shown that projects start and end at different places in the design process. Often, designers are not able to complete each and every step of the process due to external constraints. The design model must be flexible to accommodate the demands of the job, yet produce an effective product.

A design model must grow with the instructional designer. We have approached instructional design as the application of heuristics that one can apply to a variety of instructional problems. These heuristics are modified and embellished based on our own experiences, observations, and interpretations of the literature. This approach to instructional design allows the instructional designer to both modify and add to our list of heuristics.

Although we provide a strong emphasis on designing instruction in a business setting, we present an approach in this text that is applicable to instructional designers in military, medical, and government settings as well as to higher education and K–12 classrooms. Designers in each of these environments will take different approaches due to both the opportunities created and constraints imposed by each situation. For example, we do not expect a third-grade teacher to approach every lesson with the same rigor of a designer working for General Motors, Westinghouse, Motorola, or the Federal Aviation Administration. However, each designer will have the common goal of using the instructional design model to guide them in the development of effective instruction.

ORGANIZATION

Although we have avoided dividing this book into sections, one can easily identify three. The first section, Chapter 1, introduces the reader to the instructional design process. The second section, Chapters 2 through 11, provides a detailed description of the 10 steps in our instructional design model. In the third section, Chapters 12 through 15, we present the administrative, interpersonal, financial, planning, and evaluation issues that have an impact on the instructional design process.

Most of our colleagues have told us that they start with Chapter 1 and cover each chapter sequentially during the semester. Others have devised unique approaches, such as beginning with Chapter 9, then completing Chapters 12 through 14 before they teach the instructional design process in Chapters 2 through 11.

FEATURES

Each chapter starts with a series of **questions** to help focus the reader's attention on the salient points in the chapter. We have attempted to strike a balance between theory and practical applications in each chapter. A designer needs to know not only how to design instruction, but also the rationale and basis for making a decision. Our emphasis, however, is on the practical application of the instructional design process. We have included **numerous examples** based on our experiences in business, higher education, and K–12 education to illustrate these applications. At the conclusion of each chapter, we provide a **summary** of the important points followed by a list of references and relevant readings.

NEW IN THIS EDITION

We have revised and updated every chapter in *Designing Effective Instruction*. We also have significantly revised the material on preinstructional strategies and sequencing. The information on **sequencing** has been expanded and is now the only focus of Chapter 6 in this new edition. The information on **preinstructional strategies** is now part of a new chapter (8). Chapter 8 presents some basic message design principles the reader can use to improve the communication of the content.

We have also added **additional examples** in the chapters of how one might apply the instructional design process in various settings. For example, we have added new illustrations relevant to business and K–12 environments. Finally, at the end of each chapter we have added **From Here to There,** a section containing **helpful hints** for completing the task discussed in the chapter or a **case study** illustrating the application of one or more of the ideas presented in the chapter. We hope that these hints and vignettes will present a basis for an examination of the problems one might encounter when applying the instructional design process outside of a classroom and stimulate discussion in your classes.

ACKNOWLEDGMENTS

We would like to thank all of our colleagues, their students, and our own graduate students who have taken the time to talk to us at professional meetings, send us e-mail and postal mail, and called us with ideas and suggestions for improving this text. We would also like to thank three of our graduate assistants, Posey Saunders, Reneé Weiss, and Walter Baldwin, who helped with the research and provided us with insights on the student's point of view.

As with any design process, this book has gone through a lengthy formative evaluation. Our editor, Ms. Debbie Stollenwerk, reviewers John C. Belland, Ohio State University; Rita F. Braun, University of Maryland at Baltimore; Gayle V. Davidson, University of South Alabama; Gary Ellerman, Radford University; Sara Huyvaert, Eastern Michigan University; and Robert Tennyson, University of Minnesota; and Deborah Lowther of the University of Memphis provided us with many useful suggestions for improving this edition. Last, we would like to thank everyone who helped us with our examples by sharing their experiences with us.

ABOUT THE AUTHORS

JERROLD E. KEMP received his doctorate in audiovisual education from Indiana University in 1956. For 30 years he served as professor of instructional technology and coordinator of instructional development services at San Jose State University, California. Jerry first wrote *Instructional Design: A Plan for Unit and Course Development* in 1971 (Fearon), from which the present book, as the fourth version, emerged. In addition, he has authored or co-authored three other books dealing with training and technology. Jerry has been an instructional design consultant and conducts training workshops for many computer and electronics companies in Silicon Valley, California, and elsewhere.

GARY R. MORRISON received his doctorate in instructional systems technology from Indiana University in 1977. Since then, he has worked as instructional designer at the University of Mid-America, Solar Turbines International, General Electric Company's Corporate Consulting Group, and Tenneco Oil Company. He is currently a professor at The University of Memphis, where he teaches courses in instructional design. His credits include print projects, multimedia projects, and over 30 hours of instructional video programs, including a five-part series that was aired nationally on PBS-affiliated stations. He has worked on projects involving pest management for farmers, small business management, gas turbine troubleshooting, systems engineering for electrical engineers, beam pumping performance analysis, vessel design, microcomputer sales, and microcomputer repair.

Gary is a frequent collaborator with Steven M. Ross and has written more than 100 papers on topics related to instructional design and computer-based instruction, as well as contributing to several book chapters and instructional software packages. He is the associate editor of the research section of *Educational Technology Research and Development* and a past president of AECT's Research and Theory Division.

STEVEN M. ROSS received his doctorate in educational psychology from the Pennsylvania State University in 1974. He joined the faculty at The University of Memphis in 1974, and he is currently a professor in educational psychology and research there. He is the author of three textbooks and more than 100 journal articles in the areas of educational technology, computer-based instruction, and at-risk learners. He is the editor of the research section of *Educational Technology Research and Development.*

BRIEF CONTENTS

CONTENTS

CHAPTER 6
Designing the Instruction: Sequencing *90*

CHAPTER 7
Designing the Instruction: Strategies *100*

CHAPTER 8

Designing the Instructional Message   *116*

CHAPTER 9

Instructional Delivery Methods   *138*

CHAPTER 13
The Role of the Instructional Designer   *228*

CHAPTER 14
Managing Instructional Development Services   *240*

CHAPTER 15

*Using Evaluation to Enhance Programs:
Conducting Formative and Summative Evaluations*   *252*

APPENDIX

GLOSSARY

INDEX

DESIGNING EFFECTIVE INSTRUCTION

Second Edition

INTRODUCTION TO THE INSTRUCTIONAL DESIGN PROCESS

"Why examine the teaching/learning process?"

"How does curriculum planning differ from instructional design?"

"What are the components of a comprehensive instructional design plan?"

"What premises underlie the instructional design process?"

"What benefits can result from applying the instructional design process?"

"What is the value of instructional design to teachers?"

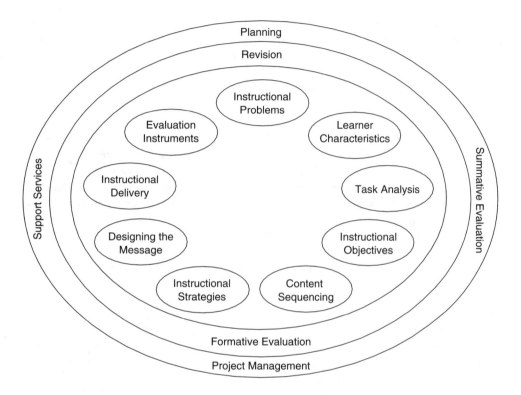

The preceding questions represent the important concepts treated in this introductory chapter. Understanding them is the basis for systematic instructional planning.

WHY EXAMINE THE TEACHING/LEARNING PROCESS?

The United States is moving toward a global, information-based economy, with an increasingly diverse work force. One result of these changes is a need for better-trained, competent managers, professionals, and technicians who are capable of using complex technologies to improve services, increase quality, and raise productivity. Also, more jobs require individuals to reason in high-level, abstract terms in order to make inferences and solve intricate problems.

The conventional structure and delivery of education, however, are at odds with these societal changes. Learning must be more effective and efficient. This need has given rise to the instructional design process, a planning method that results in successful learning and performance. Learning is haphazard; instruction is planned. Thus, our goal as designers is to create sound instruction that will lead to appropriate learning.

Before examining the elements of the instructional design process, it is useful to have a basic understanding of curriculum and its relationship to instructional design. Developing curriculum is often considered the starting point for instructional planning.

A Definition of Curriculum

The purpose of education or training is to provide a series of structured learning experiences. These may involve classes in an elementary school, courses in a secondary school or a higher education institution, or a training program in a business setting.

The term **curriculum** refers to the subject content and skills that make up an educational program. A school or curriculum includes the course offerings; at a company, the training programs may represent the curriculum. **Curriculum design** is a process of formulating a specific educational platform that defines the beliefs of what should be in the curriculum (Henderson & Hawthorne, 1995).

The emphasis of a curriculum depends on philosophical, social, and cultural forces that affect the school in terms of the broad society and the specific community it serves. For a business concern, a training curriculum reflects the organization's management policies, strategic plans, and identified needs. One caution we offer is to avoid building a curriculum in business that serves no other purpose than to offer a series of courses. All courses should serve to improve employee performance, thus supporting the mission and goals of the organization. The following questions help determine a curriculum:

1. What is the purpose or mission of the institution or department or the strategic plan of the organization?
2. What goals for education or training are necessary to serve the mission or plan?
3. How can instruction be categorized and organized to accomplish the goals?

Answering these questions can help in selecting subject areas, courses, instructional themes, or content categories. See Figure 1–1 for examples.

The Role for Instructional Design

The major goal of this book is to illustrate how to plan, develop, evaluate, and manage the instructional process effectively so that it will ensure competent performance by students. This systematic method is termed **instructional design** (often abbreviated as ID). It is based on what we know about learning theories, information

FIGURE 1–1
Organizing subject contents for curriculum

Education

Subject Areas	Courses	Themes Across Courses
Physical science	Physics	Patterns of change
Earth science	Chemistry	Scale and structure
Life science	Geology	Stability
	Biology	Systems and interactions

Training

Training Areas	Content Categories
Management development	Managing change
Employee development	Effective presentations
Product development	Project management
Marketing development	Negotiating skills
Field training	Product troubleshooting
	Economic analysis

technology, systematic analysis, and management methods. Dewey (1900) saw a need in the early part of this century for a science that could translate what was learned through research into practical applications for instruction. This science would make decisions about instructional practices that are based on sound research rather than intuition. Snellbecker (1974) and others have proposed that instructional design is the linking science described by Dewey. We agree with Snellbecker and see instructional design as the process for designing instruction based on sound practices.

The ID approach considers instruction from the perspective of the learner rather than from the perspective of the content, the traditional approach. It involves many factors that influence learning outcomes, including:

- What level of readiness do individual students need for accomplishing the objectives?
- What instructional strategies are most appropriate in terms of objectives and learner characteristics?
- What media or other resources are most suitable?
- What support is needed for successful learning?
- How is achievement of the objectives determined?
- What revisions are necessary if a tryout of the program does not match expectations?

There are other issues that also influence student learning. These issues are inherent in the instructional design process. This process is applicable for designing instruction in public education, higher education, and skills training.

The information, concepts, and procedures presented here can aid teachers and instructors, instructional designers, and planning teams—anyone who wants to develop effective, appealing instruction.

How would you answer this question: "If you were about to start planning a new unit in a course or training program, to what matter would you *first* give attention?" Here is how various individuals might answer:

Primary grade teacher: "I think first about the children. How important is the topic for them? Then, how well prepared are they to study it (physically, emotionally, intellectually)?"

High school teacher: "I'd start by writing down what I want to accomplish in teaching the unit. This becomes the goal around which I'll plan the instruction."

College professor: "My approach is to list the content that needs to be covered relative to the selected topic. This would include the terms, definitions, concepts, and principles that I feel need to be communicated to my students."

Instructional designer in industry: "It's important to start by listing the competencies I expect trainees to have after receiving instruction on the topic. These would be the outcomes or objectives to be accomplished."

The foregoing replies represent a sampling of approaches that might be taken as different individuals initiate their instructional planning. There could be other replies to the question. For example, one community college instructor always starts by writing the final examination for a new unit! He believes that passing the final exam is the students' greatest concern. Therefore, he writes questions that indicate what should receive emphasis in his teaching. His reasoning seems plausible.

As you read the replies to the question, and formulated your own answer, two conclusions should have become apparent. First, a number of different considerations appeal to educators and instructional designers as each starts planning. Second, each of us selects an order or sequence of our own in which to treat these elements.

KEY ELEMENTS OF THE INSTRUCTIONAL DESIGN PROCESS

Of the planning elements identified in the quoted statements, *four* are fundamental in instructional design. You will find them addressed in almost every planning model. They can be represented by answers to these questions:

1. For whom is the program developed? (characteristics of *learners* or *trainees*)
2. What do you want the learners or trainees to learn or demonstrate? (*objectives*)
3. How is the subject content or skill best learned? (*instructional strategies*)
4. How do you determine the extent to which learning is achieved? (*evaluation* procedures)

These four fundamental components—learners, objectives, methods, and evaluation—form the framework for systematic instructional planning (see Figure 1–2).

FIGURE 1–2
The fundamental components
of instructional design

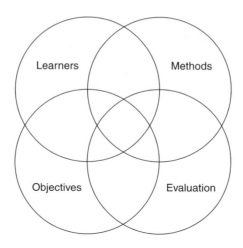

These components are interrelated and could conceivably make up an entire instructional design plan. In actuality, there are additional components that should require attention and that, when integrated with the basic four, form a complete instructional design model. The following section introduces nine elements of the instructional design process necessary for a comprehensive design plan.

THE COMPLETE INSTRUCTIONAL DESIGN PLAN

The following paragraphs describe the nine elements in a comprehensive instructional design plan:

1. Identify *instructional problems,* and specify goals for designing an instructional program.
2. Examine *learner characteristics* that should receive attention during planning.
3. Identify *subject content,* and analyze *task* components related to stated goals and purposes.
4. State *instructional objectives* for the learner.
5. *Sequence content* within each instructional unit for logical learning.
6. Design *instructional strategies* so that each learner can master the objectives.
7. Plan the *instructional message and delivery.*
8. Develop *evaluation* instruments to assess objectives.
9. Select *resources* to support instruction and learning activities.

The nine elements of this instructional design plan are illustrated in Figure 1–3.

The starting place for instructional planning should be to decide whether instructional design is appropriate for a potential project. The diagram shows this first element, *instructional problems,* at the twelve o'clock position.

Although the list of nine elements forms a logical, clockwise sequence as illustrated, the order in which you address the individual elements is not predetermined. It is for this reason that the oval pattern is used. An oval does not have a specific

FIGURE 1–3
Components of the instructional design plan

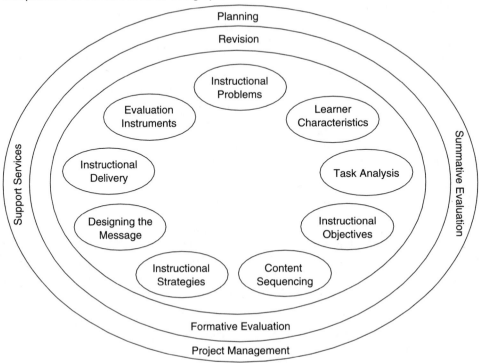

starting point. Recall the answers to the question asked of various persons earlier in this chapter. Individuals may proceed through the instructional design process in their own preferred way, starting with one element or another and following whatever order they consider logical or suitable.

In Figure 1–3, the elements are *not* connected with lines or arrows. Connections could indicate a sequential, linear order. The intent is to convey flexibility yet some order in the way the nine elements may be used. Also, some instances may not require treating all nine elements. For example, in some programs evaluation instruments may not be necessary.

Another reason for using the oval form is that a flexible interdependence exists among the nine elements. Decisions relating to one may affect others. As instructional objectives are stated, items of subject content may be added or reordered. Or, while instructional delivery methods are being chosen, the intent of an instructional learning objective may become clearer than as initially stated and require revision. Consequently, the procedure permits and encourages flexibility in the selection of elements, the order of their treatment, and back-and-forth activity among the elements. This procedure allows for additions and changes as the instructional design plan takes shape.

Many instructional design models identify and use features similar to those described in this book. Such models are often represented by a diagram with boxes and arrows as a series of steps in a set order, as shown in Figure 1–4. The intent of such a model is to establish a 1-2-3 sequential order. In actual use, the process often is not so linear. The open, circular pattern seems more appropriate and useful.

When starting to design instruction, if you feel somewhat insecure with the open, flexible format, follow the logical arrangement, starting with *instructional problems.* Then move to *learner characteristics,* and proceed clockwise through the nine elements.

As you gain experience with using this instructional design plan, you no doubt will establish your own arrangement of components for the design of a course. But even when following a sequence with which you are comfortable, you will need to make adjustments. Romiszowski (1981) refers to this as a *heuristic, problem-solving approach.* With each project, you modify your strategy, based on how things work in each situation.

The word *element* is used as a label for each of the nine parts of our instructional design plan. This term is preferable to the terms *step, stage, level,* or *sequential item,* which are expressions in keeping with the linear concept.

Another part of our diagram is the indication of *revision* around the elements. The two outer ovals illustrate the feedback feature, which allows for changes in the content or treatment of elements at any time during development. The treatment of elements may require revisions when, for example, data about learning are collected during instructional tryouts (called **formative evaluation**) or at the end of a course offering (called **summative evaluation**). If you want learners to succeed, accomplishing instructional objectives at a satisfactory level of proficiency, then you will want to improve any weak parts of the program as they are discovered.

Various expressions are used to label systematic instructional planning. In addition to the term *instructional design* used in this book, you will find reference to the following in the literature:

- Instructional systems
- Instructional systems design
- Instructional systems development

FIGURE 1–4
A typical instructional design model

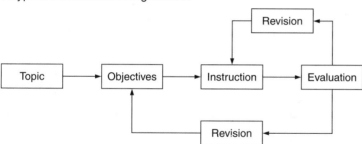

- Learning systems design
- Competency-based instruction
- Criterion-referenced instruction
- Performance technology

Another expression, *instructional development*, represents the management function in systematic instructional planning. This term includes assigning and supervising personnel, handling allocated budgets, arranging for necessary support services, and checking time schedules for compliance.

Thus, the instructional *development* procedure is used to direct and control projects, while the instructional *design* procedure plans instruction. The chapters that follow will focus mainly on the instructional design elements shown in Figure 1–3. But in Chapter 14, "Managing Instructional Development Services," the instructional development category receives attention.

PREMISES UNDERLYING THE INSTRUCTIONAL DESIGN PROCESS

We have identified seven basic premises to help you understand the ID process and apply it successfully. These premises can influence both your thinking and your treatment of the instructional design plan.

Premise 1: The instructional design process requires attention to both a *systematic* procedure and a *specificity* for treating details within the plan.

The term *systematic* refers to an orderly, logical method of *identifying, developing,* and *evaluating* a set of strategies aimed at attaining a particular instructional goal. This task is accomplished using the nine interrelated elements of the instructional design plan.

Treating each element requires exacting mental effort. Each element of the plan must be applied with attention to precise details. This means being *specific.* For example, an instructional objective is a statement that includes a particular verb that guides the development of an instructional strategy and indicates how achievement will be evaluated. The details of the instructional strategy—with the description of certain required student participation—that you choose to accomplish an objective are another indication of the specific treatment required when implementing the instructional design process.

Attention to detail is critical for the success of any instructional design work. By applying *systematic* procedures and being attentive to *specific* details, you can design effective instruction.

Premise 2: The instructional design process usually starts at the course development level.

Decisions about curricula and broad goals for a school or training program precede the design of specific courses. Although instructional designers can help administrators, managers, and committees make decisions about the purposes, directions, and emphasis of a program, instructional design work usually starts with identification of the instruction or training needs to be served. Units or topics comprising a course are then selected. This selection is followed by the development of instructional components related to the various planning elements.

> *Premise 3:* An instructional design plan is developed primarily for use by the instructor and planning team.

Some people believe that all details developed during planning (instructional needs analysis, instructional objectives, content sequencing, etc.) are to be given to learners, often in the form of a study guide. This assumption is not true. The learners will use many of the items written as elements in the plan, but not always in the form or order in which they are being developed and stated. We distinguish between the *planning* documents (instructional needs, instructional strategies, etc.) and the *instructional materials* the learners will actually see and use. The design team uses planning documents to design and develop the instructional units. Once the instructional materials are in final form, the planning documents lose their value and usually are filed.

Also, the order in which elements are treated during planning may differ substantially from the order in which they are eventually presented to learners. For example, a pretest might be developed after the final examination is devised even though students will complete it prior to the start of instruction.

> *Premise 4:* While planning, every effort should be made to provide for a level of satisfactory achievement for all learners.

A study by Bloom (1976) concluded that up to 95% of all public school students can accomplish what is required of them if each individual has suitable academic background, appropriate instruction, and sufficient time for learning. Other research has shown that if a student is prepared to learn and puts forth the effort to study but is unsuccessful in learning, a more careful design of the instructional plan can help overcome this shortcoming. This conclusion applies to training as well as to education. It justifies the need to test a plan before its implementation, as indicated by the *revision* oval in Figure 1–3.

> *Premise 5:* The success of the instructional product is dependent on the accuracy of the information flowing into the instructional design process.

To solve a performance problem, the designer must identify what the exact training needs are through the use of needs assessment, goal analysis, and/or performance. Creating instruction for a task that is not a performance problem is not likely to lead to an improvement in learner achievement. Similarly, the designer must accurately identify the target audience to design materials that are appropriate for the audience's reading and skill levels. The information obtained from the subject-matter expert must be accurate and complete. Selecting an appropriate instructional strategy for the content and objectives is essential for both efficient and effective instruction. And last, accurate information is needed from the formative evaluation of the materials to make appropriate modifications. Failure to obtain accurate information and to make the correct decisions can result in ineffective instruction.

Premise 6: The instructional design process focuses on the individual rather than the content.

Instructional design focuses on the individual and how to improve learner performance rather than on what content to cover. During learner analysis, the process focuses on individual characteristics. As we design the instruction, we consider these characteristics in the selection of the instructional strategies and delivery methods. The results can range from a highly adaptive computer-based instructional system that uses personalized information from each learner, responds in a different manner to each learner response, and is self-paced; to a group-paced classroom lecture that is carefully designed and incorporates media and supplementary materials to address the various learner characteristics. Throughout the design process, the designer focuses on the individual learner and what the learner must achieve to alleviate a problem rather than on what content to cover.

Premise 7: There is no single "best" way to design instruction.

Applying the instructional design process can reduce reliance on intuition or trial-and-error in planning. Yet the instructional design process has not reached a level of scientific exactness. Many paths can be conceived to reach the same goals and objectives. Instructors and designers are unique individuals, just as learners are unique. Each designer will formulate activities and apply elements of the instructional design plan in an individual way. The proof of an instructional plan's success will be whether a satisfactory level of learning is achieved in an acceptable period of time.

BENEFITS OF USING THE INSTRUCTIONAL DESIGN PROCESS

For any enterprise to be successful, those involved in the endeavor must derive some benefit. In a business operation the owner makes a profit, the customer is satisfied with the price and quality of the product or service, and the worker or craftsperson receives sufficient pay while feeling a sense of pride in workmanship. Those of us associated with teaching and learning must have equal benefits as well:

- The *administrator* or *program manager* wants evidence of effective, efficient learning within an acceptable cost base. The time is past when we could say, "It looks like a good program" or "It's acceptable because the students certainly enjoyed the course." We need hard evidence of success.
- The *instructional designer* wants evidence that a satisfactory program has been designed. The best indication is the accomplishment of program objectives by learners within an appropriate time period.
- The *teacher* or *instructor* wants to see learners achieve the required competencies and also wants personally to develop a positive relationship with learners.
- *Learners* want to succeed in their learning and also to find the learning experience to be pleasant and satisfying.

When the design of an instructional program follows the procedures outlined in this book or those of another suitable model, such benefits as these are realized. In other words, employing the instructional design process increases the probability of goal attainment.

In addition to enhancing learning of knowledge and skills, instructional design can foster a positive attitude toward the subject and better study habits. In our evaluation of a variety of instructional materials, we have found that well-designed instruction fosters a positive attitude and motivation. In many cases, the students inquire if more instruction will be available in the same format. We have also noticed similar responses when evaluating prototypes that present only a sample of the content.

APPLYING THE PROCESS TO BOTH ACADEMIC EDUCATION AND TRAINING PROGRAMS

Specific job training has precise, immediate requirements with identifiable and often measurable outcomes. The program must stress the teaching of knowledge and skills for the performance of assigned tasks. Academic education, on the other hand, often has broad purposes and more generalized objectives. Application of the knowledge and skills to be taught may not become important until sometime in the future.

Whether one is studying history or carpentry, the identical principles of learning apply to structuring experiences for individuals. While the emphasis, certain details, and terminology differ, both situations treat similar elements of the instructional design plan. Thus, the procedures presented in this book can be effective for either an academic or a training situation. Where particulars differ, special explanations and examples will be included in either the academic instruction or the planning for training.

Benefits of Instructional Design in Business

The benefits of the application of instructional design in business can take many forms. Results can vary from simply reducing the amount of time it takes to complete a course to solving a performance problem by designing effective instruction that increases worker productivity. In the late 1980s Motorola University conducted three limited studies of the benefits of training. They found that for every dollar invested in training, they realized a return on investment of $30 (*The Value of Training*, 1995). Although we do not have the specifics of how the return on investment was calculated, it is interesting to note that many corporations consider a return of 13% acceptable for most projects. The role of instructional design and training varies from company to company, as do the benefits. For example, Speedy Muffler King, which experienced high revenues and profits for 1994, made extensive use of training. During 1994, they provided more than 100,000 hours of employee training to improve customer satisfaction and loyalty (Canada NewsWire, 1995). Appropriate training can produce a return on investment for both tangible (e.g., increased output) and intangible (e.g., worker loyalty) measures.

Benefits of Instructional Design in P–12 Education

Do P–12 teachers have to be instructional designers in addition to their traditional roles of classroom managers, presenter-lecturers, and mentors? Our definitive answers are "to some degree" and "it all depends." By saying "to some degree," we mean that textbooks, workbooks, basal readers, and other standard instructional resources will rarely, if ever, be sufficient to satisfy formal curriculum objectives while keeping students occupied and interested. There will be numerous occasions (many teachers might say "every day") where the need for teacher-developed materials—drill-and-practice exercises, remedial lessons, or even full-fledged instructional units—will arise. Knowing the basic principles of instructional design (see the seven premises above) can help to ensure that what is produced serves a necessary purpose; meets the needs of students; is attractive and well organized; is delivered in an appropriate mode; and is continually evaluated and improved. Unlike professional instructional designers, however, the typical teacher is not likely to need formal expertise in the various instructional design processes. However, basic familiarity with major principles and procedures (e.g., how to present text, write and deliver a lecture, or prepare a test) can be extremely helpful, both for their own work and for evaluating commercial educational products.

How much teachers use instructional design will also depend a great deal upon situational factors. Teachers working in today's *restructuring* schools may find themselves increasingly involved in design activities. Specifically, in recent years, national initiatives for educational reform (Sarason, 1995) have generated support for activity-oriented, student-centered methods of teaching that stress meaningful learning applied to real-world problems. Following the classic ideas of Dewey and Piaget, modern *constructivist* theories view knowledge as primarily created (constructed) by the learner rather than transmitted by teachers (Prewat, 1995).

To promote active learning both school-wide and district-wide, comprehensive restructuring models, such as those developed by New American Schools (Kearns & Anderson, 1997), are being disseminated nationally. Nearly all of these models emphasize extensive use of project-based activities in which learners integrate concepts and skills across multiple subjects to develop products, perform experiments, and solve problems. One example is the Expeditionary Learning–Outward Bound model (Campbell, Farrell, Kamii, Lam, Rugen, & Udall, 1997). By participating in learning expeditions around the school and community (e.g., interviewing local police and citizens about neighborhood crime and presenting the findings in a group report and exhibition), the students acquire opportunities to connect learning and curriculum objectives to real-world events.

Implementing these approaches obviously requires well-designed expeditions and projects. Where do they come from? For the most part, that responsibility falls on the individual teachers. Not surprisingly, however, many find themselves unprepared for the task, and the implementations of the new strategies suffer as a result (see Bodilly, 1996). By learning more about instructional design, teachers should become better equipped to either create high-quality student-centered lessons or adapt commercial materials to fit their course needs.

WHO'S WHO IN THE INSTRUCTIONAL DESIGN PROCESS

As you prepare to study the instructional design process, you will want to view it from your own perspective. What role or roles will you assume in planning? What specific responsibilities might you have? What relationship do you have with other persons in your organization who are involved in aspects of teaching or training? These are all matters to keep in mind as you study the elements of instructional design.

In Chapter 13 we will examine in detail the roles and responsibilities of those persons engaging in instructional planning, development, implementation, and evaluation. At this point, however, you should recognize that *four* essential roles must be performed during instructional planning. You may be expected to fill one or more of these positions:

- *Instructional designer:* A person responsible for carrying out and coordinating the planning work; competent in managing all aspects of the instructional design process.
- *Instructor:* A person (or member of a team) for and with whom the instruction is being planned; well informed about the learners to be taught, the teaching procedures, and the requirements of the instructional program; with guidance from the designer, capable of carrying out details of many planning elements; responsible for trying out and then implementing the instructional plan that is developed.
- *Subject-matter expert (SME):* A person qualified to provide information about content and resources relating to all aspects of the topics for which instruction is to be designed; responsible for checking accuracy of content treatment in activities, materials, and examinations. The teacher or instructor may also serve as SME.
- *Evaluator:* A person qualified to assist the staff in developing testing instruments for pretesting and for evaluating student learning (posttesting); responsible for gathering and interpreting data during program tryouts and for determining effectiveness and efficiency of the program when fully implemented.

ANSWERING THE CRITICS

"Isn't the instructional design process actually a mechanistic rather than a humanistic method of instructional planning?" "Doesn't this procedure discourage creativity in teaching?" "Isn't teaching more of an art than a science?" These and similar questions are frequently raised and need to be answered realistically. After studying this book, you should make up your own mind about how to answer them. Following are our responses to such questions:

> *Question:* "Isn't the instructional design process actually a mechanistic rather than a humanistic method of instructional planning?"

As explained earlier, some ID models exhibit a rigidity when only a single, linear path for planning, as created with boxes and arrows, is followed without exception. Figure 1–4 illustrates this approach. The sequences should be flexible, with elements developed in different orders or arrangements as necessary. An instructional designer's style of working, the nature of a subject, or the learners' needs all can influence how the components are handled in planning. The ID process would only be mechanistic if elements were treated in a fragmented manner rather than following an integrated approach.

A *humanistic* approach to instruction recognizes the individual learner (student or trainee) in terms of his or her own capabilities, individual differences, present ability levels, and personal development. It should be apparent that these matters *do* receive attention in the instructional design process. Elements of the process include an examination of learner characteristics and an identification of readiness levels for learning. Furthermore, the application of systematic planning for designing various forms of individualized or self-paced learning also can allow for various individualized styles of learning.

Philosophically, as the planning starts, the instructional designer or instructor might have the following perspective: "I am designing a program of learning experiences for learners so that *together* we will be successful in accomplishing the stated goals and objectives. While it is important for each person to learn, it is equally important for *me* that the learner becomes proficient."

Therefore, a successful instructional program is one in which as many students as possible have succeeded, reaching a mastery level for accomplishing the specified outcomes. Grading on a bell-shaped normal curve and assigning letter grades would have no place in such instruction.

Question: "Doesn't the ID procedure discourage creativity in teaching?"

When a fine work of art is created, the artist has used a number of widely accepted design elements (unity, emphasis, balance, space, shape, color, etc.) creatively. This same principle applies to instructional planning.

Certain accepted learning principles, characteristics of individual components, and necessary relationships among elements require consideration in planning. These nine design elements, discussed earlier, can be developed and manipulated in imaginative and creative ways.

Two persons teaching the same subject or topic and targeting the same outcome goals might very well design different plans. Both can result in satisfactory student learning. The process demands dynamic interactions between students and instructor and between student and media, and different activities may be developed to satisfy those demands. This process encourages creativity, even to the extent of providing for open-ended or unanticipated learning experiences.

Question: "Isn't the main attention in ID given to low-level, immediate learning outcomes rather than to higher-order, long-term outcomes?"

Examine the test questions in a typical unit or end-of-course examination. Frequently they are multiple-choice or true/false items that involve *defining, labeling, naming, recognizing,* and other memory or recall of subject content. The ID process, in keeping with the goal to be accomplished, logically emphasizes more advanced intellectual thought processes that build on basic factual information. This emphasis may include learning related to *comprehension, application, analysis, synthesis,* and *evaluation.*

In many academic subject areas, learners achieve major learning outcomes only after they have completed a class and enroll in an advanced course or begin working on the job. Instructional design includes procedures for directly and indirectly evaluating postcourse behavior and content application outcomes.

These answers to the critics may seem unconventional. Many educators and trainers, based on their beliefs and experience, might not accept them. Often people must become dissatisfied with present practices or results before they recognize the need for change and improvement (e.g., getting beyond passive learning and rote memorization to attaining higher-level objectives and providing more meaningful educational experiences). At that point, they are probably ready to explore a fresh approach to instructional planning. Providing explanations and offering opportunities, as described in this introductory chapter, can help counter criticism of the instructional design process.

QUESTIONS . . . QUESTIONS . . . QUESTIONS

As you read and study the following chapters, you will frequently see questions being raised or referred to in relation to the topic under consideration. Such questions may appear at the beginning of a chapter to indicate the important matters that will follow. Then, as the discussion proceeds, other questions help direct thinking toward decisions that must be made.

An instructional designer continually probes for clarification, explanations, and details. You must help the persons with whom you carry out instructional planning to communicate effectively with you. This can best be done by using questions. Therefore, pay particular attention to the questions raised throughout the book. Then let questioning become a common part of your behavior as you explore and eventually practice the instructional designer role.

SUMMARY

1. Curriculum includes subject matter, skills, and courses that comprise an educational program.
2. The key elements of ID involve learner characteristics, objectives, teaching methods and activities, and evaluation of learning.
3. A complete ID plan consists of nine elements arranged in a flexible configuration and formative and summative evaluations for potential revisions.
4. A number of expressions may substitute for the term *instructional design* in the literature and in practice. The expression *instructional development* applies to the management of ID projects.
5. The ID process has the following qualities: it follows a systematic procedure with specific details, it usually starts at the course development level,

it can enhance learning at a satisfactory level, and it may result in different planning results by different designers.

6. The ID process can benefit administrators and program managers, instructional designers, instructors, and learners.

7. The ID process applies to both academic education and industrial training programs.

8. Roles involved in the ID process include instructional designer, instructor, subject-matter expert, and evaluator.

9. Criticism of the ID process that must be answered includes the opinions that it is a mechanistic rather than humanistic planning method; it discourages teacher creativity; and main attention is given to low-level, immediate outcomes.

10. Asking questions during all phases of the ID process can help direct thinking toward decisions.

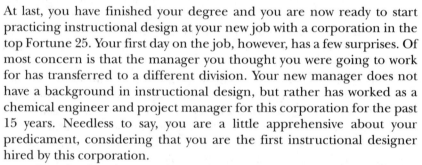

FROM HERE TO THERE

At last, you have finished your degree and you are now ready to start practicing instructional design at your new job with a corporation in the top Fortune 25. Your first day on the job, however, has a few surprises. Of most concern is that the manager you thought you were going to work for has transferred to a different division. Your new manager does not have a background in instructional design, but rather has worked as a chemical engineer and project manager for this corporation for the past 15 years. Needless to say, you are a little apprehensive about your predicament, considering that you are the first instructional designer hired by this corporation.

Shortly after the morning coffee break, your manager invites her staff in for an introductory meeting. The staff includes three trainers who have more than 35 years combined experience in teaching courses for the corporation, an administrative assistant who schedules and makes arrangements for courses, two engineers (who have worked in the department for four years each) who write new curriculum, and you. The meeting starts with each individual describing his or her background and role in the department. The other staff members can easily impress the new manager with their mastery of company lingo and number of hours of training they produce each quarter.

Turning slowly, the manager sizes you up and asks you to describe your background and your role in *her* new department. The manager and other staff members are not impressed by your degree in instructional design or the fact that you received it from a leading program in the area—probably because they have never heard of instructional design. After a brief pause and a few frowns, one of the senior trainers asks you to explain exactly what it is that you do—seems they all thought you said "interior design" and thought you were there to spruce up their offices and classrooms.

The next few minutes are critical. You can either win this manager and staff over to a new way of viewing training, or you can overwhelm them with your knowledge so they decide you are one of those intellectual types. What will you say to this group that will help ensure your longevity with the company?

REFERENCES

Bloom, B. (1976). *Human characteristics and school learning.* New York: McGraw-Hill.

Bodilly, S. (1996). *Lessons learned from New American Schools Development Corporation's demonstration phase.* Santa Monica, CA: RAND Corporation.

Campbell, M., Farrell, G., Kamii, M., Lam, D., Rugen, L., & Udall, D. (1997). The Expeditionary Learning–Outward Bound Design. In Stringfield, S. C., Ross, S. M., & Smith, L. J. (Eds.), *Bold new plans for school restructuring: The New American Schools Development Corporation designs.* Mahwah, NJ: Erlbaum.

Canada NewsWire (1995). Speedy Muffler King announces second quarter results. [On-line]. Available: www.newswire.ca/releases/August1995/03/c2085.html.

Dewey, J. (1900). Psychology and social practice. *Psychological Review, 7,* 105–124.

Henderson, J. G., & Hawthorne, R. D. (1995). *Transformative curriculum leadership.* Englewood Cliffs, NJ: Merrill.

Kearns, D. T., & Anderson, J. L. (1997). Sharing the vision: Creating New American Schools. In Stringfield, S. C., Ross, S. M., & Smith, L. J. (Eds.), *Bold new plans for school restructuring: The New American Schools Development Corporation designs.* Mahwah, NJ: Erlbaum.

Prewat, R. (1995). Misreading Dewey: Reform, projects, and the language game. *Educational Researcher, 24*(7), 13–22.

Romiszowski, A. J. (1981). *Designing instructional systems.* New York: Nichols.

Tyler, R. (1949). *Basic principles of curriculum and instruction.* Chicago: The University of Chicago Press.

Sarason, S. B. (1995). Some reflections on what we have learned. *Phi Delta Kappan, 77,* 4–85.

Snellbecker, G. (1974). *Learning theory, instructional theory, and psychoeducational design.* New York: McGraw-Hill.

The value of training. (1995). [On-line]. Available at: http://tidbit.fhda.edu/BII/NewsNotes.html.

IDENTIFYING THE NEED FOR INSTRUCTION

"What is the problem we are asked to solve?"

"Will instruction solve the problem?"

"What is the purpose of the planned instruction?"

"Why should I design a unit of instruction?"

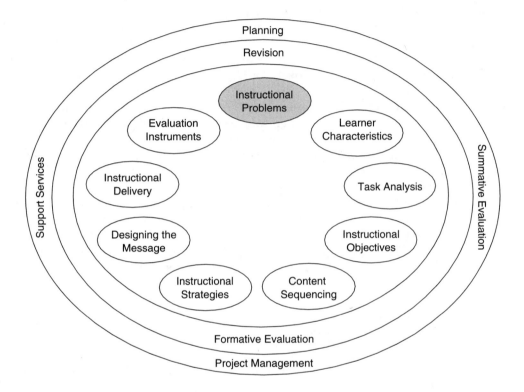

The diagram shows concentric ovals labeled from outside in: Planning, Revision, Support Services, Summative Evaluation, Formative Evaluation, Project Management. The inner circle contains: Instructional Problems, Learner Characteristics, Task Analysis, Instructional Objectives, Content Sequencing, Instructional Strategies, Designing the Message, Instructional Delivery, Evaluation Instruments.

B efore starting an instructional development project, we should ask, "Why do we need instruction? Under what conditions is it advisable to undertake a task that is both costly and time-consuming?" Let's examine some situations that might require an instructional intervention.

First, suppose performance is not meeting expectations. For example, emergency personnel who answer 911 phone calls are not providing accurate, complete information to the police and fire departments responding to emergency situations; or the mean score for a fifth-grade class on the fractions section of an achievement test is below the national, state, and district means. In these two situations the operators and students are not performing to expectations.

Second, the work environment can change as a result of modifications in procedure or the installation of new equipment. When one corporation purchases another corporation, there will likely be procedural changes for minor operations such as requesting travel or completing travel expense forms. More complex procedures can also change—for example, preparing packages for exportation. In an elementary school the principal may decide to adopt a whole-language approach, requiring staff development and changes in teaching methods. Or a school might receive money to purchase five computers for every classroom. Teachers would then need training on not only how to operate the computers, but how to integrate this technology into their curriculum.

Third, a company or industry can expand so rapidly that qualified personnel are in short supply. In the 1970s the petroleum industry grew faster than the industry could prepare engineers for higher-level positions and faster than universities could provide qualified graduates. The solid-state electronics industry experienced similar growth in the late 1970s and early 1980s, which created problems. Inexperienced professionals were often hired, promoted to higher-level positions, and advised to learn through experience on the job.

In situations like the three just described, training interventions might help improve productivity or achievement. More specifically, instructional design would provide a means for developing appropriate training or increase the cost-effectiveness of existing training. For example, a corporation may hire an outside consulting group to teach a course on time management. Could a similar course be designed in-house to reduce costs and more directly reflect the corporation's work environment? Similarly, an existing course might require an employee to attend for five full days. Perhaps a mixture of self-paced instruction and classroom instruction would reduce time away from the job.

IS INSTRUCTION THE ANSWER?

At first glance, it seems that the 911 operators mentioned earlier need training in how to record correct information, and the fifth-grade students need to study one or more units on fractions. But do we know that more instruction will solve these problems? Considering the 911 operators, could something in the environment account for their inaccuracies? A careful analysis of the situation might reveal that earpieces on the phones may not fit the operators properly or that transmissions have an unacceptable level of static. Training for the operators would not solve any of these problems, while the fifth-graders' low test scores may be the result of the students' taking the year-end achievement test *before* they have completed the planned unit on fractions.

The purpose for identifying the problem is to determine whether instruction should be part of the solution. A company that developed new training for the 911 operators or required them to repeat existing training would squander company resources. Similarly, simply rescheduling the teaching of fractions or the achievement test might easily solve the fifth graders' performance problem.

The instructional design process begins with the identification of an instructional problem or need. Why is performance below expectations? Once we know the root cause of the problem, we can determine whether an instructional intervention will solve the problem. Instructional designers can use three different approaches to identify instructional problems: needs assessment, goal analysis, and performance assessment.

NEEDS ASSESSMENT

Kaufman and English (1979) and Kaufman et al. (1993) describe **needs assessment** as a tool for identifying the problem and then selecting an appropriate intervention. If the designer fails to identify the problem properly, then the intervention may address only the symptoms, with no resultant change in the target audience's performance.

The needs assessment process serves four functions:

1. It identifies the needs relevant to a particular job or task, that is, what problems are affecting performance.
2. It identifies critical needs. Critical needs include those that have a significant financial impact, affect safety, or disrupt the work or educational environment.
3. It sets priorities for selecting an intervention.
4. It provides baseline data to assess the effectiveness of the instruction.

Gathering baseline data is not always possible or cost-effective. For example, a designer may determine that one cause of meter damage is water-meter inspectors using the wrong technique for turning off meters. Is it feasible or cost-effective to observe a number of individuals to document the incorrect procedure, since no records exist that indicate the cause of the damage? Or could the designer simply record the total number of meters replaced before and after the training is implemented?

Needs are defined as *a gap between what is expected and the existing conditions*. Instructional designers are primarily interested in gaps when actual performance does not equal or exceed expected performance. The next section will describe how to plan and conduct a needs assessment.

Types of Needs and Data Sources

Six identifiable categories of needs (Burton & Merrill, 1991) are used for planning and conducting a needs assessment. These six categories provide a framework for designers to determine the type of information to gather and a means to classify needs.

Normative Needs.   A normative need is identified by comparing the target audience against a national standard. Normative needs in education include national achievement test norms such as performance on the California Achievement Test (CAT), the Scholastic Aptitude Test (SAT), or the Graduate Record Exam (GRE).

Normative data for identifying training needs in industry often do not exist because of the lack of record-keeping at the national level. Some normative data exist for safety records (e.g., plant safety and transportation) and sales (e.g., projected sales of a product or service for a metropolitan area). A normative need exists when the target population's performance is less than the established norm. Thus, a fifth-grade class that scores 15 points below the norm on the math section of the CAT has a defined normative need. A trucking company that averages six more accidents than the industry norm per 10,000 miles driven has an identified normative need.

The first step in defining a normative need is to obtain the normative data. The test administrator's handbook or test publisher typically provides test norms. Norms related to specific industries (e.g., insurance, transportation, etc.) may be available from professional societies, trade groups, and government agencies (e.g., the Department of Transportation). Once the norm is defined, the instructional designer must collect data from the target audience for comparison with the norm. Again, summarized test data are often available in schools. Sales, manufacturing, and safety data are often included in company reports, databases, internal newsletters, and annual reports.

Comparative Needs.   Comparative needs are similar to normative needs in that both are defined by comparing the status of the target audience to an external measure or status. A comparative need, however, is identified by comparing the target group to another school or company as opposed to a norm. In education, a comparative need is identified by comparing one class to another equivalent class (e.g., two sixth-grade classes) or comparing two equivalent schools to identify differences such as available equipment or test scores. For example, public schools in Tennessee administer the Tennessee Comprehensive Assessment Program (TCAP) each spring. School districts can prepare profiles for all of their schools for the different subtests. Administrators, teachers, and parents can then compare their school to comparable schools to identify comparative needs. Many universities and colleges maintain a list of institutions they use for comparisons of faculty salaries, class size, and budgets. Businesses often study competitors to define training needs, facilities, and incentives. A comparative need exists when there is a gap between the groups. This difference, however, may not reflect a true need that can be addressed through training but rather the attitude of wanting to "keep up with the Joneses."

To identify comparative needs, the designer must first determine areas for comparison (e.g., math scores, facilities, management development, etc.). Data are then collected on the target audience to determine the current status. Next, data are collected from the comparative audience. In education, this process may be as simple as calling the other school and requesting the information. The data gathering is usually not as simple in the business environment because of the proprietary nature of information and government antitrust regulations, which often prohibit such discussions between different companies. A designer may need to revert to interviewing employees who have a knowledge of other organizations and to reading journals (e.g., *Performance and Instruction, Training and Development*) to obtain the comparative data. When identifying comparative needs, the designer must make sure that the need is a *viable* training need as opposed to a *status* need.

Felt Needs.   A felt need is an individual desire or want that an individual has to improve either his or her performance or that of the target audience. Felt needs express a gap between current performance or skill level and desired performance or skill level. When searching for felt needs, designers must identify needs related to improving performance and individual wants that are motivated by a desire other than performance improvement. For example, one company offered a training course that involved travel to several interesting locations in the United States and ended with a snorkeling trip in the Bahamas. The training manager had to determine who had a need for the course to improve job performance and who had a need to travel to interesting places. Another example is a college professor who decided to revise a course. She "felt" the need to add the new information to the course to make the course current, which would result in an improvement for the learners.

Felt needs are best identified through interviews and questionnaires. Face-to-face interviews are often more effective, since the designer can alleviate anxieties and probe for additional details. Questionnaires are only effective when individuals are willing to express their needs on paper. Typical questions to elicit felt needs are "What could be done to improve your work performance?" or "What could be done to improve the performance of (target audience)?" Such a question may open a Pandora's box of problems; the designer would need to separate needs into those that are addressable by training (e.g., "a better understanding of the accounting system") and those that are related to management problems (e.g., "reduce the amount of paperwork").

Expressed Needs.   Bradshaw (1972) defines an expressed need as a felt need turned into action. People are often willing to pay to satisfy expressed needs (Burton & Merrill, 1991). An individual who chooses one of two or more options—for example, enrolling in a specific course or workshop—is also demonstrating an expressed need. Again, instructional designers are primarily interested in expressed needs that improve the performance of the target audience or person. An example of an expressed need is the list of students who are placed on a waiting list for a course. The students have expressed a desire to enroll in the course and wait for an opening. The expressed need is the waiting list, which indicates a need for another section, a larger room, or a change in course formats to allow more students to take the course. In industry, professionals are often encouraged to attend one or more training courses a year as part of their professional development. Expressing an interest in attending such a course or having a manager recommend that an employee attend a specific course are means of identifying expressed needs.

Recently, a number of principals and teachers have requested workshops and inservice training on how to integrate the use of microcomputers into the curriculum. This request is an expressed need.

Data on expressed needs come from a variety of sources. A need for more sections of a course is expressed in the enrollment data. Individual personnel files and performance reviews often include goals in the form of either expressed or felt needs. Although the right to privacy may restrict an individual designer from reviewing files, a designer could ask the appropriate supervisor or manager to review the files and report any needs. Finally, expressed needs are often identified in suggestion boxes and in-house publications with a question-and-answer or suggestion column.

Anticipated or Future Needs.   The instructional design process often focuses on identifying needs related to existing performance problems. Anticipated needs are a means of identifying changes that will occur in the future. Identifying such needs should be part of any planned change so training can be designed *prior* to implementation of the change. For example, a school principal and supervisors might decide to implement a new instructional technique (e.g., cooperative learning) next year. An anticipated need is the knowledge teachers require to use the cooperative learning method effectively in a classroom. By anticipating the need, a designer can prepare appropriate training *before* the teachers start the new year and difficulties develop with the method. Similarly, the introduction of new software for a customer service center at Federal Express, MCI, or AT&T would require training for customer service representatives. Anticipating this need as the software is developed will allow the designers an opportunity to design the training so that it is ready prior to the transition to the new software. The customer service representatives are then knowledgeable of the new software and better able to do their job when they start using it.

Anticipated needs are often identified through interviews and questionnaires similar to those used with felt needs, but with additional questions about what changes the employee anticipates in the future that will affect the way the job is done. A second approach to identifying anticipated needs is to identify potential problem areas. For example, assume that a manually-controlled drill press will be converted to a computer-controlled machine in five years. An analysis of this change might find that the maintenance staff will need training on repairing and replacing the digital controllers on the drill presses.

Critical Incident Needs.   Mager (1984a) identifies critical incident needs as failures that are rare but have significant consequences—for instance, chemical spills; nuclear accidents; medical treatment errors; and natural disasters such as earthquakes, hurricanes, and tornadoes. A typical reaction to a critical incident need was the planning and education that occurred in Memphis in 1990 in the wake of the 1989 San Francisco earthquake. An earthquake was predicted to occur in Memphis in December 1990. Several government agencies, schools, and corporations developed earthquake awareness programs in anticipation of the disaster by analyzing the events associated with the 1989 San Francisco earthquake.

Critical incident needs are identified by analyzing potential problems. For example, chemical plants and petroleum refineries often develop employee training programs for handling emergencies such as fires, explosions, or spills. Other critical incident needs are identified by asking "what if" questions; for example, what would happen if the main computer or phone system failed?

Conducting a Needs Assessment

There are four phases to conducting a needs assessment: planning, collecting data, analyzing data, and preparing the final report. Figure 2–1 identifies the individual steps under each of these four phases.

FIGURE 2–1
Needs assessment process

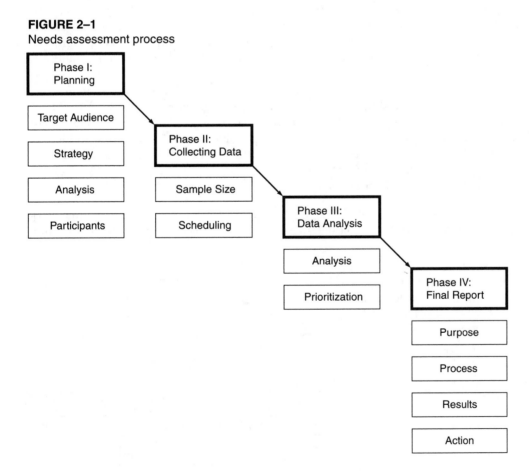

Phase I: Planning.   An effective needs assessment focuses on one job classification or target audience. Once the audience is defined, a strategy is developed for collecting the needs data. The designer first determines whether data are required for each type of need. For example, normative needs might not be essential when identifying anticipated needs due to a change in telephone systems.

Common data-collection techniques include questionnaires, rating scales, interviews, small-group meetings, and reviews of paper trails. Needs assessment results are often reported as frequencies (e.g., 60% of the employees indicated they did not know how to complete an expense advance request). Identification of the analysis methodology early in the process will aid in designing the instruments and ensure that appropriate data are collected.

The last step of the planning phase is to determine who will participate in the study. In industry, the participants (i.e., individuals to interview) might include a sampling of the target audience, supervisors and managers of the target audience, and experienced individuals who once were members of the target audience but have received promotions to a higher level. Figure 2–2 illustrates a sample organizational chart for a telephone company and identifies target participants (installers). Members of this target audience and the managers are asked to share their perceptions of the current needs. The line workers and repair people are also interviewed because they once worked as installers (the target audience) and can provide a different perspective. Experienced individuals provide another perspective based on their experiences and their interactions with the target audience.

Similar decisions are also required for school-based needs assessments. Major participants in those assessments are parents, students, and outside consultants. For example, we recently completed a technology assessment for a school to identify teacher training needs and hardware and software needs. We focused primarily on felt and anticipated needs. We collected data by interviewing teachers and asking teachers, parents, and students to complete surveys.

Phase II: Collecting the Data.   Careful consideration of the sample size and distribution are required when collecting data. It may not be logistically or economi-

FIGURE 2–2
Needs assessment partici-
pants (boldface box indicates
individuals participating in
needs assessment)

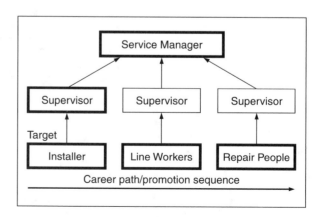

cally feasible to interview participants at each company site, plant, or division. Thus, the sample must include individuals from representative sites and regions. Also, manufacturing companies produce a variety of products at a number of different locations. Interviewing employees in only one area could provide a false picture of the training needs for a company-wide target audience. Data collection also includes scheduling appointments, making travel arrangements, and distributing and collecting questionnaires. Individual experience will determine the optimum number of interviews to plan per day and the return rate for questionnaires. Note that a 100% return rate is often unrealistic. Although a 75%–85% return rate would be desirable, the acceptable level would depend on the context. Also, unlike experimental or basic research, large samples may be less important than samples that are representative relative to the target population of employees or students.

Phase III: Analyzing the Data.   Once the data are collected, they must be analyzed. The output of the analysis is a prioritization of needs. Needs can be prioritized on the basis of economic value (e.g., cost value to the company), impact (number of people affected), a ranking scale, frequency of identification, or timeliness. One method for prioritizing the needs, the Delphi method, is an iterative process: we might mail a list of goals to a group of managers and ask them to rank the goals. In a second mailing, we might send the same group the top 40 goals and ask them to rank them again, and then the top 20 in a third mailing. This process is repeated until it establishes a focus. The advantage to the Delphi approach is its systematic and thorough data-gathering process; its disadvantage is its relative high effort and time demands. Another method for prioritizing is to use the identified needs as an input to a goal analysis (see Goal Analysis later in this chapter), which is then used to set the goals for training intervention.

Phase IV: Compiling a Final Report.   The last phase of needs assessment is to prepare a final report. A needs assessment report should include four sections:

1. Summarize the purpose of the study.
2. Summarize the process by describing how it was done and who was involved.
3. Summarize the results with one or more tables and a brief narrative.
4. Make the necessary recommendations based on the data.

The recommendation does *not* need to include prescriptions for training unless the problem is addressable by training.

Example

The Electronic Phone Company (EPC), based in St. Louis, offers discounted daytime phone rates for domestic and overseas calls to business customers. EPC has customer service and operator information centers in New York, Chicago, Atlanta, St. Louis, and San Francisco. The caller information department consists of information operators (entry level), operator supervisors, and chief operators. Information operators are promoted to operator supervisors. Operator supervisors monitor operator activity, provide coaching to entry-level operators, and handle problem situations for 10 to 15 operators. Chief operators monitor the activities of 5 to 10 operator supervisors and have the final authority and responsibility for all actions. EPC has decided that training is needed to improve the skills of the operator supervisors.

Phase I. A decision was made to collect data on all five types of needs: comparative, felt, expressed, anticipated, and critical incident. The decision was made in part because of an international conflict that began at the beginning of the needs assessment. Operator supervisors are the target audience (approximately 74 in the four locations). Face-to-face interviews were selected as the primary method for data collection. Two operators at each of three levels were interviewed individually.

Phase II. A decision was made to interview employees at all four locations, since the New York and San Francisco locations had a greater percentage of overseas calls and the St. Louis and Atlanta locations primarily handled domestic calls. The designers scheduled two days in each location to conduct six interviews (two operators at each of three levels) for a total of 24 at the four locations.

Phase III. A frequency count was made for each need identified in the interviews. The needs were categorized as either customer oriented or employee oriented. Customer-oriented needs were ranked by estimated loss of income (e.g., inability to find a phone number, misdirection of customer complaints, etc.).

Phase IV. The final report identified three training problems. First, operator supervisors needed training in the use of advanced searching techniques to identify phone numbers. Second, they needed training in handling difficult customers. Third, they needed training in coaching entry-level operators in communication techniques.

Needs assessment is a useful tool for identifying training needs. It is particularly effective when very little is known about an organization. Interviewing a number of individuals provides a broad perspective for correctly identifying the problem or needs.

GOAL ANALYSIS

Sometimes, conducting a needs assessment is neither practical nor feasible. An alternative approach is to use a goal analysis to define the problem. Mager (1984a) describes goal analysis as a method for "defining the undefinable." Some designers consider goal analysis as an integral part of the needs assessment process. Unlike needs assessment that seeks to identify *problems*, a goal analysis begins with input suggesting a *problem*. For example, a manager might determine that supervising operators are having a problem coaching the information operators. Goal analysis is then applied to the "need" to develop the goals for the training intervention. Applying goal analysis to a need suggested by one individual assumes that the need exists and that a training intervention is required to address the need. For example, a principal might ask you to conduct an inservice workshop on desktop publishing for the teachers in her school. Since you are unfamiliar with the teachers, you might attend a faculty meeting and conduct a goal analysis to determine what the teachers feel they would like to accomplish in the workshop.

A goal analysis could also use the data from a needs assessment to set priorities. Take, for example, a needs assessment that identifies the need to train managers in how to conduct hiring interviews. A goal analysis would use this need, interview training, to determine goals for the instruction.

Six Steps of Goal Analysis

Klein et al. (1971) and Mager (1984a) have suggested similar steps for conducting a goal analysis. Our six steps for a goal analysis are a synthesis of theirs.

Identify an Aim.   Using a group of experts familiar with the "problem," determine one or more aims related to the need. An aim is a general intent that gives direction. Example: Conduct an effective interview for a real estate sales position.

Set Goals.   Have the group of experts generate a number of goals for each aim. These goals should identify behaviors that describe learner performance. Examples:

> Prepare an agenda for the interview.
> Prepare a series of questions to ask during the interview.
> Prepare a structured interview form.
> Identify people to take the interviewee to lunch.
> Identify individuals to provide transportation for the interviewee.
> Identify a realtor to work with the interviewee.
> Obtain benefits information.
> Identify the steps for conducting an interview.
> Determine the type of questions to ask.

Refine Goals.   Sort through the goals and delete duplicates, combine similar goals, and refine those that are vague. This step is primarily a refinement stage to clarify the goal statements. Examples.

> Prepare a series of questions to ask during the interview.
> Prepare an agenda and transportation for the interview.

Identify a realtor for the interviewee.
Obtain benefits information.
Identify the steps for conducting an interview.
Determine the type of questions to ask.

Rank Goals.   Rank and select the most salient goals. Ranking can be by order of importance, items most likely to cause problems if ignored, or other relevant criteria. Some goals may be eliminated and others identified as critical to job performance. Examples:

1. Prepare an agenda and transportation for the interview.
2. Obtain benefits information.
3. Prepare a series of questions to ask during the interview.
4. Determine the type of questions to ask.
5. Identify the steps for conducting an interview.
6. Identify a realtor for the interviewee.

Refine Goals Again.   Identify discrepancies between the goals and existing performance. This step verifies that the need exists and that the goals are related to the job task(s) by identifying differences between existing performance and the goals. Examples:

Goal 2 was dropped because the Personnel Office handles benefits information.
Goal 6 was dropped because it was not considered part of the interview process.

Remaining goals represented existing performance problems.

Make a Final Ranking.   Develop a final ranking of the goals. Determine how critical or important the goal is to performing the tasks. Second, consider the overall effect of the goal. Relevant factors may be the cost of not doing the training, the probability the need will disappear if ignored (e.g., an impending change in the system), or the number of people affected by the training intervention. The final ranking is then used to design the training. Examples:

1. Determine the types of questions to ask.
2. Prepare a series of questions to ask during the interview.
3. Identify the steps for conducting an interview.
4. Prepare an agenda and transportation for the interview.

Comparing Goal Analysis and Needs Assessment

Although goal analysis takes less time than a needs assessment, its focus is typically much narrower. A goal analysis is typically conducted with a few individuals who are knowledgeable of the problem and target audience. The designer is relying on this small group of individuals to provide accurate input rather than gathering a variety of data from a number of sources as with a needs assessment. Deciding which method to select depends on a number of factors, including cost, time, scope of the project, and validity of the information the designer obtains from the participants. Typically, a needs assessment is reserved for projects that can justify the time and cost involved. A goal analysis is used when a problem is identified and the designer has confidence that the problem is valid. For example, a university implements a new online record system so that faculty and advisors can access student and class information. Since this system is new, training of some sort is needed. A goal analysis with appropriate individuals could be used to further define the training.

PERFORMANCE ASSESSMENT

Instructional designers often receive requests to design a training program to solve a perceived problem. A manager, chairperson, principal, or vice president may offer additional funding or rewards as an incentive to complete the project. Although it is often tempting to "take the money and run" with the project, the first step prior to initiating design is to determine whether training intervention will actually solve the problem.

Some problems, for example, may result from a failure to follow procedures rather than the execution of a task. An overnight shipping company saved thousands of dollars on training by recognizing such a problem. One facility had a consistently large number of package-sorting errors. Initial reaction might have been to design a training program to improve the sorters' skills. After careful observation of the process, however, the manager found that the crew members loading the packages on the conveyor were starting the sort earlier than scheduled and before the full complement of sorters arrived. The few sorters who arrived early were overwhelmed by the packages and made errors trying to keep up with the conveyor. Simply enforcing the procedure that the sort would not start until the designated time solved the sorting problem.

Similarly, a request was made to develop a course to help petroleum engineers plan an acid treatment on an oil well to increase oil production. An analysis of the problem indicated that treatments were adequately planned, but they were used on wells that were already producing as much oil as possible given the pipe diameter. Any additional flow would not be physically possible or economically feasible for the cost of the treatment. The training emphasis shifted from planning the treatment to determining whether it was needed.

For training to be effective, it must address the appropriate problem and not a symptom. Mager (1984b) has developed a performance analysis flowchart as an aid to identifying performance problems (see Figure 2–3). The left side of the chart addresses performance problems related to skill deficiencies, while the right side of

FIGURE 2–3
Performance Assessment Model

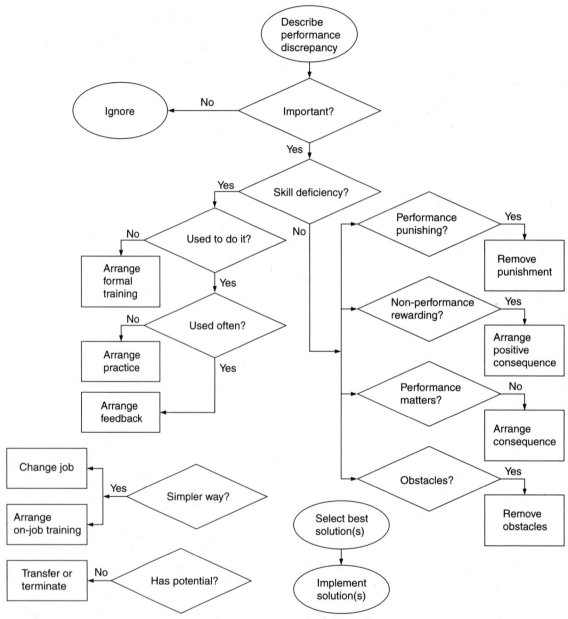

Note: Reprinted with permission from *Analyzing Performance Problems, Second Edition* by Robert F. Mager © 1984. Published by The Center for Effective Performance, 4250 Perimeter Park South, Suite 131, Atlanta, GA 30341. (770) 458–4080.

the chart addresses performance problems related to the job environment. Our first example of the missorts was solved by tracing down the right side of the chart to the obstacles question. By holding the start time of the sort to the established time, the manager removed the performance obstacle (too many packages to sort) so that the system would work as designed.

Mager cautions designers to use the flow diagram not as a rigid sequence but rather as a guide and to make intuitive leaps when appropriate. The time frame for conducting a performance assessment can range from an hour or less to several days if exhaustive observations are needed. Performance assessment is an excellent tool for determining whether a problem addressable by training does indeed exist. In contrast to needs assessment, performance analysis uses an identified need or problem as input to determine whether instruction is an appropriate solution.

Another technique, job analysis, is a listing of all the tasks an individual performs in a job. Such an approach is useful for developing a curriculum for training rather than identifying performance gaps or problem areas. While this method is very time-consuming, it does yield a complete task listing for a job. The use of job analysis to define a program assumes that training is needed on the tasks. Such an approach is appropriate for certain environments, such as a trade school or military training, that involve entry-level learners who have little knowledge or skill in the area. The outcome is typically a series of courses based on a body of knowledge the learner must master.

SUMMARY

1. Like a good problem-solving model, instructional design begins with identification of the training problem. Needs assessment, goal analysis, or performance assessment can help identify the problem. In practice, problem identification often involves a combination of these techniques rather than just one.
2. Needs assessment is an effective tool for identifying a range of problems in an organization, particularly if the designer is unfamiliar with the organization.
3. A needs assessment can identify six types of needs: normative, comparative, felt, expressed, anticipated, and critical incident.
4. A goal analysis can use either a needs assessment or a request for instruction as a starting point to establish priorities. The goal analysis process first identifies aims, then establishes, refines, and prioritizes the goals.
5. Performance assessment helps determine whether the goals of the training program actually address a training problem or whether management needs to make a change in the environment.

You have just been transferred to the U.S. Division of Deep Well Chemical Company. This company supplies chemicals for oil well work in the United States for land and offshore oil rigs. When you arrive, your manager is very agitated because he has a problem. They have had two deaths due to trucking accidents in the first eight months of this year, plus they are averaging 5.3 more accidents per 100,000 miles than the national average for trucks. The division manager has been told by the chief executive officer that he wants a perfect driving record in three months.

Your manager is convinced that the accidents are due to the drivers not obeying the speed limit and wants to initiate a program that will impose a company fine for every speeding ticket a driver receives. However, he is not sure how effective this approach will be since he does not always receive information on speeding tickets. He knows that the drivers are not performing at their best. Thus, he is giving you this problem to solve.

There are eight areas in the division (two in Texas, one in Louisiana, one in Oklahoma, one in Denver, two in California, and one in Alaska). He quickly explains that each area has a dispatcher who assigns jobs to the drivers, two to five supervisors who each manage approximately 12 to 15 drivers, and a safety manager. All training is done at Division headquarters in Oklahoma. You have permission to travel to each area where a manager will provide you with access to all personnel. Your manager would like to discuss your plan of action tomorrow morning for addressing this problem. What is your plan?

REFERENCES

Bradshaw, J. (1972). The concept of social need. *New Society, 19*(4), 640–643.

Burton, J. K., & Merrill, P. F. (1991). Needs assessment: Goals, needs, and priorities. In L. J. Briggs, K. L. Gustafson, & M. H. Tillman (Eds.), *Instructional design: Principles and applications* (2nd ed., pp. 17–43). Englewood Cliffs, NJ: Educational Technology Publications.

Kaufman, R., & English, F. W. (1979). *Needs assessment: Concept and application.* Englewood Cliffs, NJ: Educational Technology Publications.

Kaufman, R., Rojas, A. M., & Mayer, H. (1993). *Needs assessment: A user's guide.* Englewood Cliffs, NJ: Educational Technology Publications.

Klein, S. P., Hoepfner, R., Bradley, P. A., Wooley, D., Dyer, J. S., & Strickland, G. P. (1971). *Procedures for needs-assessment evaluation: A symposium.* (Report No. 67). Los Angeles: University of California, Center for the Study of Evaluation.

Mager, R. F. (1984a). *Goal analysis* (2nd ed.). Belmont, CA: Lake.

Mager, R. F. (1984b). *Analyzing performance problems* (2nd ed.). Atlanta, GA: The Center for Effective Performance.

LEARNER CHARACTERISTICS

"Why is it important to give attention to learner characteristics when planning?"

"Which characteristics are most useful, and how is information about them obtained?"

"What characteristics of special learner groups may have an important impact on instructional planning?"

"What are student learning styles, and how can we accommodate them in a lesson?"

Suppose that you had never heard about the instructional design process. You start giving the lecture at the first class meeting of your course. You have put a lot of work into developing this new introductory unit to impress students with the value of the subject. The lecture contains detailed statistical content from recent research and complex explanations. As you proceed, you sense reactions: A few students are listening intently and rapidly taking notes; others look puzzled; some appear completely indifferent. This is a one-time opportunity for all of them to get this important information! What is wrong?

Perhaps, in your preparation, you have given little consideration to the nature of the student group, their aptitudes and preparation levels, degree of motivation, or other traits that contribute to interest and success in learning. One of the key elements of the instructional design process mentioned in Chapter 1 is the need to consider the learners for whom a program is being developed. Obviously, the measure of success of an instructional plan will depend principally on the learning level accomplished by the learners involved. Learner populations, from elementary levels through high school and college and in training areas (whether industrial, business, health, government, or military) are composed of varied types of people.

Just as people differ in many respects, so do ways in which they learn differ. Some of these differences are evident in the kinds of experiences each person requires to learn and, if competence in a skill is to be acquired, in the amount of time and practice each person needs. It is essential, therefore, early in the planning process, to give attention to the characteristics, abilities, and experiences of the learners—both as a group and as individuals. To serve either an academic class or a training group, the instructional designer must obtain information about the capabilities, needs, and interests of the learners. This information should affect certain elements in planning, such as the selection of topics (and the level at which topics are introduced), the choice and sequencing of objectives, the depth of topic treatment, and the variety of learning activities.

When designing an instructional plan, decide early in the initial design stages which characteristics of your learners or trainees it would be most useful to identify. Then decide how to acquire the necessary information.

Often in learning, it is easier to understand a process by seeing an example of a final product. Here is one to consider: It is from a learner analysis that two of the authors (Ross and Morrison) conducted for a project involving the design of computer-based support tools. What follows is the summary section (using fictitious labels in places) of our final report:

- The employees to be trained are generally motivated to improve their skills and efficiency.
- New employees often start the job without adequate training.
- More employees with experience work in Section GM than in Section EO.
- Most employees are very knowledgeable about their jobs.
- Employees are generally positive about their jobs, but feel that they are inhibited by limitations of the existing computer system.
- Other employee frustrations stem from a perceived lack of understanding by other groups as to what their group needs. This is particularly strong among Section EO employees, who feel that Section A's staff needs to better understand EO's needs for orders and other tasks.
- Most users characterize themselves primarily as problem solvers.
- Employees are generally well educated and have good reading and cognitive skills.
- Employees feel great time pressure to complete their job requirements.

Based on the above characterizations and more detailed, job-specific information, we were able to make much more informed decisions about different aspects of the instructional design. For example, we decided that computer support tools requiring any substantive off-task time (e.g., receiving a CBI tutorial lesson on a particular job procedure) would rarely be used by the target employees. To derive this information, however, we needed to orient our learner analysis around characteristics most likely to impact the learning task. Let's now examine strategies and schemes for identifying these key learner differences.

TYPES OF LEARNER CHARACTERISTICS

There are countless traits that differentiate learners. In initiating learner analysis, the important task for the designer is to identify those most critical to the achievement of the specific training objectives. Also, in most applied contexts, the accessibility of learner information will be a major factor in deciding on which traits to consider. For example, where general intellectual ability is considered an important variable relating to success in the training program, administering individual IQ tests at several hundred dollars per student may be viewed as extravagant or certainly impractical relative to using some existing ability or aptitude score. On the other hand, a variable such as gender or work experience may be highly accessible but have little relevance to the particular instructional design decisions.

Heinich, Molenda, Russell, and Smaldino (1996) suggest that designers initially consider learner characteristics in terms of three categories: general characteristics, specific entry characteristics, and learning styles. Let's briefly examine each category, while remembering that on an actual design project (for example, training accountants to use new spreadsheet software) the importance of specific traits within each category will depend on both task *relevance* and *accessibility* of the learner information.

General Characteristics

General characteristics are broad identifying variables such as gender, age, work experience, education, and ethnicity. We will examine several of these variables in more detail below, but for now consider the example of training employees to use a new accounting spreadsheet. Recognizing that you have not yet conducted a needs analysis (Chapter 2) or task analysis (Chapter 4), try to form some preliminary impressions of some training approaches you might use. Would you rely primarily on a workshop or lecture? A print manual? On-the-job coaching? Job aids or guide sheets? Some combination? At this point, it's probably pure speculation, but would your "best-guess" first idea change if you were told that the employees were all novice accountants in their early 20s? What if all were disadvantaged teenagers hired for the summer on a school-to-work program? What if they were senior accountants with extensive experience on numerous spreadsheet applications? And, finally, the designer's frequent challenge—what if the employees comprised a mixture of experts, novices, and paraprofessionals with diverse job and software experiences? Given these thoughts, the importance of a prior needs (or goal) analysis and present understanding of how general learner traits may impact addressing those needs in the training design should be evident.

Specific Entry Competencies

Specific entry competencies are prerequisite skills and attitudes that the learners must possess in order to benefit from the training. Based on our experiences, we have found the analysis of such competencies is important at two stages in the design process. One stage *precedes* the design of the instruction and determines the entry characteristics of typical target students or trainees. In the example of the accounting spreadsheet project, it would certainly help to know that the majority of employees to be trained have had limited experiences in using computers in their work; or that most are highly educated with strong reading skills; or that most are extremely negative about using the new application and are likely to resist the training. Knowing learner skills or aptitudes is obviously important in determining the appropriate difficulty level of instruction. We recommend making the difficulty level *slightly higher* than that considered optimum for the average learner. Consequently, the instruction will be challenging, but not overly demanding for most learners; and it is usually easier to provide supplementary support for learners experiencing difficulty than it is to make too-easy content interesting and challenging for the majority.

The preceding sentence suggests the second stage of design during which the assessment of specific entry competencies comes directly into play. Once the instruction is designed, it is highly useful and often essential to include entry tests that determine students' readiness. For example, if one of the accounting trainees was completely unfamiliar with the computer system used in the training, a prerequisite training session to provide the needed background could prevent a situation in which that individual becomes lost and frustrated during the actual instruction. At the opposite extreme, an entry assessment may identify several trainees who have already mastered the instructional objectives and, therefore, do not need the training. Heinich et al. (1996) suggest clearly stating prerequisite competencies as part of the instructional program, such as: "The accounting trainee must be able to start up the computer and format a floppy disk for saving files."

Learning Styles

Learning styles are traits that refer to how individuals approach learning tasks and process information. Simply put, some learners find certain methods of learning more appealing and effective than others. For a long time it has been known that, rather than attending lectures and reading textual material, some individuals learn better from a visual approach to studying, and others learn from physical activities and the manipulation of objects. Attempting to identify a person's unique learning style preference can aid planning for small-group or individualized instruction.

Despite the extensive literature on learning styles, questions remain regarding the degree to which such styles can be matched to teaching methods with any benefits for learning (Knight, Halpin, & Halpin, 1992; Snow, 1992). This concern has been raised in general with regard to *aptitude-treatment interaction* (ATI) research, the attempt to systematically adapt instructional methodologies to individual learner characteristics (see review by Jonassen & Grabowski, 1993). For the designer, then, the potential value of knowing students' learning styles must be weighed against the effort required to obtain that information (e.g., administer and score a learning styles inventory) and the likelihood that useful and practical adaptations of instructional strategies can be achieved. In our view, the primary context in which you may want to consider learning styles is one-to-one instruction where materials and strategies can be easily adapted to accommodate individual needs.

On many instructional tasks, an individual's **cognitive learning style** may influence how they receive and process information. A student's cognitive learning style can be defined using inventories and questionnaires. Felder and Silverman (1988) have developed one set of common categories for analysis:

1. How information is best perceived
   - *visual*—through pictures, diagrams, and demonstrations
   - *auditory*—through words and sounds
2. Type of information preferentially perceived
   - *sensory* (external)—sights, sounds, and physical sensations
   - *intuitive* (internal)—insights and hunches
3. How information is organized
   - *inductive*—from facts and observations to infer a principle
   - *deductive*—from a principle to deduce applications and consequences
4. How information is processed
   - *actively*—through physical engagement or discussion
   - *reflectively*—through introspection
5. How progress toward understanding takes place
   - *sequentially*—as a series of related steps
   - *globally*—as a large jump or holistically

The Kolb Learning Style Inventory (Kolb, 1984, 1985) and the Myers-Briggs Type Indicator (Myers & McCaulley, 1985) are examples of self-scoring inventories that can help both individual students and instructors identify cognitive learning styles. Students who study individually and have choices can adapt activities and resources to their own styles. Instructors can use the information to address the various cognitive learning styles. Following are some useful techniques for general application (terms in parentheses refer to categories of cognitive learning-style behaviors listed earlier) as developed by Felder and Silverman (1988):

- Relate information being presented to what has come before and what is still to come (*inductive/global*).
- Provide a balance of concrete information and abstract concepts (*sensory/intuitive*).

- Balance material that emphasizes practical problem-solving methods (*sensing/active*) with material that emphasizes fundamental understandings (*intuitive/reflective*).
- Use pictures, schematics, and simple sketches along with verbal information (*sensory/active*).
- Provide demonstrations (*sensing/visual*), hands-on activities (*active*), and computer-based learning (*sensing/active*).
- Provide intervals during presentations for students to think about what they have been told (*reflective*).
- Assign drill exercises to provide practice (*sensing/active/sequential*).
- Provide open-ended problems and exercises that call for analysis and synthesis (*intuitive/reflective/global*).
- Give students opportunities to work together on assignments and group activities (*active*).
- Provide concrete examples of how a theory describes or predicts events (*sensing/inductive*); then develop the theory or formulate the model (*intuitive/inductive/sequential*); and show how the theory can be validated and deduce its consequences (*deductive*).
- Recognize students' creative solutions or activities (*intuitive/global*).

Again, you as the designer will need to weigh, on the basis of practical considerations and instructional needs, the degree to which assessing learning styles will be useful to the design project. Academic information, our next focus, will more often be a key variable for instructional planning and delivery.

ACADEMIC INFORMATION

Probably the most easily obtainable and the most often used category of information about individual learners is an academic record. This record would include:

- School grade or training level completed and major subject areas studied
- Grade-point average or letter grades for academic studies
- Scores on standardized achievement tests of intelligence and in such basic skills as reading, writing, and mathematics
- Special or advanced courses completed relating to the academic major or area of training

Much of this information is available from student records on file in a school's administrative office. Some of it is available on employment applications or in a personnel file. Confidentiality and ethical considerations must be kept in mind when referring to student or personnel records. If a specific kind of information about learners is not available, specialized tests can be obtained and administered through a testing or personnel office.

Closely associated with the academic information about learners are the knowledge and skills that learners may already possess directly relating to the subject content or skills to be learned. Obtaining knowledge and skills information is one of the purposes for the pretesting element of the instructional design process (see Chapter 10). Thus, there is a close relationship between the information gathered about learner characteristics and the data to be acquired from pretests.

PERSONAL AND SOCIAL CHARACTERISTICS

In addition to academic information, it is desirable to be aware of the personal and social characteristics of the learner for whom the program is intended. Typically, information about the following types of variables would be helpful to the designer:

- Age and maturity level
- Motivation and attitude toward the subject
- Expectations and vocational aspirations (if appropriate)
- Previous or current employment and work experience (if any)
- Special talents
- Mechanical dexterity
- Ability to work under various environmental conditions, such as noise, working outdoors during inclement weather, high elevations, and so on

Looking at this list and thinking of your recent experiences, which variables do you feel are most important for instruction or training? Much would depend on the nature and conditions of the learning activities. For many instructors, learner motivation is actually considered to be the most important determinant of success (Dick & Carey, 1996; Pintrich, Roeser, & De Groot, 1994). Learners who "just don't care" or worse, are actively resistant to the instruction, are not likely to respond in the same way to the learning activities as would highly motivated students. Design strategies that create interest and attention would be appropriate for the former group.

Learner attitude is somewhat different from motivation. For example, a learner may be interested in taking a basic electronics course, but he may feel doubtful that he can pass it based on his poor abilities. This type of self-fulfilling prophecy breeds failure by anticipating failure (Slavin, 1994). If the designer found such negative attitudes to be common for the target learner groups, she might employ strategies specifically intended to build confidence in the learner's abilities as the lesson proceeds (Jonassen & Grabowski, 1993). One possibility would be to begin the instruction with very easy content and gradually increase difficulty over time. (B. F. Skinner, in fact, employed a similar orientation, called "successive approximations" or "shaping," in designing programmed instruction.)

The manual dexterity and other special motor skills of the learner may be of major importance in certain training programs. As will be discussed in Chapter 5, the classification of motor skills has had less acceptance and less practical impact than has occurred for the cognitive and affective domains. Yet, several potential useful taxonomies exist, such as those by Heinich et al. (1996) and Kibler (1981).

The learner analysis may also reveal physical characteristics of potential students that are relevant to training decisions, such as health, physical fitness, weight, or disabilities. For example, one training program recently offered by a school district included, as a team-building exercise for administrators and teachers, an outdoor expedition requiring hiking and climbing. For several participants, these activities proved highly strenuous and produced negative feelings about the training (not to mention soreness and muscle aches the next day as a continuing reminder!).

Useful data about personal and social characteristics may be obtained by observation, interviews, and informational questionnaires, as well as from attitudinal surveys completed by learners. (See Chapter 11 for further discussion about these information-gathering methods.) If special groups comprise a significant percentage of the student population, social characteristics peculiar to each group should be given due consideration.

CHARACTERISTICS OF NONCONVENTIONAL LEARNERS

While it is important during planning to gather and use the usual kinds of information—academic, personal, and social—about all learners, attention also should be given to the special characteristics of those individuals described as *nonconventional learners,* whose preparation, behavior, and expectations may not be typical. These groups include individuals who are culturally diverse, learners with disabilities, and adult learners.

Culturally Diverse Learners

Learner groups may include members of ethnic cultures with backgrounds and behaviors that differ markedly from those of the majority of learners or trainees. Also, both the instructional designer and instructors who will deliver the instruction may differ in ethnic background from members of the student group. For these reasons, characteristics of culturally diverse learners need special attention during planning.

One obvious problem may be deficiency in the English language. If this is true, remedial training in English (or the language in which the instruction will be conducted) must be provided as needed (Ovando, 1989). Cultural and social differences should be recognized because they can affect such things as the ability to take responsibility for individualized work or to engage in creative activities. In some cultures an accepted strong authority figure, like the father in a family, influences the freedom and decision-making abilities of children. If background experiences are limited, a resulting naiveté and lack of sophistication may affect a learner's readiness for and participation in a program. In planning instruction for culturally diverse learners, care should also be given to selecting bias-free materials and providing alternative resources and activities to support instructional objectives.

To build confidence in their ability to succeed, individuals from culturally diverse groups may need more than routine teaching procedures. Such consideration can be essential, whether the learners are in an academic or a vocational training program. Some of the considerations that may be employed in helping these learners become successful in learning are:

- To provide incentives, such as personal recognition, monetary awards, or free time, as motivators for engaging in and continuing with learning
- To provide for cooperative activities, since many minority learners gain satisfaction from group projects and from assisting others. (On the other hand, some groups who are more competitive by nature may be less receptive to working in groups.)
- To employ a more visual than verbal treatment for presenting elements of a topic
- To provide extra examples as illustrations of generalizations
- To allow more time than usual for studying and completing assignments, within reasonable constraints, and more opportunity to practice a skill
- To provide many occasions for a learner to check his or her success in learning and progress toward a goal

Some of these considerations may seem to be simply common sense, but they are important for all learners. Furthermore, they are particularly valuable when preparing instruction for learners with a cultural background that differs from that of the instructor.

Information about the abilities of learners in ethnic groups can be obtained through the usual testing, interview, and questionnaire procedures, as well as from the literature (e.g., Garcia, 1991). In addition, consider getting help from counselors in an organization or the community who have had direct experience in working with such individuals.

Learners with Disabilities

The category of learners who are disabled includes individuals with physical disabilities and others with learning disabilities such as hearing and vision loss, speech impairment, and mild mental retardation. Each type of handicapped learner has unique limitations and requires special consideration. While some persons with physical disabilities can participate in regular classes, others cannot. A careful analysis of individual abilities should include observation, interviews, and testing.

Many learners with disabilities require special training and individual attention. Therefore, an instructional program may require extensive modification in order to serve such learners appropriately. Specialists who are capable of working with individuals with disabilities should be a part of any instructional planning team.

Adult Learners

An important factor reducing the homogeneity of learner populations is the increasing number of adults who have become learners in these settings: returning to colleges and universities; engaging in community adult education programs; and participating in job training or retraining for new skills in business, industry, health fields, government service, and the military.

The field of adult education, known as **andragogy,** has been studied at length. Those who work in this field recognize a number of generalizations regarding adults and their accommodation in the educational process:

- Adults enter an education or training program with a high level of motivation to learn. They appreciate a program that is structured systematically with requirements (objectives) clearly specified.
- Adults want to know how the content that will be taught will benefit them. They expect the material to be relevant, and they quickly grasp the practical use of the content.
- To adults, time is an important consideration. They expect the class to start and finish on schedule, and they do not like to waste time.
- Adults respect an instructor who is fully knowledgeable about the subject and presents it effectively. Students quickly detect an unprepared instructor.
- Adults bring to a class extensive experience from their personal and working lives. These experiences should be used as major resources by helping students relate to the subject being studied.
- Most mature adults are self-directed and independent. While some adults lack confidence and need reassurance, they would prefer that the instructor serve as facilitator to guide and assist rather than as an authoritarian leader.
- Adults want to participate in decision making. They want to cooperate with the instructor in mutual assessment of needs and goals, the choice of activities, and decisions on how to evaluate learning.
- Adults may be less flexible than younger students. Their habits and methods of operation have been developed into a routine. They do not like to be placed in embarrassing situations. Before they accept a different way of doing something, they want to understand the advantages of doing so.
- Adults like to cooperate in groups and socialize together. Small-group activities and an atmosphere for interaction during breaks are important.

For adults, as well as for other learners, the same principles of human learning and behavior must form the basis of an instructional program. (These principles will receive attention in Chapter 7.) There are differences in degree and specificity as to how the principles should be applied with certain groups during planning, when media are designed, and when instructional activities are carried out. By being sensitive and alert to the characteristics of special groups of learners, a designer can plan programs especially effective for them.

SUMMARY

1. By considering the results of task or goal analysis and the likely conditions of training (practical constraints, setting, duration), the designer needs to identify the learner characteristics most likely to have an impact on instructional outcomes.
2. Three categories of learner traits are general characteristics (gender, age, ethnicity), specific entry characteristics (prerequisite skills for the instruction), and learning styles (preferred ways of learning).
3. Knowing about students' learning styles provides a potentially valuable basis for adapting instruction, but valid learner classifications and beneficial instructional adaptations may be difficult to achieve in practice.
4. Academic records reveal the extent and quality of schooling or training that learners have already received.
5. Through observation, interviews, and questionnaires, indications of personal and social characteristics of learners can be obtained.
6. Nonconventional learners include culturally diverse learners, adult learners, and learners with disabilities. Special characteristics of such individuals should be recognized and considered during planning.

FROM HERE TO THERE

You have been asked to design a training program to improve the collaborative skills of employees at a major marketing company. It is March and the documented training design is due in late July. Time is therefore short and, as you soon discover, the target employees are very busy and not highly accessible for providing information. First, you will want to consider the needs (or goal) analysis that you already completed. Then, you will need to reflect on practical considerations involving your time schedule and the accessibility of information about the prospective trainees.

In thinking about *general characteristics*, you identify the variables of age, work experience, work level, education, and ethnicity as relevant, easily obtainable information. The personnel office promises to make these data available. For *specific entry characteristics*, you define as most critical to identify the employees' prior experiences at collaborating with others and their skills at practicing particular collaborative strategies. You then develop a plan for surveying 50 employees and interviewing 10 on these strategies; you also decide to make four site visits to observe employees' typical interactions during the work day. You consider *learning style* as an additional variable, but decide that the employees are too diverse and the prescribed training conditions too constrained to permit useful learning style adaptations.

Based on your data collection and "analysis" of findings, you begin the next phase of the design process—task analysis (Chapter 4)—with the knowledge that your learners are well educated; highly diverse in job experience, ethnicity, and age; predominantly working in high level (manager) positions; and very inexperienced in collaboration but highly motivated to improve their skills and participate in training. This information will facilitate your decisions throughout the remainder of the design process. Do you agree with the characteristics identified?

REFERENCES

Dick, W., & Carey, L. (1996). *The systematic design of instruction.* New York: HarperCollins College Publishers.

Felder, R. M., & Silverman, L. K. (1988). Learning and teaching styles in engineering education. *Engineering Education, 78*(7), 674–681.

Garcia, R. L. (1991). *Teaching in a pluralistic society: Concepts, models, and strategies.* New York: HarperCollins.

Heinich, R., Molenda, M., Russell, J., & Smaldino, S. (1996). *Instructional media and technologies for learning* (5th ed.). Englewood Cliffs, NJ: Prentice-Hall.

Jonassen, D. H., & Grabowski, B. L. (1993). *Handbook of individual differences, learning, and instruction.* Hillsdale, NJ: Erlbaum.

Kibler, R. J. (1981). *Objectives for instruction and evaluation.* Boston: Allyn & Bacon.

Knight, C. B., Halpin, G., & Halpin, G. (1992, April). The effects of learning environment accommodations on the achievement of second graders. Paper presented at the annual meeting of the American Educational Research Association, San Francisco.

Kolb, D. (1984). *Experiential learning: Experience as the source of learning and development.* Englewood Cliffs, NJ: Prentice-Hall.

Kolb, D. (1985). *Self-scoring inventory and interpretive booklet.* Boston: McBer.

Myers, I. B., & McCaulley, M. H. (1985). *Manual: A guide to the development and use of the Myers-Briggs Type Indicator.* Palo Alto, CA: Consulting Psychologists.

Ovando, C. J. (1989). Language diversity and education. In J. Banks and C. McGee Banks (Eds.). *Multicultural education: Issues and perspectives* (pp. 208–228). Boston: Allyn & Bacon.

Pintrich, P. R., Roeser, R. W., & De Groot, E. A. M. (1994). Classroom and individual differences in early adolescents' motivation and self-regulated learning. *Journal of Early Adolescence, 14,* 139–161.

Slavin, R. E. (1994). *Educational psychology* (4th ed.). Needham Heights, MA: Allyn & Bacon.

Snow, R. E. (1992). Aptitude theory: Yesterday, today, and tomorrow. *Educational Psychologist, 27,* 5–32.

TASK ANALYSIS

"What skills and information are necessary to address the identified needs?"

"What related subject content should be taught?"

"How can the subject content items be organized?"

"How is a task analyzed to identify its components and then to sequence the actions required?"

"To what other elements of the instructional design process is task analysis most closely related?"

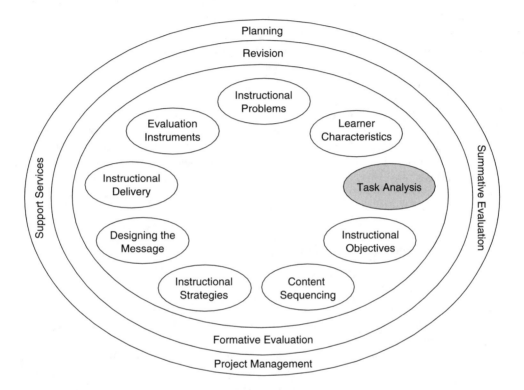

The diagram shows concentric ovals. The outermost ring contains: Planning, Revision, Summative Evaluation, Formative Evaluation, Project Management, Support Services. The inner circle contains: Instructional Problems, Learner Characteristics, Evaluation Instruments, Task Analysis, Instructional Delivery, Instructional Objectives, Designing the Message, Content Sequencing, Instructional Strategies.

T
ask analysis is probably the most critical step in the instructional design process. If a designer has not defined the content to include in the instructional package, there is little value in or need for designing an instructional strategy, producing appropriate media, or conducting an evaluation. The instructional design process depends on the concise definition of the content that is the object of the instructional materials. Jonassen, Hannum, and Tessmer (1989) consider task analysis the most critical part of the instructional design process. The analysis solves three problems for the designer:

1. It defines the content required to solve the performance problem or alleviate a performance need. This step is crucial since most designers are working with unfamiliar content.
2. Because the process forces the subject-matter expert to work through each individual step, subtle steps are more easily identified.

3. During this process, the designer has the opportunity to view the content from the learner's perspective. Using this perspective, the designer can often gain insight into appropriate teaching strategies.

Jonassen and his colleagues have identified 27 different task-analysis procedures that instructional designers can use to define the content for an instructional package. Selecting the best or most appropriate technique depends on a number of factors, including the purpose for conducting the task analysis, the nature of the task or content, and the environment in which the task is performed.

The terminology associated with topic and task analysis is often confusing. The instructional design literature frequently refers to the process of analyzing content as task analysis. Specific analysis procedures also go by a host of names. Some individuals refer to task analysis as a specific procedure for defining psychomotor skills, which leads to further confusion. In this book, we refer to **task analysis** as the collection of procedures for defining the content of an instructional unit.

INPUT FOR TASK ANALYSIS

An analysis of the content required for instruction does not begin in a vacuum. It begins with the needs or goals derived from the definition of the instructional problem (see Chapter 2). These needs or goals provide an initial definition of the breadth of the project and provide the designer a focus. For example, if you were designing a unit of instruction on cardiac care for medical doctors, would you begin with emergency-room care, bypass surgery, or rehabilitation of a patient who had suffered a heart attack? If you have properly defined the instructional problem, the problem statement and needs or goals will provide the initial direction and breadth of your analysis. Thus, a unit on cardiac care might focus only on rehabilitation as a result of the problem identification. A second input is from the learner analysis (see Chapter 3). An understanding of the learner's knowledge and background related to the topic helps the designer determine the beginning point for the analysis as well as the depth and breadth of analysis. The output of the analysis is the documentation of the content to include in the instructional materials. This output then serves as an input for developing instructional objectives (see Chapter 5).

Preparing to Conduct a Task Analysis

A task analysis can take many different forms. The methods and individuals involved will vary depending on the circumstances. Designers most often work with a subject-matter expert, an individual who is an expert in the content area. The subject-matter expert (SME) is our link to the content; we rely on this individual (or individuals) to provide accurate, detailed information to use in developing the instructional unit. Our task as designers is to help the SME elaborate on the content in a meaningful, sequential manner. The designer is responsible for obtaining a complete analysis, while the SME is responsible for providing accurate information and suggesting where gaps may exist in the original goals.

In educational settings, the instructor often serves as both the SME and instructional designer, an often difficult but necessary combination of responsibilities. The teacher/SME/designer is responsible for providing a global view ("Are all the steps and information defined?") as well as a microscopic view ("What result or condition is required before doing the next step?").

In this chapter we will describe three specific techniques for analyzing content and tasks. First, we will discuss how to conduct a topic analysis that is well suited for defining cognitive knowledge. Second, we will explain how to conduct a procedural analysis for use with psychomotor tasks, job tasks, or cognitive sequences involving a series of steps. Third, we will describe the critical incident method, which is useful for analyzing interpersonal skills.

Topic Analysis

Assume you are a student attending a lecture. As the instructor delivers the lecture, what are you doing? Probably taking notes so you can capture the essence of the content. You may take notes in detailed sentences or in an outline form, such as the following:

> *Topic: The Circulatory System*
>
> I. Types of vessels in closed circulatory system
>   A. Arteries—carry blood away from heart
>   B. Veins—carry blood toward heart
>   C. Capillaries—final division of arteries unite to form first small veins
> II. Circulation
>   A. Systemic—supplies most of body (aorta)
>   B. Pulmonary—supplies lungs
>   C. Coronary—within heart

We are all familiar with this procedure of outlining information as it is presented in a lecture. Now, reverse the procedure. You are the person who will deliver the lecture. What is your preparation? You either write out the lecture in a narrative form to read as written, or, with experience, you prepare an outline consisting of the main headings, supporting details, and examples. This outline becomes the framework for reference as a guide to your presentation.

Change the situation yet again, and imagine you are a designer working for a hardware store who must prepare a manual for customers on how to select an appropriate wood fastener. Your manager has assigned an SME to work with you on the project. You would follow a similar process to define the content so the outline becomes a reference for designing the instruction.

The topic analysis or concept hierarchy analysis is used to define the facts, concepts, principles, and rules that will make up the final instruction. Such an analysis is typically done in layers much like an archeologist excavating a site. First, the top layer of soil is scraped away. Then layers of earth are removed, and each artifact's identity and location are recorded. Similarly, a designer working with the SME carefully reveals the first layer of information while looking for indicators of content structure (facts, concept, principles, and rules). Once the structure is revealed, additional detail is gathered for each structure, and new information appears as he or she digs deeper into the content.

A topic analysis thus provides two types of information. First, it identifies the content that is the subject of the intended instruction. Second, it identifies the structure of the components. Let's first examine these content or knowledge structures and then describe the process for conducting a topic analysis.

Content Structure

Most instructional design models provide a scheme for classifying information into discrete categories (Reigeluth, 1983). These classifications are then used to identify the appropriate instructional strategy (see Chapter 7). Six structures are often associated with a topic analysis: facts, concepts, principles or rules, procedures, interpersonal skills, and attitudes.

Facts.   A *fact* is an arbitrary association between two things. For example, "Columbus discovered America" is a fact that describes a relationship between Columbus and America. Learning a fact requires only the memorization and recall of the fact. Examples of facts are listed here:

> Names, symbols, labels, places, dates
> Definitions
> Descriptions of objects or events

Most topics include many facts, since they are the building blocks or tools of any subject—the "vocabulary" the student must master for understanding. Verbal information or facts are preparation for more complex ways of organizing the content. Unless the facts are arranged in structured patterns, they will be of limited use to a student and are often quickly forgotten. Facts are easy to identify but often confused with the second category, concepts.

Concepts.   *Concepts* are categories used for grouping similar or related ideas, events, or objects. For example, we might use the concept "soft drinks" to categorize the aisle in the grocery store that contains colas, orange drink, root beer, and so forth. The concept of fruit would include apples, oranges, bananas, and dates, but not potatoes. We use concepts to simplify information by grouping similar ideas or objects together and assigning the grouping a name (e.g., fruit). Some concepts such as fruit are considered concrete concepts because we can easily show an example. Concepts such as safety, liberty, peace, and justice are abstract concepts since they are difficult to represent or illustrate.

Principles or Rules. A *principle* or *rule* describes a relationship between two concepts. In microeconomics we can derive several principles from a supply and demand curve. For example, *as price increases, the supply increases* is a principle that describes a direct relationship between the concepts (price and supply) that increase and decrease together. *As price decreases, the demand increases* describes a different relationship between price and demand that causes one to increase as the other decreases. *Stop at a red light* or *release the pressure before opening a pressure cooker* are also examples of principles.

Procedures. A *procedure* is an ordered sequence of steps a learner must execute to complete a task. For example, the back of many bank statements lists a series of steps for balancing a checkbook. This series of steps is a procedure. Similarly, a recipe for making a cake or casserole is a procedure. A procedure could be a series of psychomotor steps needed to plant a rose bush or it could be a complex series of cognitive processes required to debug a computer program.

Interpersonal Skills. Verbal and nonverbal (e.g., body language) *skills* for interacting with other people are grouped in this category. An objective for a manager training program requiring the development of interviewing skills is an example of this category. Content related to solving group conflict, leading a group, and demonstrating how to sit when interviewed are also examples of behaviors in this category. This broad category would include behaviors and objectives related to interpersonal communication.

Attitudes. *Attitudes* are predispositions to behavior. Although often overlooked, attitudes are a part of many instructional programs. For example, a training program might emphasize the safety procedures for replacing a seal on a gas valve. Corporate employees who have access to confidential financial information must complete a course that explains the misuse of this information (e.g., insider training). Such programs contain information on the laws governing the use of this information (e.g., concepts and rules) as well as a component to develop appropriate attitudes toward corporate responsibility and proper behavior.

Analyzing a Topic

Let's examine a topic analysis on wood fasteners and define each of the content structures with an example. To begin, we first asked our SME to describe the different types of wood fasteners. Our question produced the following outline:

    I. Nails
   II. Screws
  III. Bolts

Our SME considered these three major categories adequate to describe the various types of fasteners. Next, we asked the SME to further define each of these categories. He expanded our outline as follows:

I. Nails
  A. Generally made from wire
  B. Range in size from 2-penny to 60-penny
    1. Length of nails 10-penny or less is determined by
      a. Dividing size by 4 and adding 0.5 inch.
      b. Example: 7-penny nail is 2.25 inches long.
  C. Typically driven into one or more pieces of wood with a hammer
II. Screws
  A. Made of steel
  B. Size determined by the gauge (thickness) and length
    1. Length varies from 0.25 to 6 inches.
  C. Usually twisted into a hole with screwdriver
  D. Screws provide a more secure joint than nails.
III. Bolts
  A. Made from steel
  B. Measured by length and diameter
    1. Available in fine or coarse threads.
  C. Bolt is placed through a hole and then a nut is tightened from opposite side.

Let's examine the content structure identified in the outline. Some of the *facts* identified in the outline are:

Generally made from wire
Made of steel
Measured by length and diameter
Available in fine or coarse threads

The *concepts* identified in the topic analysis are:

Nail
Screw
Bolt

One *procedure* was identified in the content analysis:

Length of nails 10-penny or less is determined by dividing size by 4 and adding 0.5 inch.

Our SME helped us identify one *principle* in the content:

Screws provide a more secure joint than nails.

Next, our SME decided to provide detailed information on each fastener category starting with nails. Once we finished the analysis, we organized the content. This organization process included the following steps:

1. Review the analysis, and identify the different content structures (facts, concepts, principles, interpersonal skills, and attitudes).
2. Group related facts, concepts, principles, interpersonal skills, and attitudes. For example, in our full outline of wood fasteners, we would group all the information about nails, then the information about screws, and so forth.

3. Arrange the various components into a logical, sequential order.
4. Prepare the final outline to represent your content analysis.

The completed topic analysis on nails was as follows:

I. Nails
   A. Generally made from wire
   B. Range in size from 2-penny to 60-penny
      1. Length of nails 10-penny or less is determined by
         a. Dividing size by 4 and adding 0.5 inch.
         b. Example: 7-penny nail is 2.25 inches long.
      2. Size is written as 2d for "2 penny."
   C. Typically driven into one or more pieces of wood with a hammer
   D. Types of nails
      1. Common nails
         a. Most commonly used nail
         b. Available in sizes from 2d to 60d
            (1) 8d size is most common.
         c. Identified by flat head
         d. Used for general purposes
      2. Box nails
         a. Smaller in diameter than common nails
         b. Available in sizes ranging from 2d to 40d
         c. Also identified by its flat head
         d. Used in lumber that may split easily
         e. Often used for nailing siding
      3. Finishing nails
         a. Have a very small head that will not show
            (1) Head can be sunk into the wood and hole filled.
         b. Available in sizes 2d to 20d
         c. Used primarily for finish work and cabinetry
      4. Common brads
         a. Similar to finishing nails but much smaller
         b. Available in various lengths
            (1) Length expressed in inches or part of an inch
         c. Used for finishing work
      5. Roofing nails
         a. Similar to common nails but with a larger head
         b. Available in lengths from 0.75 inch to 2 inches
            (1) Available in various diameters
         c. Used for roofing[1]

How detailed should a topic analysis be? A designer needs to break down the content to a level appropriate for the learner. There are two sources for determining

---

[1]Information for this content analysis is based on a chapter by Phipps (1977).

the needed level of detail. First, the learner analysis describes the learner's knowledge of the content area; it is used as a general guide for the amount of information needed. A course on home repair for apprentice carpenters, for example, will require a different amount of detail than a course for homeowners. Second, the SME is often a source of information concerning the learners' entry-level knowledge. A combination of these two sources will provide a basis for determining the level of detail needed in this initial analysis. During the development and formative evaluation stages, you might find a need for additional information.

PROCEDURAL ANALYSIS

Procedural analysis is used to analyze tasks by identifying the steps required to complete them. The process breaks tasks into the size of steps needed for learning. Some designers distinguish between procedural analysis and information-processing analysis (Jonassen et al., 1989). The major distinction is that procedural analysis focuses on *observable tasks* (e.g., changing a tire), while information-processing analysis focuses on *cognitive* or *unobservable tasks,* such as deciding which stock to add to a portfolio for diversification. In recent years, the distinction between the two methods has decreased because cognitive psychology has shown the importance of cognitive steps in observable processes. We will use procedural analysis to refer to the analysis of both observable and unobservable behaviors.

Conducting a procedural analysis is a matter of walking through the steps with an SME, preferably in the environment in which the task is performed. For example, if you are conducting a procedural analysis for sharpening an ax blade, the SME should have an ax and the necessary tools. Similarly, if you are analyzing how to calculate your home's electrical bill, you will need an electric meter (or at least a picture of the dial) and the electrical rates. Each step of analysis includes three questions:

1. What does the learner do?
   - Identify the action in each step that the learner must perform.
   - These actions are either physical (e.g., loosening a bolt) or mental (e.g., adding two numbers).
2. What does the learner need to know to do this step?
   - What knowledge (e.g., temperature, pressure, orientation) is necessary?
   - What does the learner need to know about the location or orientation of the components that are a part of this step (e.g., how to position a wrench to remove a hidden nut)?
3. What cues (tactile, smell, touch, visual, etc.) inform the learner that there is a problem, the step is done, or a different step is needed (e.g., a blinking light indicates you can release the starter switch)?

In the following procedural analysis, we visited a cabinetmaker and asked him how to prepare a piece of woodwork for the final finish. During the analysis, we asked him variations of the three questions described in the previous paragraphs to identify the steps, knowledge, and cues. As part of our analysis, he informed us that someone who finishes furniture would already know the basics of sanding and using a paint sprayer. Our analysis produced the following steps:

1. Inspect all surfaces for defects.
   Tactile cue: Feel for dents, scratches, and other surface defects.
   Visual cue: Splits or cracks are normally visible.
2. Repair defects.
   a. Sand, glue, or fill minor defects.
   b. Reject pieces that you cannot repair for rework.
3. Spray two coats of lacquer sanding sealer on all surfaces.
   Visual cue: Dry, misty appearance indicates too-light application.
   Visual cue: Runs or sags indicate too-heavy application.
4. Final preparation.
   a. Allow a 20-minute minimum drying time for sealer coat.
   b. After drying, rub out all parts with #400 grit silicon carbide abrasive paper.
   c. Remove dust from all surfaces with air gun, then wipe with clean, lint-free cloth.
5. Final finish.
   a. Spray two coats of finishing lacquer on all parts.
      Visual cue: Dry, misty finish indicates too-light application.
      Visual cue: Runs and sags indicate too-heavy application.
   b. Allow a minimum of four hours for second coat to dry.

1. Inspect final finish.
   Tactile cue: Feel for grit or runs that may not be visible.
2. Rub out all surfaces with #000 steel wool.
3. Remove dust from all finished surfaces with air gun and lint-free cloth.
   a. Apply a thin coat of wax to all finished surfaces.
   b. Buff all surfaces to high gloss.
   Visual cue: Wax becomes dull prior to buffing.

In addition to an outline, designers often use flowcharts (see Figure 4–1) and tables (see Table 4–1). The table format provides a visual prompt for the designer to ask questions to obtain information about the cues associated with each step. A flowchart is useful for identifying a specific sequence of steps the learner needs to follow as well as the key decision steps. Flowcharts are also useful for helping SMEs identify missing components and for identifying alternative procedures that may have been missed in the initial analysis. A rectangle indicates an action or knowledge in the flowchart. Diamonds indicate a question or decision point with branches off each tip to another question or action. The arrows indicate the path through the flowchart.

FIGURE 4–1
Flowchart of a procedure

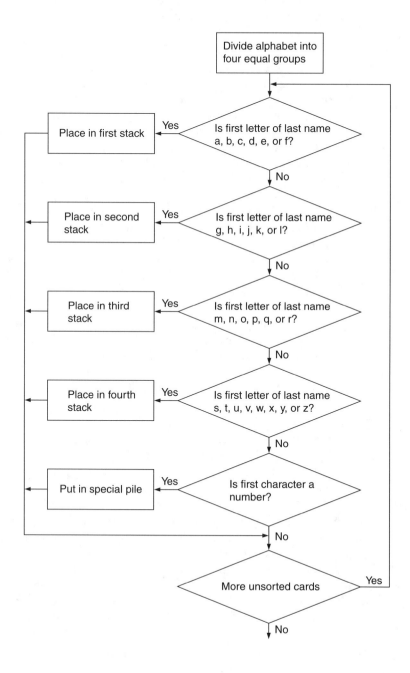

TABLE 4–1
Procedural analysis table

Step	Cue
1. Inspect all surfaces for defects.	Feel for dents, scratches, and other surface defects. Splits or cracks are normally visible.
2. Repair defects 　a. Sand, glue, or fill minor defects. 　b. Reject pieces that are not repairable for rework	
3. Spray two coats of lacquer sanding sealer on all surfaces	Dry, misty appearance indicates too-light application. Runs or sags indicate too-heavy application.

After you have collected the data for a procedural analysis, you will need to organize the information in a logical fashion. Since most procedures are sequential, they are often organized in a linear manner by the order of the steps.

We could also use a procedural analysis for a task involving primarily cognitive operations, such as alphabetizing a collection of bibliographic cards for a research paper's reference section. Again, we need to identify the steps, the knowledge associated with each step, and any cues associated with the step:

1. Divide the alphabet into four groups (e.g., a–f, g–l, etc.).
2. Sort the cards according to the first letter of the last name of the first author and place in appropriate stack.
3. When all the cards are sorted into one of the stacks, select a stack and sort the cards in the stack alphabetically according to the last name of the first author.
4. Search through the stack for duplicate cards of the first author.
5. If the duplicate card has the same authors, sort the cards by date with earliest date first.
6. If the cards have different authors after the first, sort alphabetically by second, then succeeding authors. Sort identical authors by date.
7. Repeat for each stack.
8. Sequence the stacks starting with *A*.
9. Place the cards face down on a copy machine, overlapping notes to fill the copy area.
10. Make a copy of the cards, and repeat the process until all cards are copied.
11. Attach "reference" pages to a draft of the paper.

Following is a checklist for conducting a procedural analysis:

• Are the relevant cues and feedback identified for each step of the procedure?
• Does the analysis identify the generally acceptable procedure rather than personal preferences of the SME? Tips that make a step easier are usually acceptable so long as they do not violate a safety rule.

- Are the decision steps identified (e.g., "If the blue light is on, then turn to the right; if not, turn to the left.")?
- Are all steps accurately described?
- Are critical steps that could result in personal injury, equipment damage, or other loss identified?

Procedural analyses also reveal a content structure much like a topic analysis. For the cognitive information, you need to identify the related facts, concepts, rules, and principles. Procedures or steps are grouped in several ways. One method is to classify the steps by frequency of execution (frequently, occasionally, seldom). A second method is by difficulty level (easy, moderately difficult, difficult). Psychomotor tasks may be grouped according to gross- or fine-motor skills or level proficiency (see Chapter 5).

THE CRITICAL INCIDENT METHOD

The two methods we have described—topic and procedural analysis—work well with concrete content and highly structured tasks that are easily analyzed. Analyzing a process such as how to conduct an interview, resolve an interpersonal conflict, or close a sales opportunity are more difficult because they vary from instance to instance. Although the instances share certain elements, typically the breadth of skills and techniques account for one's success. Procedural analysis works quite well for analyzing how to apply the final finish to a table, for example, because the basic process is repeated time after time, with variations due to size and type of wood. Closing a sale, however, depends on several conditions (e.g., personality of buyer, financial status of the buyer) that change with each sale. To define the content for this type of training adequately, we need a method that provides different points of view. For example, we might interview a salesperson who uses a very calm approach as opposed to another individual who uses high-pressure tactics.

A critical incidence analysis then can identify the commonalties of various approaches. The critical incident analysis provides a rich context for analyzing interpersonal skills by interviewing several individuals. In some situations, you may need to combine it with a procedural analysis to define content for designing the instruction.

The critical incident method was developed by Flanagan (1954) in World War II to determine why Army Air Force pilots were not learning to fly correctly. Pilots were interviewed to determine what conditions lead to a successful mission and what conditions lead to an unsuccessful one. A critical incident interview is based on three types of information:

1. What were the conditions before, during, and after the incident?
   - Where did the incident occur?
   - When did it occur?
   - Who was involved?
   - What equipment was used and what was its condition?

2. What did you do?
   - What did you do physically (e.g., grabbed the rudder)?
   - What did you say and to whom?
   - What were you thinking?
3. How did this incident help you to reach or prevent you from reaching your goal?

Primhoff (1973) suggests two questions to ask as part of a critical incident analysis. First, ask the SME to identify three instances when he or she was successful in doing the task. Second, ask the SME to identify three instances when he or she was not successful in doing the task. An analysis of the interviews will identify knowledge and techniques the SME used to accomplish the task. Once this information is identified, a topic and/or procedural analysis can further define the content.

The critical incident method is well suited for analyzing interpersonal skills and attitudes. If you were designing a course on classroom management for prospective teachers, you might use a critical incident analysis to determine how teachers handle a disruptive student. It is also useful for initially defining complex tasks that an SME might consider an "art." For example, a designer might use this method for initial analysis when determining where to drill an oil well, predicting successful stocks or mutual funds to purchase, or determining which type of psychotherapy to use on a patient.

CONDUCTING A TASK ANALYSIS

Your SME and the environment will influence how you conduct a topic, procedural, or critical incident analysis. If you are a classroom teacher or a part-time instructor, such as a nursing supervisor responsible for training your staff, you will most likely be your own SME. If you are an instructional designer working in a hospital, university, government agency, or business, a knowledgeable SME will most likely be assigned to work with you on the project. The environment may vary from your office to a retail store, an operating room, or an oil-drilling rig offshore. Each environment offers advantages and disadvantages.

Being Your Own SME

Being your own SME has two major advantages. First is the ease of access and scheduling meetings—you need only motivate yourself! Second, you are already familiar with the learners and the problems they have with the task. The major disadvantage is your familiarity with the content, which may cause you to skip steps and fail to identify important cues. Three techniques can counter this disadvantage. First, find another SME and assume the role of the designer. In the latter role, you will need to "forget" everything you know about the task and approach it from a naive point of view. Second, if you are conducting a procedural analysis, once you have the initial version done, ask someone else to perform the task. As the other person does the task, ask him or her to describe verbally the task. You can then check this description with yours. Third, have another expert review or actually work through your analysis to identify any missing steps, cues, or topics.

Techniques for Gathering Data

Each designer develops a repertoire of techniques for analyzing content. The first rule is to be prepared when working with SMEs. Typically they are on loan for an hour or a few days from their regular jobs. These individuals are usually experts who perform a valuable service for the organization. Adequate preparation on your part is not only courteous but shows that you respect their expertise and time. Adequate preparation includes your materials as well as adequate knowledge of the goals and problems you are trying to solve. This information was defined when you identified the instructional problem (see Chapter 2). Review those materials and, if necessary, contact some of the individuals who helped you define the problem to obtain additional clarification and understanding. The following paragraphs describe three techniques for conducting content and procedural analyses. You might use only one or a combination of all three.

Literature Research.   Reading technical manuals and other materials is the *least* preferred method of conducting an analysis. It is an inefficient way to master the content in a relatively short time. However, if the materials can give you an expert's understanding, they may be adequate for use as training materials. Reading materials to prepare for a meeting with an SME may be beneficial, but reading the materials to become an expert is often counterproductive.

Interviewing an SME.   This technique is the *most* preferred method of defining information for all three analyses. Meeting in the SME's office for an analysis that involves primarily a cognitive task has the benefit of providing easy access to the SME's resources. These resources include books as well as data to use for examples and case studies in your instruction. For example, one of the authors was developing a course on how to prepare engineering proposals. During the analysis, the SME was able to retrieve several good and bad examples from the office files. Analyzing these proposals helped in developing a procedure and checklist for proposal development as well as examples for instruction.

When conducting a procedural analysis that depends primarily on psychomotor skills, it is beneficial to schedule the SME meeting in a location where the SME can demonstrate the skills. These meetings can range from an operating room to a manufacturing plan. Sometimes a location is not available or travel or access is prohibited. For instance, one of the authors needed to analyze the tasks involved in setting the vanes on a gas turbine engine the client company manufactured but was unable to visit an installed site. After several phone calls, the SME found that each new turbine engine was run through a series of operational tests in a test cell at the plant. The SME was able to obtain the use of one of the engines for an afternoon while the analysis was conducted. For other analyses, a part was obtained from the parts warehouse, and then a meeting was scheduled with the SME in a shop to analyze the repair and maintenance of that specific part. Building and maintaining a network of key individuals is a necessary resource for an instructional designer.

Developer Modeling. This method is typically used after the initial analysis with the SME. If an instructional designer is conducting a topic analysis, the information is explained to the SME. This helps the designer check his understanding and interpretation of the content. Explaining the information to the SME will also identify topics that were not adequately explained and prompt the SME to provide additional details and examples. In a procedural analysis, the task should be demonstrated or simulated. Walking through the steps and doing the motions will help identify cues and steps that were missed in the initial analysis. For some tasks (e.g., those that are hazardous or require a great deal of skill), the designer may need to resort to only simulated actions.

Recording Methods

Another aspect of content analysis is recording the information to use in developing the instruction. Notepads and index cards are helpful for recording the topics and steps. If the task analysis is outdoors, a notepad is often preferable because it will not scatter if dropped. Index cards provide flexibility in adding new topics or steps; it is very easy to label an index card as 10A and place it in the stack between cards 10 and 11. Another method for recording information is a notebook computer, but the user should make sure it has adequate battery life or an extension cord and power source. A notebook computer with an outliner provides a very flexible method for conducting an analysis. Simply clicking at the appropriate point allows you to easily insert a new step or to rearrange other steps and information. Tape recorders are also useful for taping the analysis; however, they are difficult to reference later unless transcribed.

A 35-mm or Polaroid® camera is very helpful when conducting a procedural analysis. Taking pictures of the equipment, tools, and various steps are useful for refreshing the designer's memory. Some of the photographs can be printed in the manuals to illustrate a procedure. Designers should check first, however, to make sure they can take photographs—some locations have security regulations or may prohibit the use of flash lighting. A portable video camera is also useful for documenting a procedural analysis. The SME describes each step as it is performed. One author's project involved the development of a training program for maintaining a portable computer. The procedural analysis involved the only prototype available, and it was in a different location than the author's home. When the notes were inadequate, the tape was cued and played to review the specific steps. Still, the author called the SME several times to ask for clarification (e.g., "Do you need to rock it as you remove the board or pull it straight up?").

SUMMARY

1. One of the key steps to the design process is defining the content needed to address the instructional need or problem. This content is then used to identify the objectives, design the instructional strategies, develop test items, and create the instruction.

2. Topic, procedural, and critical incidence analyses are three methods for defining the content. A topic analysis is used to identify the facts, concepts, principles, and rules needed for the instruction. Procedural analysis is applied to a task to identify the individual steps, cues, and sequence for performing steps. Finally, critical incidence analysis is used to identify the content related to interpersonal interactions and attitudes.

3. Our experience has shown that almost every project will use at least two of these methods. The designer may switch between a topic and procedural analysis several times during an interview with the subject-matter expert.

4. When conducting a task analysis, the designer must keep accurate records of the transactions. Notepads and index cards can be supplemented with photographs or videotapes.

FROM HERE TO THERE

You are now ready to analyze the content and tasks needed for the instruction. The first step is to identify an SME who can provide you with the needed information. We always start by contacting individuals with whom we have worked in the past for recommendations. Once you have identified the expert or experts, contact them and discuss the problem. They can help you determine if you need to meet in an office or at a location that has the appropriate equipment or conditions. Also during this initial contact, inquire if any special equipment or training is needed. For example, you might need to complete a course in first aid, winter survival, or hydrogen sulfide training, or you might need special equipment such as a hard hat and safety shoes. Arriving unprepared can result in a lack of access.

Next, you need to set a time and place for your meeting. You might also mention to your SME what type of examples (e.g., written reports, diagrams, pictures, etc.) you might need for the final unit. Finally, you need to prepare for the analysis. We always like to take one or two notepads, note cards, and a camera. If the conditions are favorable, we like to take a portable computer for notetaking.

Remember to respect the expert's time during your meeting. Simply preparing a brief summary of the problem or goals and the target audience can set the stage for the analysis. While you are conducting the analysis, ask plenty of questions and seek clarification rather than wait until you return your office. Once you finish the analysis, you will develop the objectives for the instruction.

REFERENCES

Flanagan, J. C. (1954). The critical incident method. *Psychological Bulletin, 51,* 327–358.

Jonassen, D., Hannum, W., & Tessmer, M. (1989). *Handbook of task analysis procedures.* New York: Praeger.

Phipps, C. J. (1977). *Mechanics in agriculture.* Danville, IL: Interstate.

Primhoff, E. (1973). *How to prepare and conduct job element examinations.* Washington, DC: U.S. Civil Service Commission.

Reigeluth, C. M. (1983). Current trends in task analysis: The integration of task analysis and instructional design. *Journal of Instructional Development, 6*(4), 24–30, 35.

INSTRUCTIONAL OBJECTIVES

Students find it difficult to take notes during the lecture because they cannot determine what is important.

An instructional designer finds it difficult to develop a test for an instructor-led course.

After an exam, a number of students realize they studied the wrong content.

Youngsters at work are evidently having fun but seem to be learning little of value.

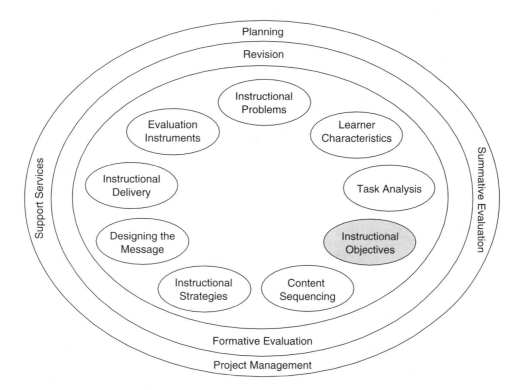

W hat do the situations listed at the opening of this chapter have in common? Each indicates the lack of a clear statement of what students are expected to learn. Unless the requirements are specifically defined, the instructor or instructional designer will not know what to include in the instruction. Also, without such a definition, the instructor has difficulty measuring the specific learning. Each of the situations is easily remedied by preparing instructional objectives. The benefits are indicated in terms of what the learner is to accomplish—hence the expression *instructional* objectives.

FUNCTION OF OBJECTIVES

Objectives perform three important functions. First, they offer a means for the instructional designer and teacher to design appropriate instruction, specifically to select and organize instructional activities and resources that will facilitate effective learning. The result is a very focused unit of instruction.

Second, instructional objectives provide a framework for devising ways to evaluate student learning. Since written tests and performance activities are the major means of measuring student achievement, objectives should guide the design of relevant testing items and procedures. Thus, the writing and use of instructional objectives can have a worthwhile impact on improving both teaching and the resultant learning.

Third, objectives guide the learner. The rationale is that students will use the objectives to identify the skills and knowledge they must master.

In this chapter, we will focus on the first function, objectives as a development tool. The use of objectives to guide learning as a preinstructional strategy is addressed in Chapter 8. Let's begin our discussion by considering the three domains or classifications of objectives. Next we will describe how to write objectives and then how to classify them for making instructional decisions.

THREE OBJECTIVE DOMAINS

Objectives are typically grouped into three major categories (or *domains,* as they are generally called): cognitive, psychomotor, and affective. These areas are often discussed in the literature related to objectives. Understanding the levels within each domain is important when planning a unit of instruction.

Cognitive Domain

The domain receiving the most attention in instructional programs is the **cognitive domain,** which includes objectives related to information or knowledge, naming, solving, predicting, and other intellectual aspects of learning. Bloom and his associates (1956) developed a widely used taxonomy for the cognitive domain. (A *taxonomy* is a method of sequential classification on different levels.) The taxonomy is organized within two major groups: (a) simple recall of information and (b) intellectual activities. Bloom labels the lowest level *knowledge,* while the higher mental abilities are classified into five increasingly more intellectual levels of *comprehension, application, analysis, synthesis,* and *evaluation.* Table 5–1 illustrates several examples of instructional objectives in each of the six levels in the cognitive domain.

Too often, major attention is given in a course to memorizing or recalling information—the lowest cognitive level. One of the challenges in instructional design is to devise instructional objectives and then design related activities that can direct students to accomplishments on the five higher intellectual levels. Although Bloom's taxonomy is used to design learning strategies, others such as Merrill (1983) have developed specific strategies for classifying objectives and then prescribing appropriate instructional strategies. We will describe these methods in Chapter 7.

TABLE 5–1
Taxonomy of cognitive objectives

Level of Bloom's Taxonomy	Course: Chemistry Topic: Gas laws	Course: Fundamentals of Electricity Topic: Connecting a Three-way Switch
Knowledge: Recall of specific information	Define pressure.	List the tools required to wire a three-way switch.
Comprehension: Lowest level of understanding	Describe the relationship between pressure and volume.	Explain the purpose for each of the three wires used in connecting a switch.
Application: Application of a rule or principle	If you have a fully inflated basketball and add more air, what is the effect on pressure inside the ball?	Sketch a diagram for connecting a three-way switch to an existing circuit.
Analysis: Breaks an idea into component parts and describes the relationships	Explain why an automobile's tire will not appear underinflated after being driven several miles at a high speed.	Determine the gauge and length of wiring needed to connect a three-way switch to a junction box.
Synthesis: Puts the parts together to a form a new whole	If you double the absolute temperature of a gas and double the pressure of the gas, what is the effect on volume?	Develop a plan for converting a dining room chandelier on a single switch to a three-way switch.
Evaluation: Makes judgments about materials and methods	Before you is a container of water vapor with a temperature of 150°C and a container of oxygen at 150°C. Which gas is more likely to behave in accordance with the gas laws?	Given a diagram of an existing two-way switch for a dining room light, determine whether it can be converted to a three-way switch.

Psychomotor Domain

The second category for grouping instructional objectives is the **psychomotor domain,** which encompasses the skills requiring the use and coordination of skeletal muscles, as in the physical activities of performing, manipulating, and constructing. Although no taxonomy is universally accepted for this domain, Heinich, Molenda, and Russell (1993) present a taxonomy based on the degree of coordination that is applicable to many design projects (see Table 5–2). Most muscular movements required for performing a task, be it doing a somersault or using a screwdriver, can be derived from this taxonomy.

Another grouping of psychomotor skills, proposed by Kibler (1981; see Table 5–3), is not a sequential taxonomy (in other words, the different levels are not sequentially organized). The value of Kibler's grouping is the recognition of separate gross- and fine-movement skills in the first two psychomotor behavior categories. Because each one requires the use of different sets of muscles, teaching such skills can be better organized by giving attention first to gross movements and then to fine movements.

From either of these two lists of psychomotor behaviors, you can classify physical skills relating to athletics, the performing arts, the manipulation of tools, and the operation of equipment. Psychomotor behaviors generally are easier to observe, describe, and measure than cognitive or affective behaviors. The details in a task analysis permit you to determine the specific muscle coordination required in a physical activity and then to state the appropriate learning requirements as objectives.

Affective Domain

The third category of instructional objectives is the **affective domain,** which involves objectives concerning attitudes, appreciations, values, and emotions such as enjoying, conserving, and respecting. This area is typically believed very important in education and training, but it is the one area in which we have been able to do the least, particularly in writing useful instructional objectives.

TABLE 5–2
Domain of psychomotor objectives

Level	Description	Example
Imitation	Demonstrates an observed action	After watching the videotape on drilling countersink holes, you will drill a countersink hole for a wood screw.
Manipulation	Performs an action	After practicing on scrap wood, you will drill a hole for connecting two pieces of wood, scoring 8 of 10 points on the performance checklist.
Precision	Performs an action with accuracy	You will catch 75% of the ground balls hit to your position.
Articulation	Performs a coordinated activity in an efficient and coordinated manner	During a tennis game, you will properly execute a backhand swing as required by the volley.

TABLE 5–3
Kibler's psychomotor skill grouping

Level	Examples
Gross bodily movements of arms, shoulders, feet, and legs	Throwing a ball for a distance, picking up a heavy object so as not to strain the body, performing a back dive
Finely coordinated movements of hands and fingers, hand and eye, hand and ear, and of hand, eye, and foot	Knitting a scarf, guiding wood through a table saw, using a typewriter, driving a car, sight-reading music while playing an instrument
Nonverbal communication through facial expression, gestures, bodily movements	Showing emotions through facial expressions, employing gestures to communicate directions, pantomiming a message
Speech behavior in producing and projecting sound, coordinating sound and gestures	Giving instructions in a foreign language or presenting a literary reading with gestures for emphasis

Krathwohl, Bloom, and Masia (1964) organize the affective domain into five levels (see Table 5–4). The levels of the affective domain, like those of the cognitive domain, form a continuum for attitudinal behavior, from simple awareness and acceptance to internalization as attitudes become part of an individual's practicing value system.

Interrelation of Domains

As you plan your instruction, keep in mind all three domains and attempt to treat the higher levels as they affect your topics and general purposes. Remember, too,

TABLE 5–4
Affective domain

Level	Description	Example
Receiving	Willing to give attention to an event or activity	Listen to, aware of, perceive, alert to, sensitive to, show tolerance of
Responding	Willing to react to an event through some form of participation	Reply, answer, follow along, approve, obey, find pleasure in
Valuing	Willing to accept or reject an event through the expression of a positive or negative attitude	Accept, attain, assume, support, participate, continue, grow in, devoted to
Organizing	When encountering situations to which more than one value applies, willingly organize the values, determine relationships among values, and accept some values as dominant over others (by the importance to the individual learner)	Organize, select, judge, decide, identify with, develop a plan for, weigh alternatives
Characterizing by a value complex	Learner consistently acts in accordance with accepted values and incorporates this behavior as a part of his or her personality	Believes, practices, continues to, carries out, becomes part of his or her code of behavior

that even though we are examining the three domains separately, they are closely related in two ways. First, a single major objective can involve learning in two or even all three domains. For example, when a technician learns to mix chemicals, he or she must first acquire knowledge about the different chemicals and their relationships as well as the psychomotor skills of performing the mixing operation. To this knowledge we might add the affective behavior of neatness and the practice of safety during the mixing procedure.

Second, attitudinal development may even precede successful learning in the other domains. Learners often need to be motivated to want to learn subject matter before instruction is successful. This step may be particularly true in a self-paced learning program, since learners in this case must take responsibility for their own learning, and both receptiveness and cooperation can, in some measure, determine their level of achievement. Once motivation is established, a well-organized program in which the learners participate successfully usually encourages them to have a positive attitude toward the subject and instructor.

DEVELOPING INSTRUCTIONAL OBJECTIVES

Some instructional designers insist that instructional objectives are defined immediately after formulating the goal or statement of general purposes for a topic. Sequentially, this approach may sound correct, but in actual practice it is not always feasible. While some subject-matter experts (SMEs) can verbalize the direction the instruction should take, others are not able to provide detailed information this early in the development process. To an instructional designer, the content may be unfamiliar and additional information may be needed to formulate meaningful objectives. Thus, the *task analysis* element is placed in the instructional design plan *preceding* the element of instructional objectives.

Writing instructional objectives is a developmental activity that requires changes and additions as the instruction is developed. Sometimes it is not until the learning activities are selected or evaluation methods stated that the "real" objectives for a topic are evident. Thus, your project may start with loosely worded objectives that you refine as development progresses. Our experiences have shown that designers often refine and modify the objectives as the SMEs refine their approach to instruction during the development process.

The Basis for Objectives

Objectives are based on the results of the task analysis and provide a refinement and implementation of the needs and/or goals for a project. If you use only a needs assessment to define your problem, the objectives will relate directly to those needs. If you use a goal analysis, the objectives will reflect a refinement of the goals. There are two cases, however, when a discrepancy may exist between the goals or needs and the objectives. First, the SME who helps with the task analysis may have a better understanding of the problem and provide different content and focus. Second, the SME may simply take a different approach to solving the problem. In either case, when this discrepancy exists, you should verify the accuracy and validity of the objectives with the group who helps you with the goal analysis or identification of the needs.

Instructional objectives identify information necessary to solve the performance problem. Deriving the objectives is a four-step process to be completed *after* the task analysis. These steps are:

1. Review the task analysis and identify the essential knowledge, tasks, and attitudes the learner must master to solve the performance problem.
2. Group the task analysis in clusters with the goals or needs you have identified.
3. Write an objective for each of the goal statements or needs.
4. Write objectives for any additional information that is essential and is not addressed by an objective.

Approaches to Objectives

Historically, instructional designers have insisted on the use of precise objectives (often referred to as Mager-style objectives) that evolved from programmed instruction. This approach is based on behavioral psychology principles that require the learner to demonstrate an overt response indicating mastery of the content. The Mager (1984b) approach was applied to writing objectives for all three domains of learning—cognitive, psychomotor, and affective. Recent trends in cognitive psychology, however, have prompted a reconsideration of the specification of objectives for each of the learning domains.

In the following sections, we will describe how to write different styles of objectives. We begin with the behavioral and cognitive approaches to writing objectives in the cognitive domain. Then we will describe how to write objectives for the psychomotor and affective domains.

WRITING OBJECTIVES IN THE COGNITIVE DOMAIN

There are two generally recognized approaches to writing objectives: *behavioral* and *cognitive*. The behavioral orientation is typically applied to writing objectives in all the domains while the cognitive approach is best suited for the cognitive domain. The following sections focus on their application in the cognitive domain.

Behavioral Objectives

A behavioral objective is a precise statement that answers the question "What behavior can the learner demonstrate to indicate that he or she has mastered the knowledge or skills specified in the instruction?" Ask yourself this question each time you start to formulate an objective; your answer will guide your efforts. To answer this question satisfactorily, you need to recognize that behavioral instructional objectives consist of at least two essential parts and two optional parts.

Essential Parts.   Start with an *action verb* that describes the learning required by the learner or trainee:

> To name
> To operate
> To arrange
> To compare

Follow the action verb with the *subject content reference* that describes the content treated:

> To name the parts of speech used in a sentence
> To operate a videotape recorder
> To arrange parts in order for assembly
> To compare points of view expressed on political issues

Taken together, the action verb (e.g., *to name*) and the subject content reference (e.g., *parts of speech used in a sentence*) indicate what the student is to achieve. Undoubtedly, you or the SME can easily choose the content for an objective. Selecting the appropriate action verb to describe the learning behavior required is the difficult part of writing objectives. For instructional objectives developed in the cognitive domain, a "shopping list" of verbs that express behaviors on each of the six levels in Bloom's taxonomy can be helpful (see Table 5–5). These verbs can assist you in recognizing (and giving attention to) the higher intellectual levels in your planning.

Affective objectives are the most difficult to write, but like objectives in the cognitive domain, they focus on a behavior that indicates the attitude. You should have little difficulty in deciding on the action verb for a psychomotor domain objective, since the skill to perform is usually directly definable.

Optional Parts.   You may feel that stating the action verb and the content reference completely expresses an instructional objective. Although these two components are adequate in many situations, sometimes it is desirable or necessary to include other parameters as part of the learning requirement. Such an objective is particularly important when the instruction has specific or minimum outcome requirements for proficiency. Objectives for such a competency-based program require two additional parts.

Level of Achievement.   The *performance standard* or *criterion* indicates the minimum acceptable performance. It answers such questions as "How well?", "How much?", "How accurate?", "How complete?", and "In what time period?" Here are ways in which the performance standard is stated:

TABLE 5–5
Observable verbs for the cognitive domain*

1. Knowledge		2. Comprehension		3. Application	
Recall of information		Interpret information in one's own words		Use knowledge or generalization in a new situation	
arrange	name	classify	recognize	apply	operate
define	order	describe	report	choose	prepare
duplicate	recognize	discuss	restate	demonstrate	practice
label	relate	explain	review	dramatize	schedule
list	recall	express	select	employ	sketch
match	repeat	identify	sort	illustrate	solve
memorize	reproduce	indicate	tell	interpret	use
		locate	translate		

4. Analysis		5. Synthesis		6. Evaluation	
Break down knowledge into parts and show relationships among parts		Bring together parts of knowledge to form a whole and build relationships for new situations		Make judgments on basis of given criteria	
analyze	differentiate	arrange	manage	appraise	evaluate
appraise	discriminate	assemble	organize	argue	judge
calculate	distinguish	collect	plan	assess	predict
categorize	examine	compose	prepare	attack	rate
compare	experiment	construct	propose	choose	score
contrast	inventory	create	set up	compare	select
criticize	question	design	synthesize	defend	support
diagram	test	formulate	write	estimate	value

*Depending on the meaning for use, some verbs may apply to more than one level.

> In proper order
> At least 8 out of 10 correct (or 80% correct)
> With an accuracy of 2 centimeters
> Within 3 minutes
> Meeting the criteria stated in the manual

The following examples illustrate objectives with an action verb, content, and performance standard:

> To arrange the six steps of water purification *in proper order*
> To troubleshoot circuit problems *with a correct solution rate of 90%*
> To measure a client's blood pressure within *±5mm Hg accuracy as determined by the instructor*
> To design a display that *received a rating of at least 4 relative to the criteria discussed in class*

Conditions of Performance. Conditions result from answers to questions such as "Is specific equipment required?", "Is access to a certain book, chart, or other reference allowed?", "Are time limitations imposed?", or "Are other specific factors set as conditions for testing?" Conditions are resources necessary for establishing evaluation requirements. They specify the conditions under which the evaluation will take place.

The following statements exemplify instructional objectives, each of which includes a condition:

> *Using the hospital's floor map as a guide,* locate all fire extinguishers and emergency exits on the floor with 100% accuracy.
>
> *Based on assigned readings,* compare the cultures of two past civilizations, enumerating at least five characteristics of each.
>
> *Given the chart showing the normal growth rate of a redwood tree,* predict within 15% accuracy the size of a tree over a five-year period.
>
> *Within a three-minute period,* set up, zero in, and operate a multimeter tester.

Mager-style instructional objectives follow the form of the objectives illustrated in these examples. When appropriate, include either or both of the optional parts. When no performance standard is included, the assumption is that only a 100% correct response or performance is acceptable. Keep your statements simple and brief. Avoid including so much detail that the effort of writing the objectives becomes discouraging and the requirements seem overwhelming to learners and instructors.

An alternative approach for specifying behavioral objectives is the use of terminal and enabling objectives. A major objective for a topic or task is called a *terminal objective.* It describes, in behavioral terms, the overall learning outcomes expressed originally as the general purpose for a topic. More than a single terminal objective may be necessary for accomplishing a general purpose. Here are examples of terminal instructional objectives:

Topic: Fetal Circulation
General purpose: To acquire knowledge and understanding of the anatomy and physiology of fetal circulation
Terminal objective: To describe the normal circulation pattern within a fetus

Topic: Renaissance and Reformation
General purpose: To understand the changes that took place in European civilization during the late Middle Ages
Terminal objective: To interpret the significant developments taking place as Europeans broke the continental bonds and established a world hegemony

Topic: The Automobile Distributor
General purpose: To clean and adjust the distributor for a smooth-running engine
Terminal objective: To service a distributor

The subobjectives that lead to accomplishing the terminal objective are referred to as *enabling* or *supporting objectives.* Enabling objectives describe the specific behaviors (single activities or steps) that must be learned or performed, often sequentially, to achieve the terminal objective. For the terminal objectives cited previously, the following enabling objectives are required:

Terminal objective: To describe the normal circulation pattern within a fetus

Enabling objectives:
1. To name the two types of blood vessels found in the umbilical cord
2. To locate the two shunts that are normal in fetal circulation
3. To label a diagram of fetal circulation, indicating differences in systolic pressure between the left and right sides of the heart

Terminal objective: To interpret the significant developments taking place as Europeans broke the continental bonds and established a world hegemony

Enabling objectives:
1. To identify economic developments that emerged in medieval Europe
2. To analyze the political, religious, social, and psychological forces that helped create the Reformation
3. To relate the intellectual and architectural accomplishments of the twelfth century to the foundations for the Renaissance

Terminal objective: To service a distributor

Enabling objectives:
1. To identify the four main parts of a distributor
2. To remove and clean the distributor cap
3. To remove and clean the rotor
4. To clean and install breaker points
5. To set breaker points

A Caution.   When instructional planners first start to write objectives, they sometimes tend to write descriptions of what is to occur *during* the instruction and consider the statements to be instructional objectives (e.g., "To view a videotape on ecological safeguards," "To teach the student how . . .," or "To read pages 45–70 in the text"). These statements are *activities;* they do *not* indicate learning outcomes. An instructional objective should focus on *outcomes* or *products* rather than on process. If you are not sure whether what you are stating is an objective, ask yourself, "Is this outcome what I want the learner to know or demonstrate after completing the topic or unit?"

Cognitive Objectives

Gronlund (1985, 1995) suggests an alternative approach to Mager's for writing instructional objectives in the cognitive domain. Both behavioral objectives and cognitive objectives specify learning as outcomes. Cognitive objectives, however, are stated in two parts. First is a statement of the general instructional objective. General objectives are stated in broad terms to encompass a domain of learning (e.g., *comprehend, understand, apply, use, interpret, evaluate*):

> Selects information using CIJE
> Understands the meaning of the terms used in the gas laws
> Interprets a graph
> Comprehends the meaning of a poem

These general statements indicate the overall outcome of the instruction. Like a behavioral objective, they focus on the products or outcomes of the instruction, not the process. Statements that include words such as *gains, views,* or *acquires* are indicators that the designer is focusing on the learning *process* instead of the *outcomes*. Thus, an objective written as "The learner will gain . . ." is focusing on the process and should be rewritten as "The learner interprets . . ." to focus on the outcome.

The second part of a cognitive objective is one or more samples of the specific types of performance that will indicate mastery of the objective. Following are examples:

Selects information using CIJE

1. Finds an article on a given topic
2. Compiles a bibliography of related literature
3. Identifies narrower and broader terms for a search

Interprets a graph

1. Determines the group that sold the most
2. Determines the groups that were below average
3. Determines the year with the greatest number of sales

Conducts effective meetings

1. Prepares an agenda prior to the meeting
2. Arranges the room for effective communication
3. States the intended outcomes at the beginning of the meeting

Why use cognitive objectives instead of behavioral objectives? If we compare the cognitive objectives to Mager-type behavioral objectives, we find they both specify a student performance in specific, measurable terms. However, with behavioral objectives the objective becomes the end rather than the means for instruction. Cognitive-style objectives overcome this problem by first stating a general objective (similar in structure to the terminal objective) to communicate the intent (e.g., "To interpret the graph"). A behavioral objective might oversimplify the intent by stating the outcome as "Identify the tallest bar on the chart." The resulting instruction from the behavioral objective, then, focuses on measuring the elements of the graph rather than interpreting it. The sample performances of the cognitive objective simply indicate behaviors that allow the teacher or instructor to infer that the learner has achieved the higher-level intent.

Behavioral objectives are particularly well suited for *mastery learning* instruction where the learner must demonstrate specific behaviors to advance to the next level. For example, a course that stresses how to produce a specific report, such as sales by departments for a given month, might best be defined with behavioral objectives. These objectives will accurately describe the outcome "The learner will print a report indicating sales revenue by department," which involves a repetitive task of entering the month and department name.

Cognitive objectives are well suited for describing higher levels of learning. For example, in a course that emphasizes labor negotiation skills, the designer might develop a cognitive objective to describe the outcome related to evaluating a contract offer: "The learner will comprehend the implications of an offer." The examples of behaviors related to this outcome could focus on specifics such as "calculating the cost of the contract to the company," "identifying possible counteroffers," and "determining long-range implications."

WRITING OBJECTIVES FOR THE PSYCHOMOTOR DOMAIN

Psychomotor skills are the most easily observed of the three domains. Objectives in this domain rely on the same four objective parts; however, the emphasis is often different. For example, the verb *demonstrate* is frequently used as the behavior. Explicitly stated conditions are often required for psychomotor objectives. For example, is the learner to use an electric drill or a manually powered drill, or are the ground balls thrown or hit by a batter? Similarly, psychomotor objectives are more likely to require specific criteria since 100% accuracy (e.g., all 10 shots in the bull's-eye) is often not expected from the novice. Thus, we might have a number of objectives ranging from hitting a large target by the end of the first practice to eventually scoring a specific number of points. Following are examples of objectives in the psychomotor domain:

Given five rounds of ammunition, the learner will shoot each round from 50 feet so that each hits within a 7-inch circle.

Given five rounds of ammunition, the learner will score a total of 30 points while firing from a distance of 50 feet.

Given two 15-inch straight needles and yarn, the learner will cast on 50 stitches of equal size and correct tension.

Time is often used with psychomotor objectives, but it may be difficult to determine whether time is a condition or a criterion. Let's examine two additional psychomotor objectives:

Students will run a quarter mile around a cinder track in under 2 minutes.

Given a malfunctioning light switch, the student will correctly replace the switch in 30 minutes.

In the first objective, time (2 minutes) is a criterion because it is conceivable that some students are not capable of running a quarter mile in under 2 minutes. Thus, the time is a standard for measurement. The 30-minute time limit in the second objective is a condition, because almost any physically able student will be capable of completing the task in less than 30 minutes.

To summarize, if the time factor is used to measure the performance, then it is a *criterion* for the objective. If the time factor is used to set a maximum time limit and there is another criterion (e.g., "correctly replace"), then time is a *condition*.

WRITING OBJECTIVES FOR THE AFFECTIVE DOMAIN

The affective domain encompasses more abstract behaviors (attitudes, feelings, and appreciations) that are relatively difficult to observe and measure. One method of developing objectives in this domain is *to specify behaviors indirectly* by inferring from what the instructor can observe. What a *learner does or says* is assumed as evidence of behavior relating to an affective objective.

Some behaviors in this area are difficult to identify, let alone to name and measure. How, for instance, do you measure an attitude of appreciating the importance of good nutrition or developing a positive relationship with company clients? Such attitudes are inferred only indirectly from secondary clues. When developing an affective objective, it is often useful to divide the objective into two parts. First, identify the *cognitive component* or "thought" that describes the attitude. Second, identify a *behavior* that when observed would represent the attitude. This behavior is then used to write the affective objective.

To measure an attitude about an activity, we must generalize from learner behaviors that indicate the student is developing or has developed the attitude. The following examples illustrate behaviors indicating a positive attitude:

The learner says he or she likes the activity.
The learner selects the activity in place of other possible activities.
The learner participates in the activity with much enthusiasm.
The learner shares his or her interest in the activity by discussing it with others or by encouraging others to participate.

If the instructional objective is "To appreciate the importance of good nutrition," accomplishment is demonstrated by the following behaviors:

Is observed eating only foods of high nutritional value (no junk foods or refined products)
Readily advises other persons about the value of nutritious foods
Voluntarily reads books and articles describing good nutrition practices
Attends lectures and workshops presented by nutrition authorities

If the instructional objective is "To develop a positive relationship with company clients," evidence of accomplishment can be shown if the employee does the following:

Is prompt for appointments with clients
Calls each client by name, is courteous, and speaks in a friendly tone
Shows an interest in the client as a person by talking about matters, other than business, that are mutually interesting

Spends extra time with a client, as necessary
Provides requested information promptly

Admittedly, these examples are only indicative of the possible successful fulfillment of an attitudinal objective and do not measure it directly. Mager (1984a) calls these attitudinal objectives *approach tendencies* toward exhibiting a positive attitude to a subject or a situation. The learner's attitude is considered negative if he or she shows *avoidance tendencies*. Notice, however, that Mager's approach to affective objectives is very close to Gronlund's cognitive approach. They both begin with a general behavior and then specific example behaviors that the instructor uses to infer the presence of the attitude.

In the book *Goal Analysis,* Mager (1984c) suggests that if employees are to exhibit safety consciousness, they are expected to practice the following behaviors: "Report safety hazards; wear safety equipment; follow safety rules; practice good housekeeping by keeping the work area free of dirt and loose tools; encourage safe practice in others by reminding them to wear safety equipment; and so forth" (pp. 46–47). This example is similar to a cognitive objective as it states a general purpose, safety consciousness, and then provides specific examples of behaviors indicating the practice of safety.

Gronlund's and Mager's approaches can help you refine ways of indicating attitudinal objectives and then setting a degree of measurement for them. [For additional help in identifying and writing affective domain objectives, refer to the work of Lee and Merrill (1972).] Table 5–6 is a list of verbs you may find useful as you state instructional objectives in this domain.

Realistically, we must recognize that there are many important objectives that cannot result in measurable outcomes. Eisner (1969) uses the term *expressive objectives* for those for which specific outcomes are not readily stated. These objectives basically identify situations for the learner. An expressive objective may allow for self-discovery, originality, and inventiveness, the result surprising both the learner and the instructor. For example, "To develop a feeling of personal adequacy in athletic performance" is an expressive objective. By stating such nonmeasurable objectives during planning, you can at least identify aspects of instructional goals that have personal or social importance and thus can make a start on deciding how to achieve them.

TABLE 5–6
Affective verbs

acclaims	cooperates	joins
agrees	defends	offers
argues	disagrees	participates in
assumes	disputes	praises
attempts	engages in	resists
avoids	helps	shares
challenges	is attentive to	volunteers

CLASSIFYING OBJECTIVES

The cognitive and affective domains comprise sequential hierarchies starting from low levels of learning or behavior and progressing through more intellectual or sophisticated levels. The psychomotor domain does not exhibit as consistent a sequencing pattern as do the other two domains.

These three domains are useful for determining the level of learning for each objective and for checking that the objectives are distributed across several levels rather than clumped as rote memory objectives. The next element of the design process is to use the objectives as a basis for developing the instructional strategies. We accomplish this task by classifying the objectives into a matrix that is then used to prescribe the instructional strategy. The three taxonomies we have just discussed are not well suited for developing instructional strategies for two reasons. First, an objective can often be classified into more than one level because the levels are not mutually exclusive. Second, the taxonomies do not provide prescriptive instructional strategies for each level. The following pages describe two different models for classifying objectives and then prescribing instructional strategies. The Mager and Beach model is particularly suited for classroom instruction, while the performance-content matrix provides a structured instructional design approach.

Mager and Beach's Model

Mager and Beach (1967) describe a performance classification approach in their book *Developing Vocational Instruction*. Objectives are classified into one of five categories or performance types and then ranked by difficulty (see Table 5–7).

Objectives that require the learner to speak in a specific manner are classified as speech performance objectives. This category is limited to *speaking;* written verbal responses are not classified in this performance category. *Manipulation* is the execution of a psychomotor skill that can range from simple skills such as dialing a phone number to complex machine operations. Objectives requiring the *rote memorization* (e.g., listing two types of screwdrivers) of information are classified in the recall category. The *discrimination* category requires the learner to distinguish between two objects (e.g., a Phillips-head and a flat-head screwdriver) or two events (e.g., a strike and a ball). Objectives that require the student to determine what to do are classified as *problem-solving performances*. Finally, each objective is classified as either easy, moderately difficult, difficult, or very difficult to perform based on the instructional designer's observations during the task analysis and input from the SME.

A Performance-Content Matrix Model

Merrill (1983) proposes another useful tool for classifying objectives in his component display theory. Although Merrill's performance-content matrix is not hierarchical like Bloom's taxonomy, it does provide a means of determining which type of instructional strategy to use to master the objective. The expanded model builds on Merrill's model to account for psychomotor, affective, and interpersonal tasks (see Table 5–8) that are not included in Merrill's component display theory. Unlike

TABLE 5–7

Mager and Beach's performance type

Objective	Performance	Learning Difficulty
1. When answering the phone, the salesperson will correctly identify the company and self.	Speech	Easy
2. Salesperson will correctly enter the customer's ID number into the computer.	Manipulation	Moderately difficult
3. Salesperson will identify to whom they transfer a customer with a problem.	Recall	Easy
4. Salesperson will determine shipping time based on zip code and package size.	Discrimination	Moderately difficult
5. When an article is out of stock, the salesperson will suggest an alternative item.	Problem-solving	Difficult

Bloom's taxonomy, this model classifies types of content and performance as opposed to levels of learning. In addition, Bloom's model is *descriptive* in that it describes different levels of learning. Instructional design models must *prescribe* optimum instructional strategies for achieving an objective. Thus, like Merrill's model, the present model uses content categories that are then used to prescribe instructional strategies (see Chapter 7).

The content aspect of the matrix provides six categories for classifying objectives. Each objective is classified into *one* category. If the objective fits into two categories, it needs to be refined and stated as two separate objectives. The following paragraphs briefly review each of the content categories.

TABLE 5–8

Expanded performance-content matrix

Content	Performance	
	Recall	Application
Fact		
Concept		
Principles or Rules		
Procedure		
Interpersonal		
Attitude		

Fact. A *fact* is statement that associates one item with another. The statement "Columbus discovered America" associates the names *Columbus* and *America*. Learning that the symbol *H* represents hydrogen in a chemical equation is also a fact that associates *H* with hydrogen. Facts are memorized for later recall.

Concept. *Concepts* are categories we use for simplifying the world. It is much easier to refer to two-wheeled, self-propelled vehicles as bicycles than having to remember the brand name of every bike. Examples of concepts are circle, car, box, woman, mirror, and tree. We can identify several different models of automobiles, but we classify each as a car just as we group maple, oak, and pine trees in the category of tree.

Principles and Rules. A *principle* or *rule* expresses a relationship between concepts. For example, "Metal expands when its temperature is increased" expresses a causal relationship between the concepts of metal and temperature. Similarly, "Providing reinforcement increases the chances the behavior will be repeated" expresses a relationship between learning (repeating a behavior) and reinforcement.

Procedure. A *procedure* is a sequence of steps one follows to achieve a goal. Procedures can describe primarily cognitive operations such as solving a quadratic equation, an operation that involves both cognitive and psychomotor operations such as taking a voltmeter reading, and primarily psychomotor operations such as driving a nail. Procedures can also vary in difficulty from repetitive tasks (e.g., driving a nail) to problem-solving tasks (e.g., debugging a computer program).

Interpersonal Skills. This category describes spoken and nonverbal (i.e., body language) interaction between two or more people. For example, an objective that describes the phone-answering skills of a telemarketing professional or the skills in making an effective presentation would be classified in this category. Similarly, a course designed to improve the skills of managers interviewed on television by improving their posture and sitting habits to project confidence would be grouped in this category.

Attitude. Objectives that seek to change or modify the learner's attitude are classified in this category. Affective objectives can vary from simply developing an awareness of different options to changes in attitudes that result in action, such as stopping theft of company materials.

The second part of the model is the performance specified in the objective. The behavior or performance specified in the objective is considered and then classified as either recall or application.

Recall. Objectives that specify that the learner simply memorize information for later recall (e.g., "Who discovered America?"; "Define reinforcement") are classified as recall performance. Recall performance encompasses those behaviors at the lower levels of Bloom's taxonomy. Verbs such as *list, define,* and *name* are often cues of recall performance.

Application. When the performance requires the learner to use or apply the information, the objective is classified as application. For example, an objective that requires the learner to demonstrate the use of reinforcement in a microteaching lesson would be classified as application. Verbs such as *demonstrate, discriminate,* and *solve* are cues that the performance requires an application of the content. Note that facts are always classified as recall because they cannot be applied.

Later chapters will use this expanded performance-content matrix to prescribe instructional strategies to help the learner achieve the objective.

DIFFICULTIES IN WRITING OBJECTIVES

One reason many people shy away from stating precise objectives is that formulating them demands much thought and effort. Each objective should be unambiguous. It must communicate exactly the same thing to all learners and to other instructors and designers. Many instructors are not accustomed to such exactness in instructional planning. For too long we have based our teaching on broad generalizations, often leaving it up to the learner to interpret what we actually mean.

Not until the importance of objectives for an instructional program becomes apparent are instructors or designers willing to put sincere effort into preparing them. Then the difficulties and frustrations are taken in stride, and we gradually develop a habit and pattern for expressing as many of the desired outcomes of effective learning as possible in specific, meaningful terms.

PROS AND CONS OF WRITING OBJECTIVES

As you studied the content of this chapter, you no doubt considered your own feelings and attitudes relative to the importance of writing instructional objectives. Some designers and instructors readily accept the position taken in this book that it is important to write observable and measurable objectives whenever possible. Others have strong views against such specificity, believing that objectives are often unnecessary or that the important outcomes of a program do not lend themselves to objective statements. These latter individuals may feel that the more important long-term outcomes of an instructional program are hard to define and often unmeasurable.

This view should not be an either/or situation. Admittedly, most objectives we write relate to short-term goals, attainable during a course or training program. Some, however, may contribute to long-term goals, such as the development of analytical skills or decision-making abilities, over which the instructor has little or no control. These high-level objectives may not be fully measurable until years later. Therefore, it is reasonable at times to assume that certain objectives cannot be completely satisfied during the planned instructional program. Instructors and designers can do a follow-up evaluation after a course to determine learner competencies relative to such important long-term objectives.

If you would like to read a rationale that examines all aspects of this topic of objectives, the reference by Davies (1976) may be most helpful. He puts objectives in perspective, based on his review of literature and research in the field of curriculum design.

SUMMARY

1. A procedure for systematically planning instruction in which the specification of instructional objectives plays a key role has been described.

2. The objectives indicate what a learner is expected to do after completing a unit of instruction, and they are expressed in precise, unambiguous terms. We have provided both a strict behavioral approach and a more flexible cognitive approach to specifying instructional objectives.

3. Objectives are important to both learners and instructors. They help learners plan their study and prepare for examinations. They guide the instructor in planning instruction and devising tests.

4. Objectives are grouped into cognitive, psychomotor, and affective domains within which increasingly higher levels of intellectual aptitude, skill ability, and emotional behavior are recognized. The domains are closely related, since a single major objective can require learning in more than one area.

5. Objectives consist of an action verb and subject content reference; they may also include a performance standard and/or conditions. Objectives on higher intellectual levels are more difficult, yet more important, to specify. Objectives in the affective domain are identified indirectly by inferring learner acceptance of an attitude from observable behavior.

6. Objectives are organized and sequenced by various methods to ensure that the more advanced objectives receive suitable attention. After the objectives are specified, they are classified into categories using one of the schemes presented. These classifications are then used to prescribe an appropriate instructional strategy.

7. The subject matter relating to instructional objectives as treated in this chapter provides the essential information to guide you in developing your own objectives and in assisting a subject-matter expert to write instructional objectives.

FROM HERE TO THERE

You have worked for a petroleum company for the past six years and are responsible for the training of civil, electrical, and chemical engineers at the various company refineries. When you visited one of the refineries recently while working on an instructional program for new engineers, you met an engineer, Ms. Calle, who had developed a program to determine the maximum output for the refinery based on the type of crude oil being refined. Ms. Calle demonstrated the program and pointed out that many engineers were requesting what she thought was unnecessary maintenance work. She had determined that the refinery was working at its maximum for the quality of crude oil input and the outputs they were producing. The problem, she said, was that the engineers were spending money for maintenance and repairs that simply were not needed. As a follow-up, you did your own analysis and verified the problem. Seeing the opportunity for fame and immediate recognition, you rushed to complete the task analysis and develop the objectives for a training program to teach engineers how to use the software to solve problems.

When you returned to your office, you showed your plan to the chief engineer who thought it was a good idea. Except, that is, for your objectives. He stated that *his* engineers knew how to solve problems and that there was no need for any problem-solving objectives. The unit should focus on how to enter the data and run the software. You pled your case with your data that clearly showed money was wasted on needless maintenance. Again, the chief engineer directed you to remove the problem-solving emphasis from the proposed training.

What would you do in this situation?

REFERENCES

Bloom, B. S., Englehart, M. D., Furst, E. J., Hill, W. H., & Krathwohl, D. R. (1956). *A taxonomy of educational objectives: Handbook I. The cognitive domain.* New York: McKay.

Davies, I. K. (1976). *Objectives in curriculum design.* New York: McGraw-Hill.

Eisner, E. W. (1969). Instructional and expressive objectives: Their formulation and use in curriculum. In W. J. Popham (Ed.), *Instructional objectives: An analysis of emerging issues* (pp. 13–18). Chicago: Rand McNally.

Gronlund, N. E. (1985). *Stating behavioral objectives for classroom instruction.* New York: Macmillan.

Gronlund, N. E. (1995). *How to write and use instructional objectives* (5th ed.). New York: Prentice-Hall.

Heinich, R., Molenda, M., & Russell, J. D. (1993). *Instructional media and the new technologies of instruction* (4th ed.). New York: Macmillan.

Kibler, R. J. (1981). *Objectives for instruction and evaluation.* Boston: Allyn & Bacon.

Krathwohl, D. R., Bloom, B. S., & Masia, B. B. (1964). *A taxonomy of educational objectives: Handbook II. The affective domain.* New York: McKay.

Lee, B. N., & Merrill, D. M. (1972). *Writing complete affective objectives: A short course.* Belmont, CA: Wadsworth.

Mager, R. F. (1984a). *Developing attitude toward learning* (2nd ed.). Belmont, CA: Pitman.

Mager, R. F. (1984b). *Preparing instructional objectives* (2nd ed.). Belmont, CA: Pitman.

Mager, R. F. (1984c). *Goal analysis* (2nd ed.). Belmont, CA: Lake.

Mager, R. F., & Beach, K. M. (1967). *Developing vocational instruction.* Belmont, CA: Pitman.

Merrill, M. D. (1983). Component display theory. In C. M. Reigeluth (Ed.), *Instructional-design theories and models: An overview of their current status* (pp. 282–333). Englewood Cliffs, NJ: Erlbaum.

DESIGNING THE INSTRUCTION: SEQUENCING

"What is the best sequence for presenting this instruction?"

O nce you have developed the objectives, you are ready to determine the optimum sequence for the instruction. As you completed the task analysis, you may have made mental notes as to how you might present the content. Instructional designers recognize that the sequence in which the subject-matter expert (SME) presented during the task analysis may *not* be the most appropriate sequence for learning the content. This chapter explains how to determine the most appropriate sequence for presenting the content related to each objective.

Sequencing is the efficient ordering of content in such a way as to help the learner achieve the objectives. For some objectives the sequence is suggested by the procedure. For example, when teaching someone how to change a tire, it would seem more appropriate to teach where the tools are located *before* teaching how to remove the lug nuts. Other topics, however, have a less obvious sequence. A course on how to write a research paper has several possible sequences, all of which are equally effective. For example, one instructor might start with how to read a research paper, while another might first teach how to use the library.

There are several general methods of sequencing content. One well-known method is the prerequisite method (Gagné, 1985), which is based on a learning hierarchy that identifies skills that are dependent on other skills. The sequence is to teach the prerequisite skills first (e.g., how to sort checks before marking them as cleared). A second approach, described by Posner and Strike (1976), is a set of strategies for sequencing the instruction based on learning-related, world-related, and concept-related content. A more recent approach is one described by English and Reigeluth (1996) as part of Reigeluth's elaboration theory. This chapter focuses on two sequencing strategies: those prescribed by Posner and Strike and those prescribed by Reigeluth.

THE POSNER AND STRIKE SEQUENCING SCHEME

We will review three sequencing schemes proposed by Posner and Strike. The first scheme, which is *learning-related*, suggests ways of sequencing the content based on learner characteristics identified in the learner analysis. This scheme considers the difficulty of the material, its appeal or interest to the learner, prerequisite information, and the learner's cognitive development. Since this scheme is based on the *needs* of the learner, it seems appropriate that the initial sequencing of the unit of instruction follows these guidelines. The next two schemes, *world-related* and *concept-related*, recommend sequencing schemes based on the *type* of content treated in the unit. For example, the world-related scheme suggests sequencing based on spatial, temporal, and physical relationships identified in the content. Similarly, the concept-related scheme suggests sequencing based on the relationships between the concepts. After the initial sequencing based on learner characteristics, you must select a "best-fit" scheme for the content from either the world-related or concept-related schemes. Thus, if you are trying to sequence a series of related concepts (e.g., herbivores, carnivores, omnivores, and examples of each), the concept-related guidelines would be most appropriate for determining which concept to present first, second, third, and so forth. The following sections describe each of the sequencing schemes.

Learning-Related Sequencing

This strategy for sequencing content is based on five student learning concepts (see Table 6–1). First, there are *identifiable prerequisites* a learner must master before demonstrating a more complex task. For example, one needs to learn the alphabet before using a dictionary or encyclopedia or before arranging data alphabetically. Second is teaching about the *familiar* or known before teaching about the unknown. When teaching a math unit on measurement in the United States, for example, you might begin with inch and foot measures before teaching centimeter and meter. A third learning-related scheme is *difficulty*. Posner and Strike (1976) state that difficulty is determined by the fineness of the discrimination the learner must make, how quickly the procedure is executed, and the amount of cognitive processing required. Guidelines prescribe teaching the easier tasks first, such as spelling short words before longer words and replacing a button before sewing a seam. Fourth is the sequencing of content based on *interest.* An introductory unit on LOGO programming might start with how to draw a design on the screen (high interest) before introducing structured programming techniques (lower interest). Fifth, the content is sequenced according to a *development theory* such as that of Bruner, Piaget, or Kohlberg. For example, following Bruner's theory, words (symbols) would be introduced only after the learner had the appropriate visual images (icons) related to the words.

Suppose a professor asks for help in redesigning a course in photography. The objectives might cover the basic operation of the camera, exposure control, depth of field, developing film, and producing prints. We might first sequence the content using learner *interest* by allowing the learners to shoot a roll of film using the exposure guide that comes with the film. Learners can enjoy immediate satisfaction with the hands-on experience. When we organize the content related to controlling the exposure, we would first teach the learner how to set the f-stop and shutter speed. Next, we would teach how to change the shutter speed and select the appropriate f-stop. Sequencing for the information on controlling exposure begins with the *easiest* step of simply setting a selected exposure and proceeds to a more difficult step of manipulating the shutter speed and f-stop to obtain different depths of field and to stop the action. Finally, we would teach how to print a picture before

TABLE 6–1

Learning-related sequencing

Phenomenon	Example/Principle
Identifiable prerequisite	• Teach a skill required to perform another skill first. • Teach addition of whole numbers before teaching addition of fractions.
Familiarity	• Begin with the most familiar information and then progress to the most remote. • Teach about mammals in the surrounding area before teaching about mammals of another country.
Difficulty	• Teach the less difficult before the more difficult. • Teach how to complete a simple income tax form before teaching how to complete a form with itemized deductions.
Interest	• Begin with the topics or tasks that will create the most learner interest. • Teach a recruit how to fire a rifle before teaching how to clean it.
Development	• Ensure that the learner has reached the appropriate developmental level before teaching a task or topic. • Teach students to recognize the color green before teaching them how to read the word.

teaching how to improve the quality of a picture through techniques such as dodging and burning. This sequencing is based on the *identifiable prerequisite* of printing a simple picture before manipulating it.

A *procedural analysis* typically reveals a temporal sequence, whereas a *topic analysis* usually reveals a logical sequence. Although the sequence identified by the procedural analysis is usable in a unit of instruction, a more effective unit might result from a different sequence or combination of sequences. A detailed analysis of basic photography techniques might proceed from reading a light meter, composing a picture, manipulating lighting, and so forth. A teaching strategy might start with how to take a picture and then how to develop the film to increase the student's interest and motivation. Thus, basing the sequence first on interest rather than a logical sequence might heighten the learner's motivation for learning.

World-Related Sequencing

Suppose you are developing a unit of instruction for automobile salespeople on the features of a new car model. Do you start at the front of the car and move to the back in your presentation? Or do you begin by describing what the drivers see when they approach the car, then what happens when they enter the door, start the car, and so on? Or do you describe the different systems in the car, such as all the safety features, the electrical system, and the power system? Obviously, there are several different ways to organize and describe the features of the car for a sales training program. Sequencing the content by walking around the car or from a driver's perspective might be appropriate for salespeople learning the features so that they can point them out to prospective customers. Describing what the driver sees in sequence is probably most appropriate for the new owner. The third approach of describing the related systems is probably more appropriate for mechanics, who require and use a different conceptualization of a car. The sequencing strategy you select, then, depends largely on the characteristics and needs of the target audience.

Content that represents *objects, people,* and *events* is presented in a sequence that is consistent with the real world. Thus, we want a one-to-one correspondence between the sequence of the instruction and the sequence of the objects and events in the real world. Sequencing is typically done according to spatial relations, temporal relations, or physical attributes that occur in the real world (see Table 6–2). A unit on a new car for salespeople might group the new features in sequence as they are found while walking around the car. Basing the organization on the physical layout of the car is referred to as a *spatial* organization. A mechanic might be more interested in the individual components of each system (electrical, power, etc.). This grouping by related features is referred to as grouping by *physical* phenomena, which is the presentation of similar items together. Finally, a unit organized on an orderly sequence of steps, such as what the driver sees when approaching the car, entering the car, and then starting it, is based on a *temporal* sequence. Temporal sequences use a time line to sequence the content.

Once a sequence is selected, the content is presented in an orderly fashion according to the scheme. For example, if we were using a temporal organization, we would *not* begin with explaining how to adjust the radio. Rather, we would start with what the driver sees when approaching the car and continue to present the content in the sequence it would occur in the real world (e.g., opening the door, sitting in the seat, putting on a seat belt, etc.). Adjusting the radio would come sometime after the key is inserted in the ignition. A spatial organization might begin with the front bumper, then the engine, the tires, the front disk brakes, the door latches, and finally the trunk. The presentation sequence follows an orderly plan from left to right, top to bottom, and so forth. Table 6–2 describes the three sequences for world-related phenomena and a sample sequence using each.

Consider how less effective the Oregon Trail (1996), a computer simulation of a wagon train trip, would be if the designers had decided to sequence the geographic locations in alphabetical order rather than in the east-to-west order as they appear on the actual trail (spatial). A unit on types of rocks might organize the rocks according to their hardness (physical). The unit, then, might start with the softest rocks and progress to the hardest rocks. Such a sequencing scheme is based on naturally occurring *physical* attributes. Following a world-related scheme for sequencing provides a concrete organization that reflects the sequence of the content as it exists in nature.

Concept-Related Sequencing

Content can also be sequenced in a manner consistent with how we organize the world conceptually or logically. Posner and Strike (1976) present four schemes for sequencing conceptual content (see Table 6–3). First is *class relations,* which groups things or events that are similar. The recommended sequence is to teach the concept to the class first and then to the individual class members. For example, a unit on

TABLE 6–2

World-related sequencing

Phenomenon	Example/Principle
Spatial	• Left to right, top to bottom, north to south • Describe a plant starting with the flower and move toward the roots in sequence.
Temporal	• Historical; first, second, third, etc.; fast to slow • When describing the mailing options at the post office, begin with the fastest and proceed to the slowest. • When describing how to give an insulin injection, describe the steps in sequence.
Physical	• Roundness, hardness, large to small, color, smoothness • When teaching the different types of wines, group them by color (e.g., white, red, blush, etc.).

TABLE 6–3
Concept-related sequencing

Phenomenon	Example/Principle
Class relations	• Teach characteristics of class before teaching members of the class. • Teach concept of central tendency before teaching about mean, mode, and median.
Propositional relations	• Provide examples first, then the proposition. • Show students examples of metal expansion (cookie sheet, bridge on a hot day, etc.), then explain that metal expands when heated.
Sophistication	• Begin with concrete or simple and then proceed to abstract or complex concepts. • Teach the concepts of mean, mode, and median before teaching analysis of variance.
Logical prerequisite	• Teach the logical prerequisite concepts first. • Teach the concept of the mean before teaching the concept of standard deviation.

computers might start with a description of the general concept of a computer (e.g., input, output, central processor, etc.) before moving on to specific types of computers (e.g., mainframe, mini, PC). In a biology unit, an instructor would begin with the definition of carnivore before giving specific examples of what a carnivore (class members) such as a dog, lion, or bear eats.

A second concept sequencing scheme, *propositional relations,* prescribes teaching the relationship between propositions before teaching the proposition. An application of this principle is the sequence for teaching the relationship among volume, temperature, and pressure of an ideal gas (Boyle's law). A prescribed sequence might be to illustrate a variety of different volume, temperature, and pressure conditions to illustrate relationships between the three variables before teaching Boyle's law.

The third concept sequencing scheme is to organize the content by *sophistication.* Examples of concept sophistication are the continuums of concrete to abstract and simple to complex. The prescription is to start with concrete, simple, or precise concepts and then proceed to abstract, complex, and imprecise concepts. For example, a chemistry instructor might start a unit with an explanation of a simple compound such as salt before discussing ionic bonding (concrete to abstract).

The fourth concept sequencing scheme is *logical prerequisite,* which prescribes that concepts necessary to understand another concept be taught first. In chemistry, an instructor would need to teach the concept of a chemical reaction before introducing the concept of an enzyme that hastens a chemical reaction.

Suppose you are developing a unit on pests for a firm that specializes in pest management for the agricultural business. One of the objectives requires the learners to identify the different types of pests, including insects, plants, fungi, nematodes, and viruses. The unit might begin with a definition of pest (class relations) and then provide examples of the different types of pests (class members). The remainder of the unit might be organized by beginning with the simplest, concrete pests (e.g., weeds) and proceeding to the more complex and abstract types of pests (e.g., viruses, bacteria) based on the sophistication of the concepts. In the section on insects, an objective might require the learner to explain the relationship between the weather (temperature) and the developmental stages of insects. Before the learners read the section on this relationship, you would present information on the life cycles of insects (logical prerequisite). Examples would then be organized showing the different life cycles of the insects in relation to the temperature. Finally, the learners would receive information about the relationship between temperature and insect development (propositional relations).

The sequence of a unit of instruction may use strategies from each of the three sequencing schemes identified by Posner and Strike (1976). The actual decision is based first on the characteristics of the learner and then on the nature of the content.

ELABORATION THEORY SEQUENCING

To determine the sequence of the instruction, the elaboration theory makes a distinction between the types of expertise the learner will develop (English & Reigeluth, 1996). *Content expertise* describes instruction that will help the learner master a body of knowledge such as chemistry or management. *Task expertise* describes a unit that will help the learner become an expert at a task such as using a bow and arrow, completing a tax form, or solving a mathematical story problem. Let's examine the sequencing schemes for each type of expertise.

Content Expertise Sequencing

A conceptual or theoretical elaboration sequence is used for developing content expertise. The *conceptual sequence* arranges concepts according to their superordinate, coordinate, and subordinate relationships. For example, in a statistics course a superordinate concept would be measures of central tendency. The coordinate concepts would be mean, mode, and median. Subordinate concepts would include scores and sum. A *theoretical elaboration* sequence organizes the content in much the same way a researcher might have followed to discover an idea. For example, when teaching Boyle's law in an introductory chemistry class, we might start with several observations of gases expanding when heated. Then, we might introduce learners to a computer-based animation that allows them to observe the pressure in a vessel as they increase and decrease the temperature. This sequence follows the recommendation by Reigeluth (1987) for starting with the readily observable and then proceeding to the more detailed and complex aspects of the theory or discovery.

Task Expertise Sequencing

The elaboration theory sequence for teaching tasks uses the *simplifying conditions method.* Sequencing for a task should start with the simplest task and proceed to the more complex. For example, when training bank tellers, we might start with a simple task such as how to accept a deposit of cash into a savings account. Next, we might show the tellers how to check the balance of a checking account. After they know how to check the balance, we could show them how to check the balance and then cash a check if there are adequate funds. Teaching these naive learners how to assess a loan application or how to react in a robbery are more complex tasks and would come near the end of the training rather than at the beginning.

FROM OBJECTIVES TO SEQUENCING

Your task analysis will provide a general outline while the classification of your objectives in the expanded performance-content matrix (see Chapter 5) will identify the types of content in your task analysis. Based on your content and performance, you can select a sequencing strategy for each objective. If your unit is primarily concerned with teaching a procedure (e.g., how to tie knots for fly fishing), you might use the same sequencing strategy for the total unit such as arranging the notes from simple to most difficult and then presenting the steps in a temporal sequence.

SUMMARY

1. Once you have completed your task analysis and written the objectives, you are ready to begin designing the instruction by determining the most appropriate sequence for presenting the information.
2. Posner and Strike (1976) suggest three sequencing strategies based on how objects or events occur in the real world, concepts and their relationships to other concepts, or the interests and needs of the learner. Organizing the content according to one of these schemes provides a systematic method for presenting the content that is likely to match the learner's expectations.
3. The elaboration theory suggests sequencing content based on whether the learner is developing task expertise or concept expertise.
4. Concept expertise sequencing presents the logical relationships between the concepts or presents the content in a sequence similar to what one might have used to discover the idea.
5. Task expertise sequencing proceeds from the simplest to the more complex tasks.

FROM HERE TO THERE

Assume that you are working for a national telecommunication corporation that employs 2,000 people in 30 call centers around the country. These individuals sell the company's services, which range from simple telephone service, to voice mail, to 800 numbers, to Internet access. This group experiences a high turnover rate of approximately 30% a year. In 12 months, the company will install a new computer system that integrates all of the services into one system (as opposed to the 14 individual computer systems needed now for the various products). You are responsible for developing the training to teach this group the products the company offers and the process for determining the pricing of each product based on past or projected usage. There are several options for sequencing the content. For example, you could organize the sequencing of the products based on their appeal to the learner (interest), or their frequency of sales or inquiry from customers (e.g., residential long distance service before voice mail). Or you could sequence them based on prerequisites such as 800 numbers before discussing the total small business package, which includes voice mail and 800 numbers. How would you sequence the information for the naive and experienced learners?

REFERENCES

English, R. E., & Reigeluth, C. M. (1996). Formative evaluation research on sequencing instruction with elaboration theory. *Educational Technology and Research Journal, 44,* 1042–1629.

Gagné, R. M. (1985). *Conditions of learning and theory of instruction* (4th ed.). New York: Holt, Rinehart & Winston.

Oregon Trail. (1996). [Computer software package.] Minneapolis, MN: MECC.

Posner, G. J., & Strike, K. A. (1976). A categorization scheme for principles of sequencing content. *Review of Educational Research, 46,* 665–690.

Reigeluth, C. M. (1987). Lesson blueprints based on the elaboration theory of instruction. In C. M. Reigeluth (Ed.), *Instructional theories in action: Lessons illustrating selected theories and models.* Hillsdale, NJ: Erlbaum.

DESIGNING THE INSTRUCTION: STRATEGIES

"What is the best way to teach a fact, concept, or interpersonal skill?"

"How can I make the instruction meaningful?"

"How can I teach an objective that focuses on interpersonal skills?"

"What is the best way to present the content so that each learner will master the objectives?"

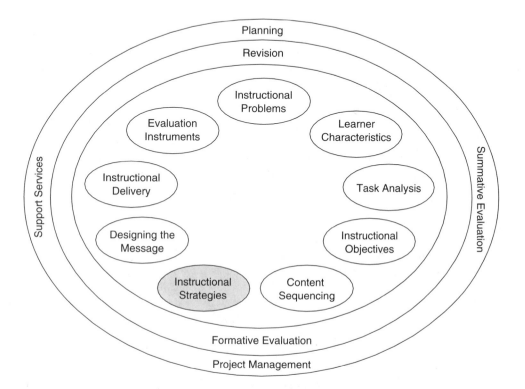

Planning

Revision

Instructional
Problems

Evaluation
Instruments

Learner
Characteristics

Support Services

Summative Evaluation

Instructional
Delivery

Task Analysis

Designing the
Message

Instructional
Objectives

Instructional
Strategies

Content
Sequencing

Formative Evaluation

Project Management

D
ecisions on the design of the instruction are made at two levels. One decision is the delivery strategy, which describes the general learning environment. General learning environments can range from a typical lecture presentation to a highly interactive computer-based instruction lesson. These strategies are often classified according to the *degree of individualization*. Individualized instruction presents the content (or objectives) to each student at an appropriate rate for the individual. Thus, one student might be on Unit 1 while another student is on Unit 5. A nonindividualized approach is the typical classroom lecture course with scheduled examinations that all students take at the designated times. Various lecture and individualized instruction approaches are described in Chapter 9.

The second decision is the *instructional strategy*, which prescribes sequences and methods of instruction to achieve an objective. These prescriptions provide guidance on how to design instructional sequences, and they are generalizable to a number of delivery strategies. These prescriptions are determined by the type of content and performance specified in the objectives (see Chapter 5). This chapter presents instructional strategies for each cell of the expanded performance-content matrix presented in Chapter 5.

WHY INSTRUCTIONAL STRATEGIES?

Prior to this stage of the instructional design process, the designer has identified an instructional problem, the content to correct the problem, and objectives for the instruction. The design of the instruction includes the sequencing of the content and the preinstructional strategy (see chapters 6 and 8). The next element in the process is to design the instructional strategies. Our primary goal is to design *effective* and *efficient* instruction that produces *reliable* results each time it is presented to the learner. We achieve this goal by developing prescriptions that describe an optimum method of instruction for different types of content. These prescriptions or heuristics are based on research; you modify them based on your experiences. This chapter provides heuristics to answer the question "How do I present the content needed to achieve this objective?"

Instructional design uses findings from educational and psychological research to develop sound instructional applications. The prescriptions presented in this chapter will provide a foundation on which you should add and develop new prescriptions based on your experience with each. This generative approach is consistent with the constructivist view (Lebow, 1994).

Designing an Instructional Strategy

Learning is an active process in which the learner constructs meaningful relations between the new knowledge presented in the instruction and the learner's existing knowledge. A well-designed instructional strategy prompts or motivates the learner actively to make these connections between what the learner already knows and the new information. Jonassen (1985) and Wittrock (1974, 1989) describe this learning process as *generative learning*. The advantages of generative learning are the learner's deeper understanding and longer retention of what is learned.

Foundations for the Prescriptions

Craik and Lockhart (1972) suggest that a learner can process new information on a continuum that ranges from phonemic to semantic processing. For example, in one study a researcher might ask one group to read through a passage and put an *X* through every *e* on the page. She might tell a second group that they will have a test on the passage when they finish. The first group, the one marking the *e*'s, would process the material at a phonemic level; that is, they are looking for *e*'s and not reading for meaning. The second group will most likely read the material for a greater depth of meaning to achieve a higher test score (especially if they are offered a reward for the performance). They will try to relate the new material to what they already know. This second group is said to process the material at a *semantic* or deeper level of processing. This type of processing produces *meaningful learning.*

Processing the new information at a deeper level allows the learner to relate the information to several existing ideas and generate more meaningful relationships. Thus, stronger memory traces are created that make the information more resistant to forgetting. One of the goals of an instructional strategy, then, is to design the instruction so that the learner is motivated to generate or construct these meaningful relationships. The design should activate the existing knowledge structures (i.e., recall of prior knowledge) and then assist the learner in altering and encoding the new structures.

This cognitive approach to instructional design is different from the traditional mathemagenic approach, which attempted to control the learner by manipulating the instructional materials. The mathemagenic approach was first suggested by Rothkopf (1960). Its most frequent implementation was the insertion of adjunct questions either before or after a paragraph. The results with a mathemagenic approach were typically rote learning or very shallow levels of processing (Jonassen, 1985).

As an alternative to the mathemagenic approach, Jonassen (1988) identifies four different information-processing strategies a learner can use *to promote deeper processing* as an alternative to the mathemagenic approach. Designers can embed these strategies into the instruction to motivate the learner to process the new information in a meaningful way. Following are descriptions of the four strategies.

The first, *recall*, is helpful for learning facts and lists for verbatim recall. Specific learning strategies that facilitate recall include *repetition, rehearsal* (e.g., mental practice), *review,* and *mnemonics.* The second type, *integration* strategies, are useful for transforming information into a more easily remembered form. Strategies that help the learner transform new content include *paraphrasing,* which requires learners to describe the new material in their own words, and *generating questions* or *examples* from the new information.

The third type of strategy, *organizational,* helps the learner identify how new ideas relate to existing ideas. Sample strategies include *analyzing key ideas,* which requires the learner to identify the key ideas and then interrelate them; *outlining;* and *categorizing.* West, Farmer, and Wolff (1991) suggest the use of tables for categorizing and integrating new information (see Table 7–1). The learner completes the table by describing the type of cut each blade makes as part of the integration process.

The fourth strategy type is *elaboration,* which requires learners to add their ideas (elaborations) to the new information. Strategies that facilitate elaboration include the *generation of mental images, physical diagrams,* and *sentence elaborations.*

TABLE 7–1
Categorization table

Saw Blade	Type of Cut
Cross cut	
Rip	
Hollow ground planer	
Combination	

PRESCRIPTIONS FOR INSTRUCTIONAL STRATEGIES

The following prescriptions are useful as basic guides for developing instructional strategies to achieve each of the content-performance types in Table 7–2. This expanded content-performance matrix was first described in Chapter 5. Each instructional objective for a unit is classified into one of the cells based on the type of content the objective treats (fact, concept, principle, procedure, interpersonal, or attitude) and the type of performance the learner must demonstrate (recall or application). Prescriptions are provided for each cell or type of objective/performance to use in developing the strategies.

Recall performance relies on rote memorization of the content. For example, the learner would recall a fact, state the definition of a concept, state a rule, list the steps of a procedure, describe a type of interpersonal behavior (e.g., how to deal with a domineering individual), and state a previously described example of a behavior indicating an attitude. *Application performance* requires the learner to apply the content (e.g., concept, principle, etc.) to a new situation or problem. For example, an application for a concept (e.g., herbivore) would be to identify new

TABLE 7–2
Expanded performance-content matrix

Content	Performance	
	Recall	Application
Fact		
Concept		
Principles or Rules		
Procedure		
Interpersonal		
Attitude		

examples as either belonging to the class (e.g., a cow) or not belonging to the class (e.g., a lion). Application objectives for rules and procedures would require the learner to apply the rule or procedure to solve a problem or explain an instance.

The remainder of this chapter presents a series of heuristics based on the research literature. Heuristics represent a problem-solving strategy rather than a set of rules that allows for a flexible approach that you can modify with each new experience. Thus, we encourage you to develop your own set of heuristics to expand and modify based on experience and your interpretation of the research literature.

These prescriptions represent a number of heuristics based on behavioral and cognitive research for each of the content-performance matrix cells in Table 7–2. A prescription is designed for *each* of your objectives based on the type of performance (e.g., recall or application) and content and is included as part of the instructional design plan. Each prescription has a minimum of two parts: (a) a description of how the information is initially presented to the learner and (b) the generative strategy to increase the depth of processing.

Prescriptions for Teaching Facts

A *fact* is a statement of association between two things (e.g., "The earth is 92.96 million miles from the sun"). Facts can only be recalled—they have no specific application (see Table 7–2). If an objective is classified as factual content and the performance is recall, then the prescriptions in Table 7–3 describe how to present the fact to the learner for optimum learning.

For concrete facts, the initial presentation should provide the student with experience with the objects of the fact (see Table 7–3). For example, to teach the fact that tomato sauce is red, we might open a can of tomato sauce and let each learner see the color. When teaching abstract facts, the designer should first attempt to find a concrete representation of the fact (e.g., a picture or other artifact) for the

TABLE 7–3

Example fact strategies

Factual Content	Example	Strategy
Concrete	Macintosh apples are red.	• Show a Macintosh apple and ask for the color. • Allow for practice/rehearsal by showing the color and asking which apple is that color or by naming the apple and asking for its color.
Abstract facts	The airport code for Memphis is MEM.	• Show luggage tag with MEM, and explain that it indicates Memphis. • Allow for practice/rehearsal by showing the tag or Memphis and asking for the city or code.
Lists	The lines of the musical staff are EGBDF.	• Show a musical staff with each line labeled. • Provide students with mnemonic to practice "Every Good Boy Does Fine."

initial presentation. To teach the learner that the capital of Indiana is Indianapolis, we might present a map of Indiana with only Indianapolis identified. The map forms a concrete representation of the fact.

Applicable generative strategies for learning facts are rehearsal-practice and the development of mnemonics (see Table 7–3). A rehearsal-practice strategy might involve covertly rehearsing by simply repeating the fact mentally, overtly practice-writing the fact, or answering questions related to the fact. Mnemonics are devices that help recall facts. For example, photography students must often learn the primary colors and their complements (red-cyan, blue-yellow, and green-magenta). A simple mnemonic (*red cars by General Motors*) will assist the learner in recalling the colors later. Mnemonics can be generated by the learner ("Can you think of a picture that will help you remember that cotton is the main export of Egypt?"), or the instruction can provide directions on how to use a mnemonic ("You can use the phrase, 'my very eccentric mother just sent us ninety parakeets' to help you remember the order of the planets from the sun").

Let's return to our earlier example of wood fasteners and assume that we are developing a unit of instruction for employees of a newly opened hardware store. One of the objectives is to teach the fact that most screws are made of steel. To teach this fact, the strategy might start with a steel screw followed by the statement that screws are made from steel. Our instructional strategy, then, gives the fact (screws are made from steel) and a concrete representation of the fact (the steel screw). Note that we are not teaching the concept of a screw; rather, we are teaching a fact of its composition. Our generative strategy might involve having the learner write this fact 10 times on a sheet of paper (practice).

Prescriptions for Teaching Concepts

A *concept* is a category used to group similar ideas or things (e.g., jewelry) to organize knowledge. Performance for a concept can be either recall (e.g., state the definition of) or application, such as identifying new examples of the concept (see Table 7–2). Recommended recall strategies for a concept are the same repetition, rehearsal, review, and mnemonics used for a fact. The instructional strategies for application-type performance, summarized in Table 7–4, are described next.

The initial presentation of the concept can include the best example (Tennyson & Cocchiarella, 1986) that illustrates the category, such as a diamond ring for the concept jewelry. Additional examples of the concept are then presented to refine the category further (necklaces, bracelets, earrings, etc.), as are nonexamples of the concept (e.g., silverware, figurines). For abstract concepts such as in chemistry, models are often used to illustrate the different types of chemical bonds. Similarly, a number of Ping-Pong balls can be glued together to illustrate the concept of hole in a chemical structure.

If the purpose of the objective is simply to remember the concept (e.g., "Define herbivore"), then the same generative strategies recommended for a fact

TABLE 7–4

Example concept strategies

Concept Example	Strategy	Implementation
Open-end wrench	Integration	• Show student the best example of the concept. • Provide student with a catalog of tools, and ask the student to identify examples of open-end wrenches.
Box wrench	Organizational	• Show student the best example of the concept. • Ask student to list the characteristics of a box wrench.

are applicable to the recall of a concept. Students could use a rehearsal-practice strategy or develop a mnemonic to help them recall the definition of the concept.

Both integration and organization strategies are useful for facilitating generative learning when learning concepts for application. An integrative strategy might have the learners generate new examples and nonexamples of the concept by making two columns on a piece of paper and writing examples in one column and nonexamples in the other. Organizational strategies include analysis of key ideas, categorization, and cognitive mapping. A strategy to induce the learners to analyze key ideas might ask them to identify the features (critical attributes) that define the concept. The instruction could direct the learner to use a categorization strategy by presenting the learners with a list of examples and nonexamples. The learners would identify those items that are examples. Finally, the instruction could encourage the learners to develop a cognitive map to determine how this new concept relates to concepts they have already learned. Table 7–4 provides examples of how a designer might use an integration and organizational strategy to design the instruction to teach two concepts.

Let's consider another objective from the training unit example on wood fasteners. The objective is to have the learners identify various types of screws. Our initial presentation would select the one best example (e.g., a flat-head wood screw) and present it as an example of a wood screw. The presentation would then include several variations of types (e.g., oval head, round head, and Phillips head) and sizes of screws. Nonexamples could include bolts and sheet-metal screws.

An organizational strategy was selected from Table 7–4 for this objective because the intent of the objective was to have learners identify a screw if a customer needed a replacement for a stripped one or additional screws of the same or different size. Organizational strategies help the learner transform the new information into a more easily remembered form by having the learner classify new examples. This approach matches our objective of having the student identify examples of screws. Our instructional strategy, then, is to send the learners through the store and have them select 25 different packages of screws, which will require the students actively to process the content and classify each package as either a screw or a nonscrew.

Prescriptions for Teaching Principles and Rules

A *principle* or *rule* is a statement that expresses a relationship between concepts such as "The sum of the angles in a triangle is 180°." Performance for learning a principle or rule can be either recall or application (Table 7–2). Principle application includes both explanation of the effect of the rule and prediction of consequences based on the rule.

There are two general approaches to principle and rule learning (Markle, 1969). The first, *rule-eg,* includes a statement of a rule followed by several examples. Using the rule-eg approach, the instruction begins with a statement of the rule or principle (the sum of the angles in a triangle is 180°), and then provides several triangles with the angle measurements listed and summed. A second, more active learning approach is *eg-rule,* which provides the learner with several examples (the triangles with their angles summed) and asks the learner to generate the rule (see Table 7–5).

If the purpose of the objective is simply to recall the principle or rule, the initial strategy would be either an example or demonstration. The generative strategies are the same as those recommended for a fact. For example, the learner might employ a covert rehearsal strategy of repeating the rule.

Integrative, organizational, and elaboration strategies can facilitate generative learning of principles and rules. The learners can paraphrase the principle using their own words or generate examples of different types of triangles to illustrate the principle as an integrative strategy. An organizational strategy might include having the learners identify key components of the principle and then compare the principle to similar principles (e.g., the number of degrees in a square). An elaborative strategy might ask the student to develop a diagram that explains the principle.

TABLE 7–5
Example principle strategies

Rule Example	Strategy	Implementation
Brush painting requires ⅓ more labor than spray painting.	Rule-eg and integration	• State the rule and then show a table illustrating the required time for each painting method.
Fusion welding is used when the base metal and weld metal colors must match	Eg-rule and organizational	• Show examples of fusion welding and bronze welding, and ask student to identify the visual difference between the two. • Have student develop a decision tree for selecting the welding process.
Metal expands when heated	Eg-rule and elaboration	• Show example of a cookie sheet warping in an oven. • Have student explain why a bridge has expansion joints. • Have student predict the effect of temperature on the expansion joints.

Returning to our example unit on wood fasteners, we find that the next objective is a rule that a nail should be driven through the thinnest piece of wood into the thicker piece. The student will use this rule to explain to customers how to select the size of the nail. Table 7–5 recommends three strategies for teaching a rule. The third suggestion, eg-rule and elaboration, was selected since this strategy is most similar to the job performance condition of explaining this principle to the customer. An elaboration strategy encourages the learner to add more information to the content, which makes the content meaningful.

The initial presentation of the rule will show several mocked-up pieces of wood nailed together. The learners are then asked to identify which piece of wood to drive the nail into first (eg-rule). An alternative would be to have the learners nail several thin and thick pieces of wood together to observe the results. The generative strategy (elaborative) asks the learners to draw a diagram for a customer to explain how to nail a $1'' \times 6'' \times 6'$ fence piece to a $2'' \times 4''$ fence rail.

Prescriptions for Teaching Procedures

A *procedure* is a sequence of steps the learner performs to accomplish a task such as threading a needle or solving a calculus problem. Like concepts and principles, the performance for a procedure can take the form of recall or application (see Table 7–2). Recall performance requires the learner to list or describe the steps of the procedure, while application requires the learner to *demonstrate* the procedure. The prescriptions for procedures are summarized in Table 7–6. The following

TABLE 7–6
Example procedure strategies

Procedure Example	Strategy	Implementation
Removing and installing piston rings	Demonstration, organization, elaboration, practice	• While watching a videotape of the process, students are encouraged to take notes on each step. • After the videotape, students are encouraged to develop a mental image of the positioning of the piston ring expander for removing and installing the rings. Then, they are encouraged to practice the procedure on an engine.
Calculating the amount of paint needed to paint a house	Demonstration, organization, elaboration, practice	• Students are presented with a worked example that illustrates how to calculate the amount of paint needed by using the square footage of the house and coverage of the paint. Learners are then encouraged to paraphrase the steps for doing the calculation. Last, they are given three examples to calculate the needed paint. When they complete an example, they compare their work against a worked example of the problem.

sections describe the strategy design for cognitive procedures and psychomotor procedures.

Cognitive Procedures. The initial instruction is the demonstration or modeling of the procedure. Since cognitive procedures are not directly observable, we must find a means of representing the procedure for the learner. Sweller and Cooper (1985) recommend worked examples (see Table 7–7) to teach cognitive procedures such as solving a math problem. The worked example shows each step of the problem-solving process. A learner studies the problem by working through each step of the example. Then, similar example problems are presented for practice.

If the purpose of the objective was simply to recall the procedure, the initial strategy would be an example. The generative strategies (e.g., recall, rehearsal of step names, mnemonics) are the same as recommended for a fact. For example, you might suggest a verbal mnemonic to help the learner remember either the steps or possibly a rule associated with a step. The generative strategy for an application performance involves two steps. First, the learner must either paraphrase the procedure or use an elaboration strategy to embellish the processes. Second, the instruction must provide the learner with practice in applying the procedure. In a classroom, the instructor can provide feedback while model answers or checklists for feedback are provided in a self-paced environment.

Psychomotor Procedures. The initial strategy for psychomotor procedures also involves modeling or demonstration of the task. For tasks involving psychomotor skills, the demonstration may need to have motion (e.g., a live demonstration or a videotape), or a series of still pictures may be adequate. Motion is often required

---

TABLE 7–7
Worked example

Problem: In baking a cake, the baker must combine 4 parts of flour with 1 part of milk. This particular cake will use 16 cups of flour. How much milk needs to be added?

Solution: Let's make Y the number of cups of milk that are needed. It is the *unknown* quantity. Now let's summarize the problem information in a table.

	Recipe	**Baker's Cake**
Flour	4 parts	16 cups
Milk	1 part	Y cups

Note that to solve the problem, we need equal ratios of milk to flour. Thus,

$$\frac{1}{4} = Y/16$$
$$1 \times 16 = Y \times 4$$
$$16 = 4Y$$
$$4 = Y$$

The baker needs 4 cups of milk.

---

for complex psychomotor tasks or when teaching psychomotor tasks to naive learners. A skilled individual such as an experienced car mechanic may find a series of still pictures (see Figure 8–4) adequate to learn a familiar procedure (e.g., replacing the brake pads on an automobile). A naive learner who is unfamiliar with the basic skills may find a more realistic demonstration, such as a videotape, more beneficial because it helps develop a model for executing the task. The initial learning for a psychomotor procedure is enhanced by encouraging the learner to develop mental images of the procedure and by adding verbal labels to the steps (Bandura & Jeffery, 1973; Anshel & Singer, 1980). Again, the generative strategy involves two steps. First, the learner is encouraged to either develop a mental image of the procedure, paraphrase the procedure, or elaborate on the steps of the procedure (e.g., connecting cues or decisions to each step). Second, the learner is encouraged to practice the procedure (see Table 7–7). Feedback can be provided by either an instructor, samples for comparison, or a checklist. If the objective is recall performance, then the generative strategies (e.g., recall, rehearsal of step names, mnemonics) are the same as those recommended for a fact.

The sample wood fastener unit has an objective for converting the length of a nail given in pennies to inches. The initial presentation is a worked example that illustrates the steps (see Table 7–8). The generative strategy involves two steps: (a) Ask the learners to paraphrase the procedure, and then (b) provide the learner with five problems to solve. The learners will then compare their answers with a worked example of each problem for feedback.

Prescriptions for Teaching Interpersonal Skills

Interpersonal skills deal with the development of communication skills. Performance for interpersonal skills is either recall or application, with a primary emphasis on application (see Table 7–2). The strategy for interpersonal objectives, based on Bandura's (1977) social learning theory, involves four steps. The first step is the initial instruction that presents the model to the learner. Models of the interpersonal behavior (e.g., how to deal with a student who is disrupting the class) are usually presented as live demonstrations or role plays, videotapes, or as printed scenarios. As part of the observation process, the learner's attention may need to be directed to identify key steps of the behavior as a generative activity (see Table 7–9).

The second step is for each learner to develop a verbal and imaginal model of the behavior. A verbal model is derived from the key steps—the process (e.g., modeling) can be paraphrased, or a cognitive map can be developed showing the

TABLE 7–8
Wood fastener worked example

Problem: Determine the length in inches of a 9d (penny) nail.
Solution: Divide the penny size by 4 and add 0.5 inch.
9d ÷ 4 = 2.25 inches
2.25 + 0.5 = 2.75 inches

TABLE 7–9
Example interpersonal skills strategies

Interpersonal Skill Example	Strategy	Implementation
Facilitate a group problem-solving meeting.	Model	Show students a videotape of a facilitator demonstrating the appropriate behaviors for a group.
	Develop verbal and imaginal model (organization)	Have students identify the key behaviors and when they are used.
	Mental rehearsal (elaboration)	Provide students with several instances that require the application of a facilitative behavior, and ask them to imagine how they would react.
	Overt practice	Provide opportunities for each student to facilitate a group as part of a role-play.

relationship between the steps. The imaginal model is developed either by offering the learner an image (e.g., "Remember how the teacher focused the student's attention on what she was explaining") or by directing the student to develop an image of the behavior.

Third is providing for mental rehearsal (covert practice) in executing the skill. Strategies for mental rehearsal can include examples or case studies presented in print or on videotape that prompt the learners to determine how they would respond.

Fourth is overt practice, which can include role plays involving two or more learners. Some environments might allow the development of interactive programs that present a situation, allow the learner to select a response, and then show the effects of the response.

If the purpose of the objective is simply to recall the interpersonal skill, the initial strategy would be a videotape or role play. The generative strategies (e.g., rehearsal of the step names, practice in reciting the names, mnemonics, etc.) are the same as those recommended for a fact.

The sample unit on wood fasteners includes a unit on sales techniques. One of the unit's objectives is for the student to demonstrate how to greet a customer correctly. The first step of the strategy is for the learner to view a videotape in which an expert demonstrates how to greet a customer. During a second viewing of the tape, words describing each of the steps for greeting a customer (e.g., making eye contact, smiling, verbal greeting) are superimposed on the video image to cue the student.

The second step is for the learner to develop the verbal and imaginal models. After viewing the videotape, students are asked to paraphrase the process (verbal model). Next, learners are directed to imagine themselves working in the wood fastener department when a customer approaches them. They are then told to visualize the scenario in their minds as to how they would greet the customer (imaginal model).

Mental rehearsal, the third step, is accomplished by presenting the learners with three scenarios with different situations (e.g., you are stocking new screws; you are busy with another customer) and asking them to imagine how they would greet the customer. The learners are divided into pairs and directed to role-play the different roles of the customer and sales associate as overt practice.

Prescriptions for Teaching Attitudes

An *attitude* consists of a belief and associated behavior or response. The strategy for teaching (changing) attitudes is similar to the strategy for interpersonal objectives. Both are based on Bandura's (1977) social learning theory. The prescription for attitudes is to model the behavior, develop the verbal and imaginal model, use mental rehearsal, and provide for both covert and overt rehearsal (see Table 7–10).

The last objective for our sales associates training concerns an attitude that all nails need to be weighed accurately. If the purchase weighs more than marked, then the store loses money; if the package weighs less than measured, then the customer loses (students learned how to weigh the nails in an earlier unit). The strategy employs the same four steps used for interpersonal skills.

In the first step, the instructor models how the exact weight of the nails is recorded on the sales slip. Second, the learner identifies the consequences of over- and undercharging the customer (verbal model) and imagines the consequences of each action (imaginal model). Third, the learner practices the imaginal model. Fourth, the learner practices the behavior of weighing the nails with an emphasis on marking the sales slip accurately.

TABLE 7–10
Example attitude strategies

Interpersonal Skill Example	Strategy	Implementation
Discussion of work projects with others may be giving away proprietary information.	Model	Have two students role-play a casual conversation between two individuals from two different companies where each describes a problem they are having with a work project.
	Develop verbal and imaginal model (organization)	Have students identify the type of information exchanged.
	Mental rehearsal (elaboration)	Provide students with several instances in which they might inadvertently give information away and ask them to imagine how they would react.
	Overt practice	Provide opportunities for each student to practice the appropriate behaviors.

SUMMARY

1. To design effective instruction, the designer must concentrate on how to present each individual objective in a manner that will help the learner achieve the objective. Designing the instructional strategies is probably the most crucial step in the process and can contribute the most to making the instruction successful. Unfortunately, however, the design of the instructional strategies is often the most neglected step of the instructional design process.

2. Instructional strategies begin with determining the content and performance type of each objective using the expanded content-performance matrix. This classification of the objectives helps the designer identify how the learner is to perform the behavior specified in the objective and the type of content the learner must master. Specific strategies are then prescribed for each cell of the content-performance matrix.

3. Each prescription involves two components. The first component is the initial presentation of the content for the learner. Our preferred form is direct, purposeful experience (concrete) with the content. Typically, the prescriptions recommend either hands-on learning experiences or the use of visuals or representations for abstract ideas.

4. The second component of the prescription is a generative strategy to make the content meaningful and to encourage active processing by the student. The generative strategies include recall, integration, organization, and elaboration. These strategies are then embedded, that is, made a part of the instructional unit so as to encourage the student to respond actively.

5. The prescriptions presented in this chapter form the basis of a set of heuristics for designing instruction. Each designer should attempt to modify and expand these heuristics based on experience.

6. The following steps describe how to design your instructional strategies:
   a. Review each objective and determine which cell it best fits in the performance-content matrix.
   b. Refer to the appropriate table of prescriptions in this chapter, and select an initial and generative strategy.
   c. Develop the instruction, which consists of the initial presentation and the generative strategy.

FROM HERE TO THERE

You are developing an introductory course on management information systems (MIS) for a company. Your task analysis has identified three different types of data bases (concepts) and information on how to determine which database is appropriate for the user's data (rules). The next step is to design the strategies for teaching the concepts and rules.

The concepts include relational, hierarchical, and multidimensional databases. You have also identified a total of seven rules that will help a user determine which database is most appropriate for the task. In your task analysis, you have identified one excellent example of an existing database for each of the three you will include in the unit. You also have two or more examples of each rule. How would you design the initial presentation and generative strategy for this instruction?

REFERENCES

Anshel, M. H., & Singer, R. N. (1980). Effect of learner strategies with modular versus traditional instruction on motor skill learning and retention. *Research Quarterly for Exercise and Sport, 51,* 451–462.

Bandura, A. (1977). *Social learning theory.* Englewood Cliffs, NJ: Prentice-Hall.

Bandura, A., & Jeffery, R. W. (1973). Role of symbolic coding and rehearsal processes in observational learning. *Journal of Personality and Social Psychology, 26,* 122–130.

Craik, F. I. M., & Lockhart, R. S. (1972). Levels of processing: A framework for memory research. *Journal of Verbal Learning and Verbal Behavior, 11,* 671–684.

Jonassen, D. H. (1985). Generative learning vs. mathemagenic control of text processing. In D. H. Jonassen (Ed.), *Technology of text: Vol. 2. Principles for structuring, designing, and displaying text.* Englewood Cliffs, NJ: Educational Technology Publications.

Jonassen, D. H. (1988). Integrating learning strategies into courseware to facilitate deeper processing. In D. H. Jonassen (Ed.), *Instructional designs for microcomputer courseware.* Hillsdale, NJ: Erlbaum.

Lebow, D. (1994). Constructivist values for instructional systems design: Five principles toward a new mindset. *Educational Technology Research and Development, 41,* 4–16.

Markle, S. (1969). *Good frames and bad: A grammar of frame writing.* New York: Wiley.

Rothkopf, E. Z. (1960). The concept of mathemagenic activities. *Review of Educational Research, 40,* 325–336.

Sweller, J., & Cooper, G. (1985). The use of worked examples as a substitute for problem solving in learning algebra. *Cognition and Instruction, 2,* 59–89.

Tennyson, R. D., & Cocchiarella, M. J. (1986). An empirically based instructional design theory for teaching concepts. *Review of Educational Research, 56,* 40–71.

West, C. K., Farmer, J. A., & Wolff, P. M. (1991). *Instructional design: Implications from cognitive science.* Englewood Cliffs, NJ: Prentice-Hall.

Wittrock, M. C. (1974). A generative model of mathematics learning. *Journal of Research in Mathematics Education, 5,* 181–197.

Wittrock, M. C. (1989). Generative processes of comprehension. *Educational Psychologist, 24,* 345–376.

DESIGNING THE INSTRUCTIONAL MESSAGE

"What is the best way to introduce the content to a learner?"

"What is the best way to implement my instructional strategies?"

"How can I cue the learner to the most important information?"

"Should I use pictures with my instruction?"

Thus far, we have focused on defining the problem and content, specifying the objectives, and designing the instructional strategies. The next step is to prepare the instructional materials by translating the instructional design plan into a unit of instruction. Translating the plan into an effective instructional unit requires more than simply "writing" the instruction. Effective instruction is developed through careful structuring and presenting the materials that both engage the learner and signal the learner to the important points. Now that we have determined the content and strategies for the instruction, we must shift our focus to the design of the message (Fleming, 1993).

In this chapter, we have divided this message design process into three sections. First is the preinstructional strategy, which is a technique for preparing the learner for the instruction. Second are strategies for signaling the structure of the text through words and typography. Third is discussion of the use of pictures and graphics in your instruction.

PREINSTRUCTIONAL STRATEGIES

Once the sequence for the instruction is established, the designer can begin to focus on how to present the information. Each unit of instruction begins with an introduction that prepares the learner for learning the task. Hartley and Davies (1976) identified four different methods or *preinstructional strategies* for introducing an instructional unit—the traditional written paragraph introduction (i.e., overview) plus three alternative approaches. Each of the four preinstructional strategies has specific applications for use in creating a better introduction for the unit.

The first preinstructional strategy is a *pretest,* which is a set of questions directly relevant to the instruction. The second type of preinstructional strategy is a set of *objectives,* which can be a simple restatement of the objectives the designer has developed, or the objectives can be modified and presented as goal statements describing the behavior the student must master. A third technique is the *overview,* which is similar to a summary. Unlike pretests and objectives, an overview is written as paragraphs of prose rather than a list of items. A variation of an overview is the graphic organizer, which uses a graphic to illustrate the content. The fourth preinstructional strategy is the *advance organizer,* which is similar to an overview but written at a higher level of abstraction.

Table 8–1 summarizes the applications and prescriptions derived from Hartley and Davies (1976) for each of these strategies. The "Function" column describes the instructional purpose we want to accomplish with the preinstructional strategy. "Content Structure" describes the nature or length of the content. Some topics are labeled as loosely structured (e.g., "How to sell a vacuum cleaner") because there is not one set method. A highly structured topic (e.g., "How to balance a checking account") has a set of well-defined steps that are easily identified and recognized by experts. A subject area such as math that is primarily rule-based is described as having a dominant structure as opposed to a topic such as visual literacy, which is more loosely structured. The "Learner" column describes the characteristics of the target audience in terms of maturity or intelligence. The last column, "Task Attributes," identifies the learning conditions best suited for this preinstructional strategy. The following sections provide guidelines for developing each type of preinstructional strategy.

Pretests

A pretest used as a preinstructional strategy differs from a pretest used to assess the learner's prior knowledge. When used as a preinstructional strategy, a pretest is designed to *heighten* the student's awareness of the content by serving as cues to the key points. These cues will help the learner identify and focus on the main ideas in the unit of instruction. Pretests work best when the instructional time is relatively short, allowing the learner to remain focused on the questions. Answers are typically not provided to the pretest questions, since the answers are derived from the instructional materials. (Additional guidelines for developing pretest questions are provided in Chapter 10.)

TABLE 8–1

Strategy	Function	Content Structure	Learner	Task Attributes
Pretests	Alert student to what is expected	Length of the instruction is relatively short and is loosely structured	Above average IQ, older or more mature learners	Learners should have some familiarity with the content if the questions are to be meaningful.
Behavioral objectives	Inform the student of *precisely* what is expected	Used to preface a passage less than 2,500 words*	Middle ability students	Works best with traditional methods such as lectures.
Overviews	Prepare the learners for the learning task	Little or no structure	Lower ability students learning ⟶ Higher ability students learning ⟶	facts concepts
Advance organizer	Clarify content for learner using conceptual framework	Should have a dominant structure	Above average ability, maturity, and sophistication	Factual information

* See Klauer (1984)

119

The following pretest might be used with a chapter on measures of central tendency:

Think about the following questions as you read this unit.

1. What are three measures of central tendency?
2. When is it appropriate to use each of the measures?
3. What are the steps to follow when calculating the mean?

Each of the questions is open-ended and serves to make the learner aware of three main points in the chapter. The designer does not expect the learners to answer the questions (if they can, then they may not need to complete the unit). Instead, the questions should direct the learner to these three key areas.

Pretest Guidelines

1. A preinstructional pretest should be relatively short so as not to delay the start of the instruction.
2. Typically, the questions are open-ended and answered mentally to stimulate the student to think about the answer as he or she reads the content.
3. If there are several objectives for the unit, the pretest items can be a sampling of the objectives rather than an item for each.

Objectives

The use of behavioral objectives has been the subject of much research in recent years (see Klauer, 1984). Davies (1976) has suggested that objectives may even be superfluous with highly designed materials such as computer-assisted instruction and other instructional design products. Another issue is whether students actually know *how* to use objectives for learning. Klauer's analysis found that learning directions and questions were more effective than specific (e.g., Mager style) objectives. One possible explanation was that the learners were better able to interpret and understand the implications of the learning directions and questions because they were presented in simpler sentences. Although the general trend continues to be the use of objectives as a preinstructional strategy, the research results suggest they are not as effective for promoting student learning as once thought. However, research and practice *strongly* support the use of objectives by teachers and instructional designers when designing instruction.

Here is an example of the use of objectives as a preinstructional strategy for a unit on job aids:

At the end of this unit, you will

- describe the difference between a job aid and a unit of instruction,
- determine when a job aid might be more appropriate than training, and
- design a job aid.

Objective Guidelines

1. Use a statement that clearly indicates the behavior the student needs to master rather than including the verb, condition, and criteria (cf., Klauer, 1984).

2. If there are several objectives for the unit, create more general statements to keep the list less than seven items long. Too many objectives will place too many requirements on short-term memory, resulting in confusion rather than mastery of the material.
3. Write the objectives in a style the learner can understand (e.g., "At the end of this unit you will. . ." as opposed to "At the termination of the instructional presentation, the learner will. . .").
4. Objectives are less effective with units of instruction that are longer than 2,500 words (Klauer, 1984). Researchers theorize that it is too difficult for learners to remember the objectives and the content for lengthy passages. As a result, the effectiveness of the objectives as a preinstructional strategy is decreased.

Overviews

Overviews and advance organizers are often referred to synonymously, although they are quite different. Overviews are written at the same level of abstraction as the unit of instruction and simply serve to introduce the student to the central themes.

Overviews are most often identified as an introduction because they are written as prose. The following is an example of an overview for a unit on job aids:

> A job aid is a step-by-step guide for performing a task on the job. Job aids are often used for complex tasks or infrequently performed tasks. An example of a task is the instructions on a pay telephone for making different types of long-distance calls. Although most individuals making such calls have received instruction on the task, the task is performed so infrequently that a job aid is used to prompt the user for the steps to perform.

Overview Guidelines

1. There are three general approaches to an overview. The first is simply to provide a summary of the content. The second is to pose a problem that the unit will help the learner solve (e.g., finding a discrepancy in your bank account). The third approach is to describe how the content will help the learner.
2. An overview should be relatively short (e.g., less than one page). A longer overview places an extra burden on the learner's short-term memory, which can interfere with the actual learning task.

Advance Organizers

An advance organizer is written at a higher level of abstraction and serves to provide a conceptual framework to increase the meaningfulness of the content. This conceptual framework is hypothesized to make it easier for the learner to grasp the new material. There are two forms of advance organizers. If the learner is familiar with the content, then a *comparative* organizer is used that compares the new content with what the learner already knows. If the learner is unfamiliar with the content, then an *expository* organizer is used that incorporates relevant information the learner already knows.

The following comparative organizer is from a study by Glover, Bullock, and Dietzer (1990). Notice how the authors compare the idea of model testing to the development of a car using a *model* car.

> Many scientific advances are the result of testing models that describe natural phenomena. Scientific models are similar in some ways to the models with which we are all familiar. For example, a model car represents a real car but is easier to manipulate and study than the real car. Consider how a car easily can be put into a small wind tunnel in order to test the means by which the car's form allows it to slip through the air. By testing the model car, engineers can quickly and inexpensively test many possible forms of new cars before settling on one. On the next several pages you will read more about how astronomy uses models (p. 296).

Advance Organizer Guidelines

1. State materials in general terms that learners can understand and remember.
2. Ideas presented should be inclusive of the content covered.
3. If the learner is unfamiliar with the content, use an expository advance organizer. Expository organizers include relevant information the learner already possesses and compares this known information to the new information in the instruction.
4. If the learner is somewhat familiar with the content, use a comparative organizer to compare the new idea to known ideas.

The selection of a preinstructional strategy should be based on the factors in Table 8–1. The process is one of finding the best fit among the function, content structure, target audience, and task attributes.

MESSAGE DESIGN FOR TEXT

An instructional unit—whether a textbook, printed manual, computer-based instruction, or videotape—is an artifact of the design process that will endure (Simon, 1981). This artifact represents the interface or interaction between the learner and the instructional materials. In Simon's terms, the artifact will serve its purpose if it is appropriate for the learner. Thus, our task as designers is to create an appropriate interface between the instructional materials and the learner. One part of this process is to design the message so that it is communicated effectively. In this section, we will consider how we can design the message by manipulating the text (e.g., structure of the writing) and the typography.

After analyzing science textbooks, Chambliss and Calfee (1989) concluded that there are three critical design elements essential to good printed instruction.

First is a set of distinctive elements such as words or typography that signal the structure of the text to the learner. For example, in this book the words at the beginning of each chapter signal the structure of the text through a series of questions and an overview. The paragraph headings signal the structure of the chapter, and bold and italics are used to signal key words. Second is the coherence of the text structure that aids the organization and recall of information. We can affect this structure by using redundancy and familiar text. Third, there must be a match between the content and the learner's background if the learner is to comprehend the text. Other research also supports the notion that we can affect cognitive process by designing the message (Britton & Gülgöz, 1991; Jonassen, 1982; Mannes, 1994; Schraw, Wade, & Kardash, 1993). Let's examine how we can manipulate or structure the text to communicate the schema or topic structure to the learner.

Signaling the Text's Schema

When learners are presented with a signal that identifies the text's structure, they can use this information to form a model of expectations that will aid comprehension (Mannes, 1994). As the learner encounters new information, this information is placed within the existing model. The preinstructional strategies described in the first part of this chapter are one means of signaling the overall structure of the text. Another approach is to alert the learner to specific information within the paragraph or section of the material. For example, how can you alert the reader that six different tools are needed to complete a task, or that a particular paragraph will compare RAM memory to ROM memory?

Armbruster (1986) identified five common text structures that a designer can use to signal important text for the learner:

- Lists of items or ideas which are in no significant order. Examples of lists in instructional materials could include the clothing you would need to take on a raft trip or the instruments needed to extract a tooth.
- Comparisons or contrasts of ideas or objects. A comparison in a seventh-grade science text is the difference between a planet and a moon. Similarly, a course on corporate finance might contrast two methods of cost accounting.
- Temporal sequences that are events connected by time or specific sequences. The steps for testing and replacing an automobile battery or for solving a quadratic equation are examples of temporal sequences.
- Cause and effect structures, or explanations, describe the relationship between two ideas or events. That is, one idea or event is explained as a result of the second. For example, an economics text explains the relationship between consumer demand and price. An instructional unit on crude oil production explains the relationship between well pipe diameter and maximum flow rate through the pipe.

- Definition and example structures are used to teach concepts by defining the concept and then offering examples of the concept. An example concept in a biology textbook is a capillary. Similarly, a concept in a database management training manual is a relational database.

Once the designer has identified the different topic structures in the instruction, the task is one of signaling these structures to the learner. These signals do not add new content to the text; rather, they provide emphasis to the structure or message the designer wishes to convey (Meyer, 1985). There are two methods for signaling these structures. First is through explicit statements that alert the learner to the structure. For example, we have signaled this list of two items by first mentioning that there are two methods, and then by starting the sentences with *first* and *second*. Second is through typographical conventions that signal the structure through change. Examples of typographic signals are the use of bold, italics, and spacing (e.g., indenting and vertical space).

Explicit Signals

Probably the most common method of explicit signaling is through the use of what Meyer (1985) calls *pointer words*. These words, such as *there are two methods* . . . , alert the learner to what to expect in the following sentence, paragraph, or chapter. By combining Meyer's pointer words with Armbruster's (1986) content structures, we can create a table of explicit signals (see Table 8–2) used as part of the message design process.

This list provides a general guide for how you can manipulate your text information to provide signals to important points for the learner. It is important that you use signals wisely and not overload the learner. Using too many signals on a page, whether in printed or electronic text, can result in too much distraction, with the learner failing to identify what is important. A second method for signaling the structure of the text is through the use of typography.

Typographical Signals

With the increased availability and ease of use of desktop publishing, the instructional designer now has greater control over the use of typographical signaling. We can use typography to signal the structure of the text by identifying changes in topic, and we can signal important words, phrases, and ideas by making them different from the surrounding text. Let's examine how we can use headings, layout, and typographical variations to signal the learner.

Headings.   Authors often use headings to signal the change of ideas and to provide the learner with a picture of how the materials are organized. The use of headings to signal changes of topics is even prominent in electronic documents. The tags used to create web pages for the World Wide Web recognizes six different levels of headings for a web page document (see Figure 8–1).

TABLE 8–2
Explicit Signals

Text structure	Example	Signaling words*
Lists	*The following* items are essential for a week long raft trip. . . . Humans *have five* senses. *First is...*	First, second, third, etc.; subsequent; another
Comparisons or contrasts	A single proprietorship is a business that is owned by one individual and typically managed by the owner. *In contrast,* a corporation is owned by a few to several thousand individuals and is incorporated under the laws of one of the fifty states.	But, in comparison, however, while, to differentiate, a distinguishing
	A prime number is divisible by itself and 1 *whereas* a composite number is divisible by at least one other whole number in addition to itself and 1.	
Temporal sequence	Hold down the Command key *while* pressing S to save the document.	Beginning with, after, next, then, first, second, etc.
	Finally, switch the main breaker to "on" and close the fuse box door.	
Cause and effect	*If* the application works properly with the extensions off, *then* there is probably a conflict with an extension.	Consequently, as a result, if/then, the reason, one explanation
	One result of increased recycling is the development of new industries to convert these items into new products.	
Definition and example	Assets are items or resources of value that are owned by an individual or business. *Examples of* assets include cars, buildings, a home, furniture, and computers.	For example, include, another
	Hibernation is a period of inactivity in cold-blooded animals. Animals that hibernate include snakes, rodents, and bees.	

* See Meyer (1985) for a detailed list.

Headings are key words or short phrases that identify the content of the sections of text information. We have found that most instructional materials need between two and three levels of headings. A heading level corresponds to the different levels in an outline you might use for writing a paper. For example, first-level headings would correspond to the points listed as Roman numerals I, II, III, etc. Second-level headings would refer to the A, B, and C, points under each of the Roman-numeral headings. The third level of headings would correspond to the points under the 1, 2, and 3, points under the A, B, and C headings.

FIGURE 8–1
Using headings as signals

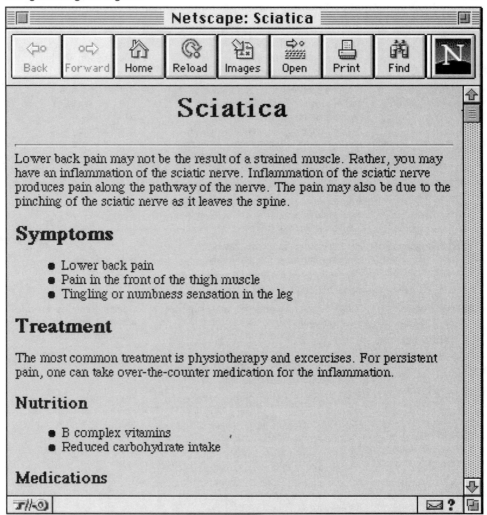

Each level of heading has a different typographical design. For example, in the manuscripts for this book, the first-level headings were 18-point bold type centered on a line. The second-level headings were left justified (i.e., against the left margin) and in 14-point bold type. Finally, the third-level headings were the first few words of a paragraph and were printed in bold. This style is one that is similar to the method used when writing articles for publication using the American Psychological Association's (APA) Style Manual and works well for manuscripts or documents that are desktop published.

To design headings for instructional materials, we suggest that you start with the objectives for the unit. Often, the objectives can function as the first level of headings. The second-level headings will signal the major ideas or steps needed to achieve the objectives. For complex content, you may want to also add a third level of heading that identifies specific ideas, tasks, or concepts in the unit. Next, you will need to select a typographical style that signals the heading. If you look through various books, magazines, and instructional materials, you will find a variety of styles used to identify the various levels. Your style should be easily recognizable by the learner. For example, using subtle changes in type size (e.g., 14, 12, and 10 point) with left justified headings might be a unique typographical design, but may be confusing to the learner. Again, we prefer a design based on the APA manual with minor variations used to create a unique design. A unique approach that does not signal the changing level of headings for the learner is likely to result in ineffective communication of the structure of the information.

If your materials are designed by a graphic designer, you may want to meet with this individual before you start creating your materials and seek his or her input on the design. In some instances, you may not have any decision-making authority on the typographical design of the final document. For example, a textbook author seldom has any input in the actual typographical design of the book. Yet, an instructional designer working in industry may have total control of the typographical design. Similarly, many graphic designers and editors are requesting that authors (including instructional designers) use a style template that assigns a specific style to text and graphics in a document. The graphic designer can then take the disk copy of the manuscript and easily create a layout on a microcomputer by assigning different typographical styles (e.g., bold, italics, type size, and spacing) to the document. This process can greatly reduce the production process and cost of the materials.

Layout. A designer can also use the layout of the page to signal structure of the information. For example, you can divide the page into vertical spacing and horizontal spacing, which graphic designers refer to as "white space." By increasing the number of lines between a heading and the previous and next paragraphs, you can create an emphasis on the heading. Similarly, you can indent a list of items from the left margin to signify that the items are grouped together.

Typographical Variations. Another means of signaling the structure of the information is by varying the type by adding bold, italics, underscore, or a change in type size, which creates a difference in the pattern of the page. Out of curiosity the human eye is drawn to this difference. Thus, type variations are used to signal important words and new information. There are three factors to consider when using typographical variations. First, using too many variations on a page can overwhelm the reader, making it difficult to determine what *is* important. Second, the use of a single variation must be consistent throughout your materials. For example, you should not use bold to identify new terms in one chapter of a book and then switch to italics in another chapter. Decide on how you will use a variation, if any, *before* you start writing, and then be consistent. Third, the mixing of different typefaces or fonts on a page requires an understanding of concord and contrast in typography. Designers who lack experience in typography should avoid mixing typefaces and rely primarily on the use of bold, italics, and size variations of one type font to signal the structure of the text.

PICTURES AND GRAPHICS IN INSTRUCTION

The final consideration is the use of pictures and graphics in instruction. There is considerable research (e.g., Levie & Lentz, 1982) and books (e.g., Willows & Houghton, 1987) devoted to the study and use of pictures in instruction. In this section we will describe the effectiveness of pictures in instructional materials, the functions pictures can serve, and some general design considerations for using pictures for instruction.

Effectiveness

There is a general consensus that illustrated text is conducive to learning the related text information. Pictures help readers learn the text information that *was illustrated* (Levie & Lentz, 1982). The pictures neither helped nor hindered the learning of textual information that *was not* duplicated in the illustrations. Pictures are particularly helpful when used to show spatial relationships described in the text (Peeck, 1987). For example, in a text describing the relationship between the position of the moon relative to the earth and sun during a lunar eclipse, a picture of these spatial relations would benefit the reader. Pictorial representations are also beneficial when used to illustrate abstract material and the main ideas in the text. However, no one type of information benefits more from illustrations than another.

Extensive research on the effectiveness of different types of illustrations was the subject of much of Dwyer's (e.g., 1970, 1972) work. A series of his studies has focused on the use of photographs, realistic drawings, and simple line drawings in instruction. He concluded that if the learner has limited time for viewing the illustration, such as in an externally paced presentation like a videotape or lecture, then a simple line drawing tends to be most effective. If the learning environment is self-paced, then the learner is more likely to take advantage of the details in a more realistic picture such as a photograph. However, there is always the possibility that the learner may focus on inappropriate parts of an illustration with too much detail.

Simply placing an illustration in the instruction, however, does not guarantee that the learner will examine the illustration and gain any benefits. Directing the learner's attention to the illustration through prompts such as "examine the difference . . ." are not always effective (Peeck, 1987). Researchers, however, have had more success when the learner interacts with or studies the illustration (Dean & Kulhavy, 1981; Winn & Holliday, 1982). For example, the designer might require the learner to label parts of a diagram or picture, answer questions about the picture, or trace and study a picture. A balance is needed between the picture and the activity, as overprompting the learner is also detrimental to learning from a picture (Winn & Holliday, 1982).

The Function of Pictures

One can examine almost any textbook with pictures and often see a variety of styles (e.g., simple to complex, black and white or color, line drawings or color drawings). Upon a more careful examination of the pictures and prose, one can identify pictures that serve different functions in a textbook. Levin (1981) has identified five different learning functions that pictures can perform in text. He also suggests that these functions are not equal in their effects on learning. Following is a summary of his categories with examples of how you might use each in designing instructional materials.

Decoration. Pictures at the beginning of a chapter often serve no other purpose than to decorate and to signal that a new chapter is about to start (see Figure 8–2). From a publisher's standpoint, the inclusion of these pictures increases sales by making the text appealing. An instructional designer might view the pictures as

FIGURE 8–2
Decorative picture

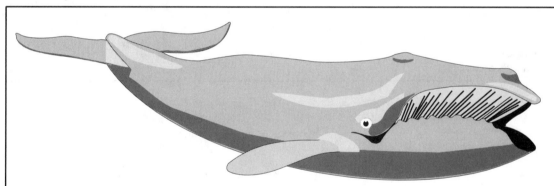

From a unit by Reneé Weiss, used with permission.

motivational for the student. Graphic designers also use decorative pictures in the text to "break up" the page so that it is appealing to the reader. The general idea is that a full page of text is threatening to the reader. Decorative pictures have no direct connection to the text information.

Representation.   When a picture is used to represent people, tools, things, or events in the text or other media, they are classified as representational. These pictures illustrate a major portion of the important textual information (Figure 8–3). For example, a designer might use two pictures in a science text to illustrate the difference between rotation and revolution of a planet. Representational pictures provide a concrete reference for verbal information, which makes the information easier and more meaningful to the learner. These pictures are often used in children's books to illustrate poems, fairy tales, and stories. They are also used in technical training materials to illustrate new ideas.

Organization.   If you have ever purchased a car repair manual, you have probably seen a series of pictures that performed an organizational function. Designers can use pictures, such as step-by-step, how-to pictures to provide a framework for the text (see Figure 8–4). The pictures in a manual on how to program a VCR or set up an

FIGURE 8–3
Representational picture

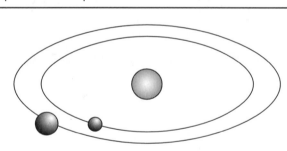

Planets orbit the sun. We can also say that planets revolve around the sun. All the planets revolve around the sun in the same direction. The time it takes a planet to revolve around the sun is known as one year on that planet.

Planets also spin or rotate on their axes, which causes day and night. If we were to draw an imaginary line through the center of the earth, we would call it an axis. The earth spins or turns on this axis. The planets all rotate on their own axes at different speeds. The earth rotates on its axis once every 24 hours.

FIGURE 8–4
Organizational picture

The Surgeon's Knot

The surgeon's knot is used to tie different diameter lines. Although it is not a very neat knot, it is very strong and easy to tie. It can be used to add tippet to the end of your line. This is especially useful when modifying your line to imitate dry flies, and when you want to do it quick, use the surgeon's knot.

Lay the new line parallel to the end of the leader, so that the lines overlap about four inches.

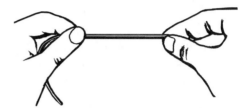

Make an overhand knot by forming a loop, bringing the tippet and leader around and through the loop. Keep the strands together.

Bring the same double strand around and through the loop once more, forming a double overhand.

Wet the knot, and then tighten by pulling all four ends to set the knot. Apply equal tension to both sides as you pull. Trim the tag ends as close as possible.

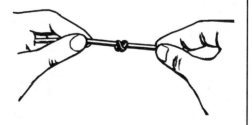

From a unit by Elizabeth Mathis, used with permission.

answering machine provide a map or path for completing the process. In many cases, the pictures provide more information than the few words associated with each picture. Pictures that perform an organizational function are not limited to procedural tasks. They are often used to describe the various attributes or features of an object (e.g., a new car) or a concept (e.g., a tornado).

Interpretation.   Pictures that help learner understanding of difficult or abstract information are classified as performing an interpretation function (see Figure 8–5). Carefully selected pictures can add comprehensibility to a passage by providing visual interpretation of the content. For example, a science book that uses pictures to explain Ohms Law by comparing it to the flow of water, or compares the heart to a water pump are examples of interpretative pictures. According to Levin, Anglin, and Carney (1987), the distinction between the representation, organization, and interpretation functions is one of the underlying mechanism (i.e., how the picture is used). Representational pictures add concrete representations to familiar information and organizational pictures add coherence to easy-to-process material. Interpretation pictures, on the other hand, provide added comprehensibility to difficult or abstract materials.

FIGURE 8–5
Interpretation picture

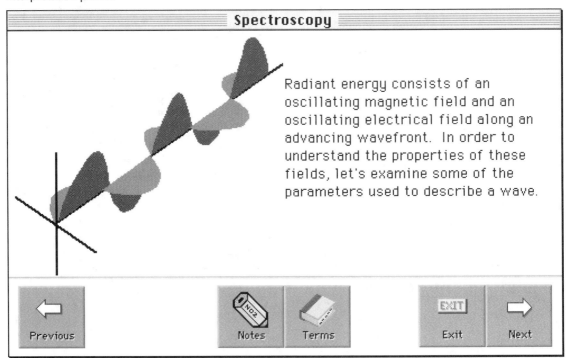

Transformation. Pictures that provide the learner with a mnemonic learning aid perform a transformation function (see Figure 8–6). Transformational pictures are useful in passages that require the memorization of facts by providing the learner with a visual anchor for recalling the fact. A transformation picture often combines concrete images to help the student recall an abstract idea.

Using Pictures in Instruction

The decision to use pictures in instruction is influenced by three factors. The first and most influential is to enhance learning. Second is the availability of the picture or illustration. Third is the cost of reproducing the materials with the added pictures. We have examined the first factor in the previous sections and will now address the last two factors.

Availability. With the advent of desktop publishing, computer-based instruction, and multimedia productions came the introduction of new technologies and processes for incorporating pictures and illustrations in instructional materials. For our purposes, we will classify pictures into three categories—original art, clip art, and photographs.

FIGURE 8–6
Transformation picture

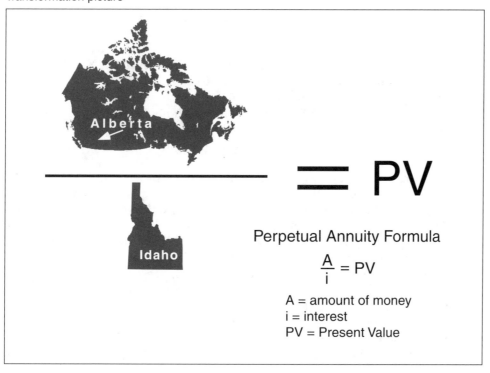

Original art is typically drawn by the instructional designer, artist, or graphic artist. The work can be a simple pen-and-ink line drawing, a watercolor, or a computer drawing. Original art requires someone with the artistic ability to render the picture. Computer drawing and drafting programs make it relatively simple for an individual with limited artistic ability to produce an illustration. More complex illustrations require more expertise. Thus, the use of original art can substantially increase the cost of your materials.

Clip art is widely available on CD-ROMs for most computer platforms. A designer can find a wide variety of photographs and line art (e.g., line drawings). Some of the materials are available for little or no royalty, and any royalty paid is often less than the cost of creating an original drawing. One problem with clip art is that it is generic and may not fit a designer's needs without some alteration. Also, the art may be outdated, depicting, for example, computers that are several years old or different from those used in the designer's organization. However, for those with limited artistic ability and limited access to a graphic artist, clip art provides a viable alternative.

Designers have the option of hiring a photographer to take specific photographs, purchase stock photographs, or select photographs from a CD-ROM. Again, CD-ROM photographs are often generic in nature and may not fit the specific need. Digital cameras have made it relatively easy for a designer to take a picture and incorporate it into the instructional materials whether distributed on paper or electronically via computer. The quality of the photograph will also depend upon the skill of the individual taking the picture.

Cost of Reproducing. The cost of reproducing the instructional materials is the final factor that influences the use of pictures in instructional materials. The cost of reproducing pictures is seldom a factor when the materials are distributed electronically such as in computer-based instruction, web publishing, or on CD-ROM. Typically, cost is only a factor when a large number of pictures require additional disks. Cost, however, is often a factor when preparing print materials that use either color and/or photographs.

Accurate reproduction of photographic images typically requires the use of the printing process (e.g., offset printing) as opposed to photocopying. Before a photographic print can be reproduced, it must be converted to a screened image, which is an additional cost. Each photograph must be individually screened and prepared for printing. Digital photographs do not require this process and may produce an acceptable photocopy.

Black-and-white line drawings add no additional cost to the duplication of materials. These drawings can be scanned into a computer and included with text or simply pasted in if they are clip art or computer drawings. Documents comprised only of text and line drawings can be reproduced by photocopying or offset printing. The addition of color either for text or drawings will add cost for any method of reproduction.

SUMMARY

Once you have completed the design of your instructional strategies, you are ready to concentrate on how to present the information. In this chapter, we have described how to create a preinstructional strategy to focus the learner's attention on the instruction, how to signal different aspects of the instruction through words and typography, and, finally, how to use pictures to enhance learner understanding. This message design process provides a means for effectively communicating your instructional strategies.

FROM HERE TO THERE

You have worked diligently on an instructional project, including creating the design of the graphics and printed page. At the last minute, your manager decides that your project is just the thing to showcase the training department. He makes arrangements for you to meet with a production house that will transform your document into something to rival a *National Geographic* publication, at least in looks. During your first meeting with the graphic designers, you explain your design scheme with the headings and indentations, stressing their importance for communicating the structure of the text. You also stress the importance of keeping the graphics very simple so as not to confuse the learner with too much detail. The graphic designers agree and promise to follow your suggestions.

Two weeks later you receive the page proofs from the production house. After a cursory examination, you can find absolutely no trace of the original structure that you conveyed to the graphic designers. In addition, the artists have turned your carefully crafted drawings into balloon-style cartoons, which detract from the potential dangers of working the high-voltage electrical equipment. In fact, the unit looks more like a comic book than either your original design or *National Geographic* magazine. Having seen the invoice included with the work (which makes you wonder why you suffered through an instructional design program), you wonder if you should mention the problems to your manager. Assuming that you have your anger and surprise under control, how would you approach this problem and correct it?

References

Armbruster, B. B. (1986). Schema theory and the design of content-area textbooks. *Educational Psychology, 21,* 253–267.

Britton, B. K., & Gülgöz, S. (1991). Using Kintsch's computational model to improve instructional text: Effects of repairing inference calls on recall and cognitive structures. *Journal of Educational Psychology, 83,* 329–345.

Chamblis, M. J., & Calfee, R. C. (1989). Designing science textbooks to enhance student understanding. *Educational Psychologist, 24,* 307–322.

Davies, I. K. (1976). *Objectives in curriculum design.* New York: McGraw-Hill.

Dean, R. S., & Kulhavy, R. W. (1981). The influence of spatial organization in prose learning. *Journal of Educational Psychology, 73,* 57–64.

Dwyer, F. M. (1970). Exploratory studies in the effectiveness of visual illustrations. *AV Communication Review, 18,* 11–15.

Dwyer, F. M. (1972). *A guide to improving visualized instruction.* University Park, PA: State College, Pennsylvania State University, Learning Services Division.

Fleming, M. (1993). Introduction. In M. Fleming and W. H. Levie (Eds.), *Instructional message design: Principles from the behavioral and cognitive sciences* (pp. *ix–xi*). Englewood Cliffs, NJ: Educational Technology Publications.

Glover, J. A., Bullock, R. G., & Dietzer, M. L. (1990). Advance organizers: Delay hypothesis. *Journal of Educational Psychology, 82,* 291–297.

Hartley, J., & Davies, I. K. (1976). Preinstructional strategies: The role of pretests, behavioral objectives, overviews, and advanced organizers. *Review of Educational Research, 46*(2), 239–265.

Jonassen, D. (1982). *The technology of text.* Englewood Cliffs, NJ: Educational Technology Publications.

Klauer, K. J. (1984). Intentional and incidental learning with instructional texts: A meta-analysis for 1970–1980. *American Educational Research Journal, 21,* 323–339.

Levie, W. H., & Lentz, R. (1982). Effects of text illustrations: A review of research. *Educational Communications and Technology Journal, 30,* 195–232.

Levin, J. R. (1981). On the functions of pictures in prose. In F. J. Pirozzolo & M. C. Wittrock (Eds.), *Neurospychological and cognitive processes in reading* (pp. 203–228). New York: Academic Press.

Levin, J. R., Anglin, G.J., & Carney, R. N. (1987). On empirically validating functions of pictures in prose. In D. M. Willows & H. A. Houghton (Eds.), *The psychology of Illustration: Volume 1. Basic research* (pp. 51–85). New York, NY: Springer-Verlag.

Mannes, S. (1994). Strategic processing of text. *Journal of Educational Psychology, 86,* 577–588.

Meyer, B. J. F. (1985). Signaling the structure of text. In D. J. Jonassen (Ed.), *The Technology of text, volume 2* (pp. 64–89). Englewood Cliffs, NJ: Educational Technology Publications.

Peeck, J. (1987). The role of illustrations in processing and remembering illustrated texts. In D. M. Willows & H. A. Houghton (Eds.) *The psychology of Illustration: Volume 1. Basic research* (pp. 114–151). New York, NY: Springer-Verlag.

Schraw, G., Wade, S. E., & Kardash, C. A. (1993). Interactive effects of text-based and task-based importance on learning from text. *Journal of Educational Psychology, 85,* 652–661.

Simon, H. A. (1981). *Sciences of the artificial* (2nd ed.). Cambridge, MA: The MIT Press.

Willows, D. M., & Houghton, H. A. (Eds.). (1987). *The psychology of Illustration: Volume 1. Basic research.* New York, NY: Springer-Verlag.

Winn, W. D., & Holliday, W. G. (1982). Design principles for diagrams and charts. In D. Jonassen (Ed.), *The technology of text, volume 1* (pp. 277–299). Englewood Cliffs, NJ: Educational Technology Publications.

INSTRUCTIONAL DELIVERY METHODS

"Should I lecture on this content, or is there another way to present it?"

"Is a group discussion the best method to accomplish these objectives?"

"Shall I do role-playing somewhere in this unit since my students are likely to benefit from such an activity?"

"Which method of self-paced learning would be appropriate for this topic?"

"Is it better to perform the demonstration before the class or put it on videotape for students to watch on their own?"

"They tell me it's best to include some activity for students during a lecture. How can this be done?"

"My company operates offices in several states and overseas. What would be the best method for delivering the instruction to these individuals?"

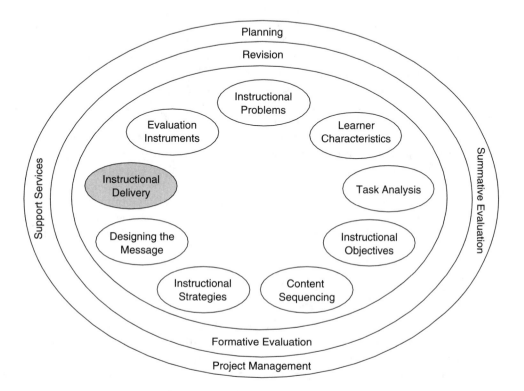

O nce the instructional strategies are designed (see Chapter 7), the instructional designer must make a decision on how to deliver the instruction to the target audience. In education, the most common means of delivery is the lecture, while in training programs there is typically a mix of lecture-type courses and self-paced courses. A designer can most likely design the same content for effective delivery in either a lecture format or a self-paced format. The key issue is which delivery approach will be more efficient. We can measure the efficiency of the program in terms of how much learning takes place relative to the time a student is engaged in the instruction (some companies include all time away from work for the training), the time the instructor is involved, the effort of the instructional design team, and the cost of the delivery system.

The selection of a delivery method is constrained by the objectives and the instructional environment. For example, objectives require different instructional strategies (see Chapter 7) and different delivery methods. A course or unit that focuses on the development of interpersonal skills is not well suited for delivery in a totally self-paced environment. Rather, a mix of self-paced instruction and small-group methods might be more appropriate.

Tessmer and Harris (1992) suggest an environmental analysis to identify the constraints of the instructional environment. After completing an environmental analysis, an instructor might decide to change the format of a course because the facility has only one large auditorium. Plans for extensive small-group activities would need to be modified, or a different facility would be required.

Similarly, a designer working for a large corporation with divisions in several states has different constraints. Schedules and/or costs might prohibit the use of large-group delivery methods. The designer would then need to identify either small-group or self-paced formats that would work within the constraints. If the appropriate technology were available, the designer might instead consider distance learning. Using two-way video and audio transmissions, employees at different sites could simultaneously listen to the same presentation and interact with an instructor and other students who may be thousands of miles away!

This chapter focuses on three different instructional delivery methods: group presentations (lectures), self-paced instruction, and small-group activities. Examples of each method are described, followed by a discussion of its strengths and limitations.

GROUP PRESENTATIONS

In the group presentation or lecture method, the instructor tells, shows, demonstrates, dramatizes, or otherwise disseminates subject content to a group of learners. This pattern can be utilized in a classroom, an auditorium, or a variety of locations through the use of radio, amplified telephone, closed-circuit television transmission, interactive-distance television, or satellite communication (teleconferencing).

While lecturing, the teacher may include media materials, such as transparencies, recordings, slides, video recordings, or computer-generated images, either singly or in multi-image combination. The presentation can also take place without the teacher being present (e.g., using slides with accompanying audio recording or in a video format).

These activities illustrate the one-way transmission of information from instructor to learners, often for a set period of time (generally a 40- to 50-minute class period). In small classes there may be some degree of two-way communication between teacher and learners, but most frequently learners are passively listening and watching.

Strengths

The benefits of choosing a group presentation method to accomplish certain learning objectives include the following:

- A lecture format is familiar and conventionally acceptable to both instructor and learners. This method is the most common form of instructional delivery.
- Lectures can often be fairly quickly designed since the instructor is familiar with the material and will make the actual presentation. The designer often provides the instructor with a list of objectives and a topic outline with the unwritten agreement that the instructor will follow the outline. The assumption is that the instructor can make the necessary strategy decisions. This strength is a particular advantage when instruction is needed to address a critical, short-term need.
- A lecture places the instructor in direct control of the class and in a visible authority position. For some instructors and in many teaching contexts, these factors are advantageous for achieving the objectives.
- Large numbers of learners can be served at one time with a lecture. The group is limited only by the size of the room; thus, lectures can be highly economical.
- As instructional needs change, a presentation can be easily modified by deleting content or adding new content just before or even during the delivery. Also, the presentation can be easily adapted for a specific group of learners (e.g., made longer or shorter, more or less difficult, etc.).
- Lectures are a feasible method of communicating when the information requires frequent changes and updates or when the information is relevant for only a short time period, such as the implementation of a new travel policy.
- A good lecture can be motivating and interesting for the students.

Limitations

The group presentation method of instruction suffers from the following limitations:

- Learning is typically very passive, involving listening, watching, and taking notes, with little or no opportunity for exchanging ideas with the instructor.
- To maintain learners' attention during a presentation, the lecturer needs to be interesting, enthusiastic, and challenging.
- When an instructor lectures, demonstrates, shows a video, or otherwise presents subject content to a class of learners, the assumption is made that all learners are acquiring the same understanding, with the same level of comprehension, at the same time. They are forced to learn at a pace set by the teacher. Thus, lectures are not adaptive to individual differences.
- If questioning is permitted, instruction stops and all learners must wait until the question is answered before the presentation can proceed.

- In a large lecture class, it is difficult for the instructor to receive individual feedback from learners pertaining to misunderstandings and difficulties encountered during the presentation. Thus, some learners may leave the class with incorrect learning.
- A presentation may be inappropriate for teaching psychomotor and affective objectives as these objectives typically require some form of practice or active learning environment.
- A large-group presentation may vary from presentation to presentation. Thus, the consistency of information and topics covered may not be the same for any two groups. This problem is particularly relevant when the training needs to be consistent, such as when teaching policies or procedures.
- Students who have difficulty with auditory learning will be at a disadvantage throughout the presentation.

Applications

There are specific situations and times at which a presentation to a group of learners is most valuable:

- As an introduction, overview, or orientation to a new topic
- To create interest for a subject or topic
- To present basic or essential information as common background before learners engage in small-group or individual activities
- To introduce recent developments in a field, especially when preparation time is limited
- To provide such resources as a one-time guest speaker, a video, or other visual presentation that can most conveniently and efficiently be shown to the whole group at one time
- To provide opportunities for learners to make their own presentations as reports to the class
- As a review or summary when the study of the topic or unit is concluded
- To teach a large group of learners in a highly economical manner

Guidelines for Effective Lecturing

Keep in mind that learning is enhanced when learners are actively involved. Therefore, it is important to develop a plan for including learner participation activities when lecturing. Also, to facilitate learners' understanding of the material, lectures should be clear and well organized. We recommend the following components:

- *Active interaction with the instructor.* Prepare questions to use at various points during the verbal presentation; encourage or direct learners to answer and enter into discussion with the instructor. Decide on places to stop a presentation (often at the conclusion of a section, or the end of information presented on a concept) and ask questions to measure understanding and encourage discussion.

- *Note taking.* Encourage note-taking by learners so that they will actively work with the material. Notes taken in the students' own words are useful in producing meaningful learning rather than rote memorization.
- *Handouts.* Consider preparing structured notes on topics requiring the learner to (a) fill in an outline of content (e.g., structured notes), (b) complete diagrams that accompany visuals used in the presentation, (c) write replies to questions, (d) solve problems, and (e) make applications of content and concepts as the presentation proceeds. Learners can also complete self-check exercises or quizzes over the content presented. The key is to stimulate active processing of the information. For this reason, detailed notes are generally *not* recommended, since they eliminate the need for the students to generate their own.
- *Other mental activity.* Encourage thinking by helping learners verbalize answers mentally to rhetorical or direct questions that you or another learner pose. You can also ask learners to formulate their own questions relating to the materials for use in follow-up small-group sessions.
- *Terminology.* Use clear terminology and meaningful examples to illustrate concepts.
- *Organization.* Organize the lecture by constructing an outline. Bring the outline (or note cards) to the presentation and talk "from" it rather than reading it verbatim (a guaranteed painful experience for listeners). Unless you are very accomplished as a lecturer and highly familiar with the presentation, do *not* try to speak extemporaneously; a frequent result is a disorganized and rambling presentation.
- *Enthusiasm.* Show enthusiasm and interest in your subject.
- *Format.* A standard model (adapted from Slavin, 1994) is as follows:
  1. Orient the students to the topics (an outline, story, or overview).
  2. Review prerequisites.
  3. Present the material in a clear, organized way.
  4. Ask questions.
  5. Provide independent practice.
  6. Review and preview.

Distance Learning as a Special Application

As telecommunications technology becomes more advanced and cost-effective, distance learning is receiving increasing attention as an instructional delivery system. As Simonson (1995) points out, although few students prefer to learn at a distance relative to being in the same room with the instructor, there are times when the convenience of distance education outweighs other factors. In the typical distance-learning setting, there is a *host* classroom or studio in which the instructor will actually present the instruction. *Remote* sites contain one or more video monitors, TV cameras, or microphones, along with other, optional equipment (e.g., a FAX machine) to permit the two-way transmission of voice, video images, written communications, and computer animations and simulations. In essence, the students at the remote site can hear, see, and interact with the instructor as he/she presents material in real time. Naturally, differing degrees of instructor-to-student interaction will be possible depending upon the number of remote sites to which the instruction is transmitted.

A newer type of distance learning is one using the Internet to deliver the instruction. Although not well developed or widely used yet, Internet instruction can be delivered by web pages that students visit to read text, view animations and graphics, and view digitized video clips. A second form of Internet instruction is the use of a listserv that distributes to all other students e-mail messages submitted by each member of the class. Although it is not real time, the listserv may function as a substitute or extension of a seminar class where the discussion transpires over a week or more rather than during a short meeting.

Strengths. Distance learning has additional strengths beyond the traditional classroom lecture and self-paced instruction for both training and education environments:

- Students can "attend" a lecture or group presentation without being present.
- Very large audiences situated miles apart can potentially be served.
- Quality communications equipment at the host site can transmit professional-level, multimedia presentations.
- Unlike conventional video presentations, students can experience instruction as it happens, thus permitting updates, announcements, and the spontaneity of live events.
- Unlike conventional instructional television, students can interact with the instructor by asking questions or making comments.

Weaknesses. There are also additional weaknesses associated with distance learning that one would not encounter in a traditional classroom. These weaknesses are:

- Depending on the sophistication of the telecommunications system and other resources, the quality of the video and/or audio transmission may be inferior to a presentation given in the same room (e.g., video images that are not well synchronized with the sound may be distracting to learners).
- Despite the two-way communication capabilities, interactions between individuals at the host and remote sites are more constrained and less fluid than would take place in the same room. To the extent that such interactions interrupt the main presentation or are difficult to follow aurally and visually, students may lose interest in the instruction.
- Distance learning is still a relatively expensive mode of education.

Guidelines for Effective Learning. The following heuristics can help you plan an effective distance learning lesson.

- Due to its expense, use distance learning selectively, where it fits special instructional conditions and needs (i.e., enables you to reach learners who are geographically dispersed).
- At the remote site, use multiple monitors rather than a single monitor where appropriate to achieve greater closeness between students and the presentation (Gopalakrishnan Jayasinghe, 1995).
- At the host site, favor an eye-level rather than high-angle camera position to increase eye contact by the presenter (Gopalakrishnan Jayasinghe, 1995).
- Carefully balance the amount of two-way communication permitted so that appropriate opportunities for interactivity are provided without compromising the pace or continuity of the lesson.
- Where appropriate, integrate multiple media (e.g., professional-quality videos or software presentations) to increase variety and impact, so that the distance instruction is more than watching essentially a TV-type lecture.

SELF-PACED LEARNING

Self-paced learning has received the most attention in instructional design. As the principles of learning indicate, much evidence supports the belief that optimum learning takes place when a student works at his or her own pace, is actively involved in performing specific learning tasks, and experiences success in learning.

Self-paced learning methods are also called *individualized learning* or *self-instruction.* While these terms may have different meanings, the important features for the learner are responsibility, pacing, and successful learning based on specific learning objectives and a variety of activities with accompanying resources.

Most frequently, the instructor selects the learning objectives and sets the requirements learners must follow. A "true" individualized learning or learner-controlled program would require the design of separate objectives and learning activities for each learner according to that individual's own characteristics, preparation, needs, and interests. Implementation of such a system usually requires a computer-managed instructional system to track the progress of each student and to select the appropriate objectives. Self-paced instruction, however, can occur at several different levels. Classic models from the literature are mastery learning (Block, 1971) at the precollege level and the Personalized System of Instruction (PSI) at the college level (Keller & Sherman, 1982). In school contexts, comparable approaches are sometimes referred to as continuous-progress grading, in which students' evaluations depend on the number of units they complete in a given time period (Slavin, 1994).

Drawing from these models, a quality self-paced learning program includes the following specific features:

- Learning activities are carefully designed to address specific objectives. A typical self-paced unit is organized into comparatively small, discrete steps, each one treating a single concept or segment of content. The size of the steps can vary, but it is essential that they are carefully sequenced.
- Activities and resources are carefully selected in terms of the required instructional objectives.
- The learner's mastery of each step is checked before he or she proceeds to the next step. Therefore, it is necessary to require the learner to demonstrate mastery of the content.
- The learner then must receive immediate confirmation of mastery of the objectives. With each success, the learner confidently advances to the next step.
- When the learner has difficulty understanding the material or fails to master the objectives for a unit, further study may be necessary, or the learner may ask the instructor for help. Thus, the learner is continually engaged in active learning and receives immediate feedback.

Most objectives in all three domains can be treated through some form of self-paced learning activities. In some learning environments, the instructor and students may feel more secure using a mixture of self-paced and group-paced instruction. The instructor and designer *must* determine the most appropriate delivery method for each of the objectives. In some situations, background and factual information might be assigned to a self-paced mode to ensure that all learners have mastered the basic information. Then, the group presentation (lecture) can build on this foundation. In another situation, the lecture might provide the background material, and some form of individualized instruction treatment would help the learners achieve the higher-level objectives. The instructor can then work with individual students who have difficulty mastering the material, while the faster learners can proceed to the next unit. Today, the greater emphasis being placed by educators on cognitive theory and self-constructed knowledge has altered thinking that self-paced units must be highly rigid in content and linked to highly specific mastery criteria. That is, units that are project-based and discovery-oriented would certainly represent desirable types of self-paced instruction (e.g., using the Internet as an information source for creating a classroom exhibition on world-renowned natural history museums).

Strengths

Evidence suggests that in many situations, learners participating in self-paced learning programs work harder, learn more, and retain more of what is learned than do learners in conventional classes. Self-paced learning offers a number of unique advantages as an instructional method:

- Both slow and advanced learners can complete the instruction according to their own abilities and under appropriate learning conditions.
- The self-reliance and personal responsibility required of learners by a self-paced learning program may carry over as habits to other educational activities, job responsibilities, and personal behavior.
- Increased attention by instructors can be given to the individual learner.
- The activities and responsibilities of an instructor involved in a self-paced learning program change because less time is spent in making presentations and more time is devoted to addressing learners in group sessions, consulting with individuals, and managing the learning environment.
- While major approaches to self-paced learning are not always immediately cost-effective, as the lessons and resources are employed over time with additional classes, the cost of a program can be reduced appreciably. (For a consideration of program costs and measuring program efficiency, see Chapter 12.)
- The information presented to each learner remains consistent (i.e., each learner receives the same basic ideas) over time, which reduces variations caused by lectures presented on different days.

Limitations

There are also some limitations to self-paced learning that make it less suitable for some environments:

- There may be a lack of interaction between instructor and learners or among learners if a self-paced program is the sole method of instruction in a course. Therefore, it is important to plan for periodic instructor-learner, small-group activities as appropriate.
- If a single-path, lockstep method is followed, learning can become monotonous and uninteresting. On the other hand, open-ended (discovery-type) projects may allow for too much divergence in what learners experience and accomplish.
- Lack of self-discipline combined with procrastination can result in delaying the completion of required study by some learners. Many learners must develop new habits and patterns of behavior before they are successful in self-paced learning. Setting deadlines (weekly or monthly) within which learners can adjust to their own study pace is often required and beneficial for some learners.
- The self-paced method often requires cooperation and detailed team planning with the faculty involved in the course. Also, coordination with other support services of the organization (facilities, media, reproduction, etc.) may become necessary or even critical. Such an effort is in

contrast to the usual single-person operation characteristic of conventional teaching.

- More preparation and expense is typically involved in developing self-paced units compared to lecture presentations.

Procedures

A self-paced unit typically includes a great deal of active learning. If existing materials (e.g., textbook, films, videotapes, etc.) are adapted, then the designer needs to develop materials to encourage active learning. These materials can include study guides, worksheets, and exercises. The Keller Plan (PSI) is a good example of how an instructor can adapt existing materials for use in an individualized program.

Since individuals learn at different rates, there should be time to study when it is convenient for them and also time in which to pace themselves. An individual may want to linger over some material and speed through that which they understand quickly. A preferable way to plan for individualized learning is to start with a variety of materials serving the objectives and then plan more than one instructional sequence to provide for differences among individual learners. Depending on preparation and need, some learners may take the fast track, even skipping ahead and using few materials before concluding their study. Other learners may require a slower track that contains a greater number of concrete illustrations or examples, more review exercises, or even smaller segments of subject content with a repetition of explanations in different contexts. A designer needs to include a management system into the course design to accommodate these learners.

Individuals also differ in their learning styles (see Chapter 3). Some learners respond best to visual materials, while others work better with printed resources or hands-on experiences. Therefore, it may be advisable to collect or prepare a variety of materials to treat a set of learning objectives, and then allow each learner to select a preferred way to study. For example, if an objective requires the operation of a piece of laboratory equipment, the program for mastering this objective may include printed instructions, a set of still photographs, a short film or videotape, and the equipment. One learner may choose to begin with the video demonstration and then go immediately to practice with the equipment; another learner might prefer to read the instruction sheet and then examine the still pictures before attempting to practice; a third might go immediately to the equipment and learn in a trial-and-error fashion.

By recognizing that active participation is a key element for learning, instructional planners can design a variety of experiences for learners. These can range from a carefully structured program that allows learners to proceed at their own pace, to one that gives individuals virtually complete freedom and responsibility for choosing their own activities and materials according to their own learning styles or preferences.

Examples

Following are descriptions of several procedures for implementing self-paced learning. They range from the use of simple prepared materials, to adaptations of commercial materials, to systematically planned, full-scale programs.

Learner Contracts. The learner enters into an agreement with the instructor to achieve acceptable objectives, often by completing a project in exchange for rewards (credit points, participation in special activities, or free time). Either the teacher suggests resources, or the learner takes responsibility for deciding what to do to achieve the objectives and carry out the project.

Textbooks/Worksheets. At times, to effectively study the content of a textbook or other printed resources used as an integral part of a course, a learner may need guidance when reading or language skills are limited. First, objectives are developed from the textbook content. Second, a worksheet directs the study of text chapters and provides review exercises, questions, and other activities. Third, a self-check test or a project to apply the content may be provided at the conclusion of each chapter review. After completing this work, a learner will be better prepared to participate in class work requiring both understanding and application of the textual content.

Computer-Based Instruction. A computer-based instruction (CBI) unit offers several options. It can offer a drill-and-practice routine to improve associations such as math facts, a tutorial to present new information, or a simulation that allows the learner to manipulate a system and observe the results. Some CBI programs are adaptive. One type of adaptation is through branching and presentation of information based on the learners' performance. A second form of adaptation is through the use of personalized information (e.g., learner's birth date, best friends, favorite food, etc.) in the examples and problems (Dorsey-Davis, Ross, & Morrison, 1991).

Audiotape/Worksheets. With an audiotape and worksheets, a learner reads information, refers to diagrams or other visuals, solves problems, and completes other activities under the direction of the instructor's voice on tape. The recording provides directions, information, explanations of answers, and other "tutorial" assistance.

The tape/worksheet combination is often developed to treat specific course topics for which other instructional materials may not exist or that require a unique approach. Tapes that contain the instructor's voice are typically a personal, often informal method of presenting course material in an interesting way. The audiocassette tape and worksheet combination form a compact package that learners can conveniently use wherever or whenever they choose.

Visuals/Guide Sheets.   Visuals with a guide sheet may be used when learners need directions or instructions in order to operate equipment, carry out a process, or complete a precise activity. Visuals in either still or motion picture form can guide learners through the steps necessary for completing a specific task.

A careful task analysis of the steps is a necessary prerequisite to developing a guide sheet. When visuals are combined with printed guide sheets that summarize an operation or provide other necessary factual or supplemental information, a complete self-instructional package on a topic can result.

Multimedia Package.   As the name implies, a multimedia package consists of several types of media resource materials that are used concurrently or sequentially in a self-paced learning situation. A package usually treats a single topic within a course. It can best provide the instruction for topics that require the realism of photographs or the symbolism of diagrams along with verbal explanations.

Commercially prepared multimedia packages are available in several formats: slides or a set of filmstrips with correlated audiocassettes and printed materials; a videocassette or motion picture film and printed materials; an interactive CD-ROM; and an interactive videodisc. The materials may include combinations of readings, worksheets, illustrations, animations, and real-time demonstrations. In addition, equipment and tools may be part of the kit with which the learner carries out performance activities.

As part of these packages, a syllabus or guide should describe (a) the learning objectives of the package, (b) the directions for use, and (c) the methods for evaluating how well the utilization of the package satisfies the instructional objectives.

Personalized System of Instruction (PSI).   The PSI method of self-paced learning (developed by psychologist Fred Keller [Keller & Sherman, 1982] and often called the Keller Plan) is an approach that may be applied to a complete course. Most frequently, it is based on a textbook with study units consisting of readings, questions, and problems. Instructional resources need not be limited only to written material. Other media of a visual and/or audio nature may be incorporated.

After studying and completing prescribed activities for each unit of material, a learner reports to a course proctor to be tested on the unit of instruction. The complete test is immediately graded by the proctor (usually a learner who previously completed the course successfully), who then shows the results to the learner. With satisfactory accomplishment of the test (often a competency-level requirement of 80%–90%), the learner proceeds to the next chapter or unit. If the specified level of learning does not result, the learner studies the material again and takes another form of the test when ready.

This procedure is repeated until the learner achieves success on each unit. Thus, completion times will vary between learners. Where *course* completion time must be fixed (e.g., at the end of a semester), grades may be based on the number of units completed. While some study is undertaken individually, not all learning has to occur in isolation. Some instructors meet with a class or small groups of learners to conduct special lectures and discussions. In addition, the contact between individual learners and proctors, for the purpose of evaluation and imme-diate feedback, can encourage further study. Although these days the Keller Plan is less frequently used as a comprehensive, intact design than in the 1970s, its basic elements offer viable strategies for self-paced instruction that can be adapted for use in a variety of contexts.

Audio-Tutorial Method.   Another complete, systematic approach to a self-paced learning course is the audio-tutorial method, designed by the botanist Samuel N. Postlethwait (Postlethwait, Novak, & Murray, 1972). The process usually includes three major components: (a) a large group meeting of the whole class, usually weekly, for a number of purposes—introducing a new topic, presenting a guest speaker, showing a film, or administering an examination; (b) self-paced learning activities in a learning lab appropriate for the course; and (c) group discussion ses-sions in which learners may ask questions, make reports, and engage in other forms of interaction.

A study guide is prepared that contains learning objectives, activities, exer-cises, and self-check tests. Audiotapes are used during the self-paced learning period to lead the learner through the learning experiences. The recording is not a lecture. The instructor's voice on the tape provides some information, tutorial guidance, and directions for the learner. Activities directed by the tape may include completing readings in books and from articles, studying visual materials, completing worksheet questions, and performing laboratory work as appropriate. The tape also provides the learner with answers as feedback on learning. The instructor or a teaching assistant usually is available in the learning lab to assist learners and answer questions. As with the Keller Plan, the audio-tutorial method is more likely to be seen today in adapted forms, all involving, in some way, self-paced completion of audio-taped lessons as primary or supplementary instruction.

Self-Instructional Modules.   The self-instructional module is a package that treats a single topic or unit of subject content. It includes a study guide containing all nec-essary information for a learner to proceed through the assigned material. Impor-tant components of a module are (a) carefully stated directions; (b) instructional objectives; (c) descriptions of activities and exercises (often with alternative choices so that a learner may select a preferred method of study); (d) a list of resources; and (e) one or more tests, with answers, so the learner may check progress in learning.

The module may refer the learner to other resources in the library or lab. Activities are not necessarily limited to the study of written materials alone. Video and audio media resources are often used to augment, clarify, or enhance printed information. A series of self-instructional modules may comprise an entire course or be used as part of a course to cover topical areas. Study time for individual modules may vary from less than an hour to a day or more of work.

A Planning Checklist. If you are developing a self-paced program, the following checklist of questions for evaluating your planning may prove useful:

____ 1. Is the program adaptable to the characteristics of learners who have different cultural and ethnic backgrounds?

____ 2. Are learners who need remedial help identified before starting on a unit or module?

____ 3. Are learners allowed to skip ahead if they already show competencies in part of the topic being treated?

____ 4. Are low-level cognitive knowledge and psychomotor skills mastered before requiring higher-level learning experiences and practical applications of subject content?

____ 5. Is adequate attention given to affective objectives? That is, are learners developing positive attitudes toward the subject or its applications?

____ 6. Are options provided so that a learner may select learning experiences and resources?

____ 7. Are learners permitted or encouraged to progress at their own rates?

____ 8. Do learners have opportunities for checking their progress as they proceed through a program?

____ 9. Do learners have opportunities to share their learning or otherwise interact among themselves and with the instructor?

____ 10. Do instructors consult with or assist individual learners and small groups?

____ 11. How will self-pacing for the particular unit impact other activities in the course?

Changing Roles. Finally, as a planning team designs a self-paced learning program, the instructors involved should recognize that not only are they changing their methods of instruction, they also must change their own roles in working with learners. These changes can become both stimulating and more demanding. Some of the changes that can be anticipated are:

- Freedom from routine teaching of basic facts and skills
- More time spent with individual learners in diagnosing their difficulties, giving help, and monitoring their progress
- More opportunities to interact with learners on higher intellectual levels concerning their problems, interests, and uses of the subject content
- More time required for preparing, gathering, and organizing materials for use by learners
- More time required to orient and supervise aides, tutors, proctors, and other assistants

SMALL-GROUP FORMATS

In the small-group teaching/learning format, teachers and learners, or learners themselves, work together in groups of 2 to 10 or so individuals to discuss, question, pursue problems cooperatively, and report. This approach provides students an opportunity to synthesize the content and improve their communication skills.

Strengths

Small-group formats have the following strengths:

- A small-group format can engender synthesis of content by allowing individuals to discuss materials, share ideas, and problem solve with others.
- Learners acquire experiences in listening and oral expression through reacting to others' ideas and presenting their own. The more able learners can strengthen their own learning by explaining points or principles to other learners (also known as "peer teaching").
- By listening to students' discussion in a small-group session, an instructor can gain an increased awareness of the successes or shortcomings of various phases of an instructional program as well as obtaining suggestions from learners for revisions.
- Small-group sessions promote active learning.
- Learners develop social skills by working with others.

Limitations

Small-group learning may have the following drawbacks:

- Students need to complete the assigned readings before the small-group activities so that they will be ready to participate.
- Instructors who are not prepared or who are inexperienced with small-group activities may fall back on lecturing for their own security or provide too much input at the expense of the discussion.
- Careful planning of group composition and management are required to create an atmosphere that encourages all group members to participate.
- Individual groups require feedback on their progress and often prompting to help them cover the planned information.
- Students are not trained instructors; thus, the group activities should be used to supplement rather than replace other forms of instruction (lecture or individualized).

Formats

A number of different techniques are available to encourage and provide for interaction within small groups. These eight techniques are useful in both large-group and self-paced formats.

Discussion.   Discussion is the most common form of face-to-face teaching in which facts, ideas, and opinions can be exchanged. As learners think about a subject under discussion and present their views, learning can take place on higher intellectual levels (specifically analysis, synthesis, and evaluation) than is possible solely with the recall of information.

Discussions can take three forms:

1. *Instructor-directed* discussion is characterized by questions posed by the instructor and answered by individual learners. Such a format provides for a limited exchange of ideas within the group.
2. *Group-centered* discussion allows for a free-flowing exchange of ideas without the controlling influence of the instructor. Cooperation between participants provides their own direction and control of the pace. This method is open-ended, as the discussion can go in any number of directions depending on learner interactions and reactions.
3. *Collaborative* discussions often focus on solving a specific problem. The instructor has neither a dominant nor a passive role but serves as a resource person and also as a contributor. All participants share decision-making responsibilities and are obliged to accept and integrate the ideas presented and critically evaluate alternative solutions. This method is the most difficult form of discussion to implement; it is best used after a group has experience with the previous two forms of discussion.

Panel Discussion.   In the panel discussion, three to six qualified persons (from the community or a professional group) present information or their views on an assigned topic in front of the class. The individuals may represent different viewpoints, various interest groups, or special experiences. Learners may research topics and comprise the panels themselves to present their findings. Following the presentations, learners in the class are encouraged to ask questions of the panel members.

Guided Design.   The guided design method, developed by Charles E. Wales (Wales, Nardi, & Stager, 1987) of West Virginia University, focuses on developing the learners' decision-making skills as well as on teaching specific concepts and principles. Learners work in small groups to solve open-ended problems that require them to gather information (outside of class), think logically, communicate ideas, and apply steps in a decision-making process. Learners are required to look closely at each step in the decision-making operation, apply the subject matter they have learned, exchange ideas, and reflect on solutions developed by others. The instructor acts as a consultant to the class.

Case Study.   In a case study, learners are provided with detailed information about a real-life situation. All related circumstances, issues, and actions of persons involved are carefully described. Learners must study and analyze the situation as presented. They decide what was done correctly and what mistakes might have been made in terms of principles and accepted practices in their field of specialization. During discussion, each person must explain, justify, and defend his or her own analysis of the case situation. This method is widely used in the business management field.

Role-Playing.   Role-playing involves the spontaneous dramatization by two or more persons of a situation relating to a problem. The incident might have to do with interpersonal relations or an operational problem within an organization. Each person acts out a role as he or she feels it would be played in real life. Other learners or trainees observe the performance and then, when the performance ends, discuss the feelings expressed and actions observed. This process promotes an understanding of other persons' positions and attitudes as well as the procedures that might be used for diagnosing and solving problems.

Simulation.   Simulation is an abstract representation of a real-life situation that requires a learner or a team to solve a complex problem. The instructor creates aspects of the situation that are close to reality, and the learner must perform manipulations, make responses, and take actions to correct deficiencies or maintain a proper status. Many simulations are computer controlled, such as a mock-up simulator of an airplane cockpit for pilot training. The simulator allows the instructor to set up appropriate conditions that require specific responses by the trainee. The participants become deeply involved, undergoing the same stress and pressures they would experience in reality. The instructor discusses and evaluates the results of the activity with the learners.

Games.   A game is a formalized simulation activity. Two or more participants or teams compete in attempting to meet a set of objectives relating to a training topic. The game takes place under a set of rules and procedures, with information being provided that requires decision making and follow-up actions. The subjects of most instructional games are typical real-life situations as related to a training topic. Periodically, the results are evaluated by the instructor, other learners, or a group of judges. A wide variety of prepared games is available for use in many areas of instruction.

Cooperative Learning.   Cooperative learning is a specific type of group activity that attempts to promote both learning and social skills by incorporating three concepts (Slavin, 1994) into the instruction: (a) group rewards, (b) individual accountability, and (c) equal opportunity for success. Consideration of these components suggests that cooperative learning needs to be carefully planned and systematically implemented. It is much more than assigning learners to groups and telling them to "tutor each other" or complete a project.

Two major forms of cooperative learning involve having students work in groups to (a) help one another master material and (b) complete a project, such as a written report, presentation, experiment, artwork, and so forth. In both situations it is desirable to follow these guidelines:

- Limit group size to three to five students.
- Compose groups so that they are heterogeneous in ability level, gender, and ethnicity.
- Carefully plan the activities with regard to room arrangement, task materials, and time frame.
- Establish some reward (recognition or something tangible, depending on the age level of the learners) to motivate the groups.
- Ensure that everyone in the group has a specific task with which they can succeed with appropriate effort. Otherwise, shy or lower-ability students may defer to others and not benefit from the activity.
- Teach the lesson using an instructor presentation or appropriate individualized approach; use cooperative learning as a supplement for review, practice, remediation, or enrichment.
- Monitor and assist the groups as needed.
- Base grades as much as possible on individual group members' personal contributions or achievement; use the group reward as the means of recognizing the group's success.

Cooperative learning has proved very successful in research studies. Several models, such as Student-Teams Achievement Divisions, Co-op Co-op, Cooperative Controversy, and Jig Saw, have become quite popular in recent years. Also consider that the way cooperative learning is designed may depend on the conditions of instruction. In a computer-based learning context, for example, the lack of sufficient computers for all students may necessitate employing some form of cooperative groupings. However, the availability of space around the computers may further dictate how many students can work together at the same time.

As Sherman and Klein (1995) recently demonstrated in a research study, strategies for making cooperative learning more effective may be integrated with the main instruction. Specifically, they designed a computer-based unit to cue students working in groups to perform various interactive cooperative activities (e.g., "Yulanda, explain to Gerry why the first statement below is an example of an observation, but the second statement is not.") Their findings indicated that both learning interactivity and achievement increased relative to a non-cued condition. For more ideas on cooperative learning, the books by Slavin (1995) and Johnson and Johnson (1986) should be valuable in suggesting alternative approaches and outlining implementation procedures.

SUMMARY

1. The three patterns we have examined—presentation to class, self-paced learning, and small-group interaction activities—provide the framework for delivering a variety of instructional formats. As you consider the selection of methods, the following important questions should be asked:
   a. Is there subject content or other material that can best be uniformly presented to all learners at one time?
   b. Is there subject content that learners can better study on their own, at their individual paces?
   c. Are there experiences that would best be served by discussion or other group activity, with or without the instructor being present?
   d. Is there need for individual learner-instructor discussion or consultation in private?
   In considering these questions, the planning team should consider some degree of balance among the three delivery patterns.
2. Although the large-group presentation format is still the most widely accepted method in schools, it keeps learners in a generally passive mode and may not be cost-effective in training contexts where learners are geographically dispersed or highly varied in experiences and training needs. Distance learning is gaining popularity as a mode for reaching many learners located at remote sites.
3. In business, many companies are switching to a self-paced delivery format to reduce travel costs and time away from the job and to increase the efficiency of the instruction. Greater access to computers by businesses and schools is making self-paced instruction more practical and potentially more powerful.
4. In many situations, there are no clear-cut divisions among the three patterns. A presentation to a regular-sized class can incorporate questions and discussion. A self-paced learning period may be supplemented periodically with tutorial interaction as one learner helps another or as the instructor replies to a trainee's question. Combining orientations to fit instructional conditions and individual needs is a sensible approach that can potentially yield benefits much greater than could be attained by using any one method alone.

FROM HERE TO THERE

The city police department requests the development of a training unit to teach officers a new protocol for testing drivers for possible intoxication (DUI). Because of the officers' highly varied schedules and differing degrees of prior experience with the new procedure, you (as the designer) decide that group presentations will be impractical and inefficient. Instead, after conducting careful task and learner analyses, you select self-paced instruction as the primary delivery mode. Given the department's lack of computers for training purposes, and the expense of developing (and possibly revising at some later point) computer-based units, you further decide to make the primary instruction print-based. Using the main strategies from mastery learning and PSI, you develop three sub-units, each covering a different major area (identification-apprehension, testing, decision-debriefing). Each sub-unit includes a set of objectives, instructional materials pertaining to each objective, and an assessment. For two of the sub-units, you include audiotapes to supplement the print instruction, and for the sub-unit on testing, you include a video to demonstrate the testing procedures. At the completion of the entire unit, the officers take a cumulative test. Failure to achieve a score of 90% or higher necessitates review and retesting on a parallel test form. Thus, although the unit employs the self-pacing mode, it incorporates a variety of instructional approaches to address the project's specific training needs and conditions. Do you think this design will meet the needs of your client?

REFERENCES

Block, J. H. (Ed.). (1971). *Mastery learning: Theory and practice.* Englewood Cliffs, NJ: Prentice-Hall.

Dorsey-Davis, J. D., Ross, S. M., & Morrison, G. R. (1991). The role of rewording and context personalization in the solving of mathematical word problems. *Journal of Educational Psychology, 83,* 61–68.

Gopalakrishnan Jayasinghe, M. (1995). *The impact of camera angle, single versus multiple monitors, and incentive on instructor credibility, immediacy and interaction in a simulated distance learning environment.* Unpublished dissertation, University of Memphis, Memphis, TN.

Johnson, D. W., & Johnson, R. T. (1986). *Learning together and alone.* Englewood Cliffs, NJ: Prentice-Hall.

Keller, F. S., & Sherman, J. G. (1982). *The PSI handbook: Essays on personalized instruction.* Lawrence, KS: International Society for Individualized Instruction.

Postlethwait, S. N., Novak, J., & Murray, H. (1972). *The audio-tutorial approach to learning.* Minneapolis: Burgess.

Sherman, G. P., & Klein, J. D. (1995). The effects of cued interaction and ability grouping during cooperative computer-based science instruction. *Educational Technology Research and Development, 43*(4), 5–24.

Simonson, M. (1995). Does anyone really want to learn at a distance? *Tech Trends, 40*(5), 12.

Slavin, R. E. (1994). *Educational psychology* (4th ed.). Needham Heights, MA: Allyn & Bacon.

Slavin, R. E. (1995). *Cooperative learning: Theory, research, and practice.* Englewood Cliffs, NJ: Prentice-Hall.

Tessmer, M., & Harris, D. (1992). *Analysing the instructional setting: Environmental analysis.* London: Kogan Page.

Wales, C. E., Nardi, A. H., & Stager, R. A. (1987). *Thinking skills: Making a choice.* Morgantown, WV: Center for Guided Design.

THE MANY FACES
OF EVALUATION

"How can I determine whether this course is teaching what it is supposed to?"

"Which parts of this lesson are working well, and which need improvement?"

"What are some ways to measure the accomplishment of performance skills besides observing a person at work on a job?"

"If all students satisfactorily accomplish all the objectives I set for a topic, shouldn't they all receive an A?"

"When is it appropriate to use a performance test instead of an objective test?"

"The questions on this test don't relate to the objectives the teacher gave us at the beginning of the unit. Shouldn't they?"

"Should I pretest my students? If so, how can that information be used to improve instruction?"

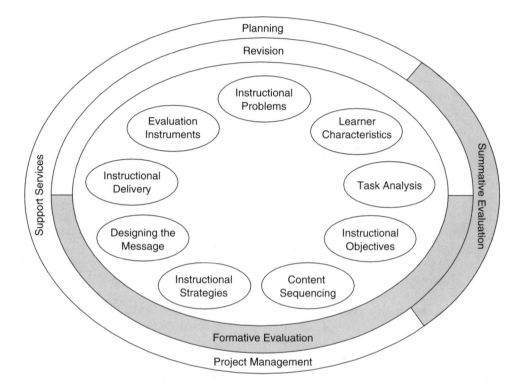

As reflected by these questions, evaluating learning is essential in the instructional design process. After examining learner characteristics, you identified instructional objectives and selected instructional strategies to accomplish them. Now, finally, you must develop the testing instruments and materials to measure the degree to which learners have acquired the knowledge, can perform the skills, and exhibit changes in attitudes as required by the objectives.

In this chapter we examine the purposes and major forms of evaluation and important concepts concerning its role in the instructional design process. In Chapter 11 we will focus on specific procedures for constructing different types of tests and instruments to evaluate student learning.

Purposes of Evaluation

Before initiating an evaluation, you must determine its goals. The overall goal is to determine *student success in learning*. But will the evaluation results be used primarily for *improving* how the course is taught or for identifying the *effectiveness* of the course? These two functions clearly go hand in hand, but the nature of the evaluation process is likely to differ depending on which function is assigned greater importance. We refer to these complementary approaches as *formative evaluation* and *summative evaluation*.

Formative Evaluation

Even the most talented and conscientious designer is not likely to develop the "perfect" lesson or course the first time through. What seems excellent as a concept or idea may not work as well as planned when actually put to use in the classroom. Formative evaluation thus becomes an important part of the instructional design process. Its function is to inform the instructor or planning team how well the instructional program is serving the objectives *as it progresses*.

Formative evaluation is most valuable when conducted during development and tryouts. If the instructional plan contains weaknesses, they can be identified and eliminated before full-scale implementation. Test results, reactions from learners, observations of learners at work, reviews by subject-matter experts, and suggestions from colleagues may indicate deficiencies in the learning sequence, procedures, or materials.

Formative testing and revision (and retesting and further revision, if necessary) are important for the success of an instructional design plan. They should relate not only to the suitability of objectives, subject content, learning methods, and materials but also to the roles of personnel, the use of facilities and equipment, schedules, and other factors that together affect optimum performance in achieving objectives. Remember, the planning process is highly interactive—each element affects other elements.

The following questions might be used to gather data during formative evaluation:

1. Given the objectives for the unit or lesson, is the level of learning acceptable? What weaknesses are apparent?
2. Are learners able to use the knowledge or perform the skills at an acceptable level? Are any weaknesses indicated?
3. How much time did the instruction and learning require? Is this acceptable?
4. Did the activities seem appropriate and manageable to the instructor and learners?
5. Were the materials convenient and easy to locate, use, and file?
6. What were the learners' reactions to the method of study, activities, materials, and evaluation methods?
7. Do the unit tests and other outcome measures satisfactorily assess the instructional objectives?

8. What revisions in the program seem necessary (content, format, etc.)?
9. Is the instructional context appropriate?

We will more closely examine the procedures for conducting formative evaluations in Chapter 15. For now, consider the purposes of the formative approach in comparison to those of an alternative orientation, summative evaluation.

Summative Evaluation

Summative evaluation is directed toward measuring the degree to which the major outcomes are attained by the end of the course. Key information sources are therefore likely to be the results of both the unit posttests and the final examination for the course. In addition to the effectiveness of student or trainee learning, interests of summative evaluations also frequently include:

- efficiency of learning (material mastered/time)
- cost of program development
- continuing expenses
- reactions toward the course or program
- long-term benefits of the program

Long-term benefits may be determined by following up on learners who complete the program to discover whether and when they are using the knowledge, skills, and attitudes learned. (Summative evaluation receives full attention in Chapter 15.)

RELATIONSHIP BETWEEN FORMATIVE AND SUMMATIVE EVALUATION

At this stage, you probably have noted some similarities as well as differences between formative and summative evaluations. Let's now take a closer look at how these approaches compare.

The Role of Instructional Objectives

For both evaluation approaches, what is evaluated is determined directly by instructional objectives. If one objective, for example, is to teach trainees how to file an accident report correctly, then assessing how well they do this becomes an essential part of an evaluation regardless of whether the primary interest is to improve the instruction (formative) or judge its effectiveness (summative). If improving student *attitudes* toward the accident reporting process is *not* an instructional goal, there will be little rationale for including an attitude measure (although, as we will see, attitude assessments can be valuable in interpreting why particular objectives are or are not achieved successfully).

Instructional objectives, however, provide only part of the basis for determining evaluation objectives. Broader educational or training goals may suggest looking at "summative" impacts of instruction on personnel, administration, resource allocation, and cost-effectiveness (see Chapter 15). As will be discussed later, analyzing processes of instruction (e.g., teaching methods, student behaviors, or student feelings) becomes especially important in conducting formative evaluations to describe how well particular course features are operating.

Multiple Data Sources Equal Increased Information

Because most units of instruction have multiple objectives with different focuses, both formative and summative evaluations will require varied sources of outcome data. Examples would include measures of knowledge, skills, behaviors, attitudes, and completion time, as well as information about the instructional delivery, learning activities, resources, teacher characteristics, and so on. The more the designer knows about the instruction and its outcomes, the more confidently he or she can make conclusions and recommendations. Generally speaking, there is a greater need for multiple data sources in formative evaluations, since the interest is not only to determine the effectiveness of particular elements but also how to improve those that are not working as planned.

Processes and Products

Formative evaluation asks, "How are we doing?" while summative evaluation asks, "How did we do?" (Slavin, 1994). To answer these questions, different types of measurement orientations are needed. Specifically, formative evaluation will emphasize the measurement of outcomes as instruction evolves (or "forms"). Interest is *as much with process as with product.* Summative evaluation will stress measurement of criterion outcomes that occur at the end of instruction. Interest is *more with products than with processes.*

Time of Testing

For formative evaluations, testing is important at all phases of instruction—*pretesting* (before), *embedded testing* (during), and *posttesting* (after). Although all three types of testing may be used in summative evaluation, posttesting is clearly the most critical and the main basis for forming conclusions about the instruction. (In the final section of this chapter, we will examine uses of pretesting in more detail.)

When to Evaluate

Formative evaluations are most valuable *before* instruction is fully developed, when it is inexpensive to make changes. As will be discussed more fully in Chapter 15, some common modes of formative evaluation are *connoisseur-based (expert) review, one-to-one trials, small-group testing,* and *field testing.* All of these are used to refine instruction at different developmental stages. Summative evaluations, in contrast, are designed to examine the effectiveness of completed versions of instruction. While summative evaluations come toward the end of the instructional development process, formative evaluations appear at different phases.

RELATIONSHIP BETWEEN EVALUATION AND INSTRUCTIONAL OBJECTIVES

There must be a direct relationship between instructional objectives and assessment measures. In the case of knowledge testing, some authorities even suggest that as soon as a subject content list and the details of a task analysis are first completed, you should *immediately* write examination questions relating to the content. In turn, the questions can be reworded as instructional objectives. This procedure may seem to be a backward way of planning, but it points to the importance of relating evaluation directly to instructional objectives.

Usually, once you are satisfied with the extent and completeness of the instructional objectives, you are ready to develop ways for evaluating them. For accomplishing this, two key ideas are crucial. First, obtain a good match between types of instruments and types of objectives. Second, consider using several data sources to gain as complete a picture as possible about the degree of learner attainment of each objective and the processes involved. Remember, not all instructional objectives lend themselves to direct, precise measurement that leads to a simple "success/fail" answer.

Matching Measures to Objectives

In Chapter 5 we discussed that various forms of objectives are useful for describing different types of learning outcomes—for instance, cognitive objectives for knowledge, psychomotor objectives for skills, and affective objectives for attitudes. To complete the cycle, those objectives, coupled with the evaluation goals, in turn suggest certain types of evaluation instruments or measures. Finding the measures that best fit each objective is an important evaluation task. Note the following real-life examples, where such fits could be seriously questioned:

- A corporate training course on group leadership skills included objectives that were nearly all performance- or skill-based. For example: "The student will distribute an agenda for the meeting." Yet, the sole evaluation measure employed was a 25-item multiple-choice knowledge test administered as a pre- and post-assessment! Not surprisingly, students "significantly" improved their scores across the two testings (after all, they were taught new material). Should the course be viewed as successful in meeting its objectives?
- A college professor evaluated achievement on the midterm and final exams of a history course by asking students to list the "major developments" that led to the Vietnam War. Scoring was based on how closely the students' listings matched the one given in class; these assessments accounted for about 85% of the final course grade. Does this evaluation approach appear valid given instructional objectives that emphasize *analysis* and *synthesis* of historic events?
- A department chairman wanted to evaluate the effectiveness of teaching in a certain core course. Toward the end of the year, he scheduled sessions in which he would visit a class, dismiss the instructor for 20 minutes, and ask

class members to react in a group discussion to the teaching methods and teacher qualities. Was he likely to obtain an accurate picture of teaching effectiveness in that course?

The answer to the questions in all three illustrations is a definite no. Inappropriate instruments were employed in each situation. For the corporate training evaluation, improvement on the knowledge test says little about trainees' abilities to perform the desired skills. Similarly, verbatim recall of historic facts from a listing appears to be a trivial, lower-level measure of learning in the history course. Finally, although the department chairman was on the right track by employing student attitudes as a data source, the specific measure used (a group discussion) likely will generate invalid results because students may feel pressured and self-conscious about speaking openly in front of a group and the department chairman.

Suggested Measures for Alternative Outcomes

Suggested instrument selections for assessing different types of instructional outcomes are provided in Figure 10–1. For now, we will simply identify the instruments and save discussion of the procedures for developing them for Chapter 11. Keep in mind that the ultimate choice of evaluation measures will depend on a variety of factors other than what is considered in an ideal sense to be most desirable and valid. These factors include costs, time, skill required for test administration, instrument availability, and accepted practices in the educational or training context concerned.

VALIDITY AND RELIABILITY OF TESTS

Once you have determined the types of measures for evaluating objectives, selecting or developing the instruments becomes the next major task. Whichever route is taken, it is important to ensure that those instruments possess two necessary qualities: validity and reliability.

Validity

Attention was previously given to the validity of testing when the necessity for a direct relationship between instructional objectives and evaluation items was indicated. A test is considered valid when *it specifically measures what was learned, as specified by the instructional objectives for the unit or topic.*

In Chapter 5 we described the benefits of developing a performance-content matrix that relates objectives to learning levels. One way of ensuring a high degree of test validity is to devise a second table of specifications that relates test items to objectives. Such a table can serve two purposes. First, it helps verify that outcomes at the higher learning levels (application, analysis, synthesis, and evaluation) receive adequate attention. Second, it shows the number of questions needed for measuring individual instructional objectives or groups of related objectives.

FIGURE 10–1

Various evaluation instruments for different outcomes

A. Knowledge

Data Sources: **Objective Tests**

Objective test questions have one correct answer and thus can be easily ("objectively") graded.

1. Multiple choice

Example: *Which state is the farthest west in longitude?*

> *a. Hawaii*
> *b. California*
> *c. Alaska*
> *d. Washington*

2. True-False

Example: *In the sentence "The boys enjoyed the movie," the subject is "movie." (T/F)*

3. Matching

Example: *Match the choice in column B that describes the term in column A.*

> *A*   *B*
> Mean   Midpoint
> Mode   Most frequent score
> Median   Variability
>   Average

Data Sources: **Constructed-Response Tests**

Constructed-response tests require the learner to generate ("construct") responses to questions. Thus, alternative answers and/or solution strategies are usually possible.

1. Completion (fill-in-the-blank)

Example: *Instructional objectives that describe the use and coordination of physical activities fall into the _____ domain.*

2. Short essay

Example: *Define formative and summative evaluation and describe two ways in which they might differ procedurally.*

3. Long essay

Example: *Discuss the purposes of instructional evaluation. Using an example lesson or course, describe the considerations and steps that would be involved in such evaluations with regard to (a) planning, (b) implementation, and (c) interpretation and dissemination of results.*

4. Problem solving

Example: *Complete each of the following math problems, showing the correct formula, your work, and the solution.*

1. *Four electricians install 1,327 outlets in 70 apartments. What is the average number of outlets in each apartment?*

(continued on next page)

FIGURE 10–1
(Continued)

B. Skills and Behavior

Data Sources: 1. Direct testing of performance outcomes

Example: *A test of tying different types of knots used in sailing*

2. Analysis of naturally occurring results

Examples: *Number of accidents, attendance, sales increases, etc.*

3. Ratings of behaviors based on direct observation

Example: *Rate teacher clarity on a five-point scale.*

4. Checklists of behavior based on direct observation

Example: *Check each safety precaution exhibited by trainees while wiring circuits.*

5. Ratings or checklists of behavior based on indirect measures

Example: *Peer evaluation of the student's communication skills while dealing with clients*

6. Authentic tests

Examples: *Portfolios or exhibitions that display students' work in meaningful contexts.*

C. Attitudes

Data Sources: 1. Observation of instruction

Examples: *What percentage of the students are attentive? How frequently does the typical student participate in class discussion? Do students appear to enjoy the lesson?*

2. Observation/assessment of behavior

Examples: *How many plays do students attend following an arts appreciation course? What percentage of students enroll in Algebra II following completion of Algebra I?*

3. Attitude surveys

Examples: *Ratings of instructor preparedness, lesson difficulty, clarity, and organization, open-ended evaluation by hospital patients of the bedside manner of the nurses who cared for them*

4. Interviews

Examples: *What appear to be the strengths of the instruction? Why? What appear to be the weaknesses? Why?*

These frequency values reflect the relative importance of each objective or the proportion of emphasis it is given during instruction.

Table 10–1 indicates the nature and number of test questions for instructional objectives in a knowledge-based unit. Table 10–2 relates the number of test items to the instructional objectives on a task involving different cognitive levels and psychomotor performances. By designing such tables, you can be reasonably certain you will test for all instructional objectives and give each the proper amount of attention.

Although validity is typically associated with knowledge tests, it has the same importance for all types of evaluation measures. The key idea is that *the test assesses what it is supposed to measure.* Thus, course attitude surveys need to measure reactions to the course (and not primarily instructor popularity or some other incidental variable); performance tests need to assess processes and outcomes relating to the skills or competencies of concern; observations of instruction need to describe events and impressions that accurately capture what occurred when the instruction was delivered.

Validity is not always easy to measure or quantify. Several different types exist and are discussed in most measurement texts (e.g., face, content, predictive, concurrent,

TABLE 10–1

Topic: Community Services for the Elderly
Specifications relating number of test items to learning objectives on cognitive levels

Objective	Knowledge	Comprehension	Application	Analysis	Synthesis	Evaluation
1. Recognize misconceptions and superstitions about the elderly.	3					
2. Differentiate between facts and opinions about physical and social behaviors of the elderly.		2				
3. Describe attitudes toward the elderly as practices by various ethnic groups.		2				
4. Locate information relative to community programs for the elderly.		4				
5. Classify community organizations according to types of services offered for the elderly.				2		
6. Develop a plan for judging the value of individual community programs for the elderly.					3	
7. Assess the merits of a community program for the elderly.						2
8. Given a hypothetical or real situation, analyze the needs of a senior citizen and recommend one or more community programs.			4			

TABLE 10–2
Specifications relating number of test items to learning objectives on cognitive levels for psychomotor performance
Task: Measuring Electrical Values in Series Circuits

Objective	Knowledge	Comprehension	Application	Psychomotor
1. List symbols used to identify components in an electrical circuit.	2			
2. Recognize the makeup of a complete series circuit.		3		
3. Identify a series circuit in a schematic diagram.		1	2	
4. Assemble a series circuit on a board using component parts.				2
5. Set up and adjust a multimeter for measuring each of three electrical values.				1
6. Measure and calculate voltage, current flow, and resistance in a series circuit.			3	3

construct validity). The two most important types for the instructional designer are face validity and content validity, which both involve judgmental processes. *Face validity* is supported by the judgment (often by an expert panel) that the measure appears ("on the face of it") to assess the measure of interest. *Content validity* is similar to face validity but typically involves a more specific examination of individual items or questions to ensure that each "content domain" is appropriately addressed. For example, a final achievement exam that draws 90% of its items from only one out of four primary course units would have questionable content validity. Tables of specification (see Tables 10–1 and 10–2) are especially useful in making content validity judgments.

Reliability

Reliability refers to a test's ability to produce consistent results whenever used. If the same learners, without changes in their preparation, were to take the same test or an equal form of the test, there should be little variation in the scores. Certain procedures can affect the reliability of a test:

- The more questions used relating to each instructional objective, the more reliable the test will be. If only one question is asked about a major objective or an extensive content area, it can be difficult to ascertain whether a learner has acquired the knowledge or guessed the correct answer. (See the previous procedure for developing a specification table relating the number of test questions to the objectives.)
- The test should be administered in a standardized way. If more than one person directs testing, similar instructions must be given to each group of individuals who take the test over a period of time.

- Everyone should be tested under the same conditions so that distractions do not contribute to discrepancies in the scores.
- Testing time should be the same length for all learners.
- Possibly the most important factor that can affect test reliability is the scoring method, especially when marking an essay test or judging performance on a rating scale. Despite attempts to standardize how different persons score tests, criteria can be viewed in various ways, and variations are unavoidable. The less subjective the scoring, the more reliable the test results will be. As will be discussed later, ensuring adequate reliability has been the main challenge for instructors using performance assessments (e.g., evaluating students on the quality of their oral reports) and authentic measures (e.g., portfolios showing the students' work in mathematics over the last six weeks).

There are a number of different methods for assessing reliability:

- The *test–retest* method correlates students' scores on two different administrations of the same measure.
- The *parallel forms* method correlates scores on similar ("parallel" or matched) tests taken at different times.
- The *split–half* method correlates students' scores on half of the test with those on the other half. (The split should be every other item, rather than the first versus the second half, to ensure similar content and difficulty.)
- When computed by popularly used formulas such as KR 20 and coefficient alpha, *internal consistency* reliability is comparable to performing all unique split-half correlations. High internal consistency means that different test items are measuring the same abilities or traits.

Relationship Between Validity and Reliability

A final question to consider is the relationship between validity and reliability. Does validity require reliability? Does reliability require validity? The answers to these two questions are yes and no, respectively.

For an assessment to be valid, it must be reliable. Think about it: How could a test measure what it is supposed to if the scores vary from testing to testing (without any change in testing conditions or learner states)? On the other hand, you could have reliability without validity. For example, an instructor might attempt to assess students' ability to design lessons by giving them a 50-item true/false test on learning theories. The scores might remain consistent from one testing to the next, but they would hardly reflect instructional design skills, the outcome of major interest.

STANDARDS OF ACHIEVEMENT

Suppose you have completed planning your evaluation. Not only have you identified the types of measures needed, but you also have outlined the domains to be assessed and the amount of weight to be given to each one in order to establish high content validity. Before you develop the actual tests, there is another decision to be made—how to judge achievement.

Two standards of achievement can be applied when interpreting test scores and assigning grades: *relative* or *absolute*. Understanding each standard, as well as its particular implications within the instructional design process, is an important part of evaluation.

Relative Standards

In most conventional educational programs, the performance of one learner is compared with those of other learners in the class. A test based on relative standards will indicate that one learner has learned more or less than other learners have, which results in a relative rating of each learner within the group. The rating does not necessarily signify the level of proficiency of any learner in the group with respect to a specific standard of accomplishment.

For example, assume that scores on an 85-point test range from 44 to 73. The instructor would assign grades, starting with the 73 score as the highest A. It might then be decided, for example, to have about 7.5% of the learners receive a grade of A, 17.5% a B, 50% a C, 17.5% a D, and 7.5% an F (see Figure 10–2). This approach is called a *normal distribution*, or "grading on the normal curve." Grades are assigned in a relative or normative fashion.

Note the characteristics of the normal distribution. It is symmetric (you can fold it in half); the mean (average), mode (most frequent score), and median (halfway point or 50th percentile) are identical and positioned in the exact middle of the distribution; and the frequency of scores decreases as you move from the middle to the extremes of the distribution in either direction. Many human characteristics (height, weight, and intelligence) tend to be normally distributed. Note, however, that normal distributions facilitate the use of (but are not required for) *norm-referenced grading*. Regardless of the distribution, the critical element is that *people are being compared with each other rather than against a standard.*

FIGURE 10–2
Grading on the normal curve

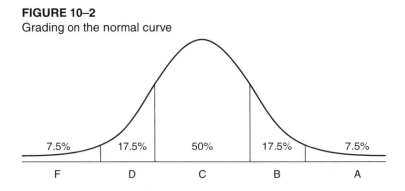

| 7.5% | 17.5% | 50% | 17.5% | 7.5% |
| F | D | C | B | A |

Norm-referenced scoring, grading, and reporting conventions are therefore designed to convey these comparisons. But, under norm-referenced systems, it cannot be assumed, for example, that a learner who received an A this year in Biology 101 is comparable in achievement to another learner who received an A in the same course last semester. The high grades convey that both students did well *relative to their classmates,* but they do not indicate which specific competencies or skills the students have mastered.

Standardized scores, such as those for the ACT, SAT, and GRE exams, also illustrate norm-referenced scores. Perhaps the type of relative score with which you are most familiar is percentile scores. If you know that Micah scored at the 89th percentile on the geometry final, what have you learned? Essentially you know that Micah performed well, surpassing close to 9 out of 10 of his classmates. What you do not know from that information alone is how he did in terms of his actual score (number or percentage correct) or types of learning demonstrated.

Norm-referenced testing procedures are important in comparing the overall accomplishments of individuals or a class to established local, state, or national norms. They are also useful when the purpose of evaluation is to select individuals who stand out from the group (at the high or low extremes) for special programs. For example, there seems to be good reason to want one's heart or brain surgeon to be someone who not only passed all the competencies but also excelled in the knowledge and skills required relative to other medical students. Because of this property, norm-referenced testing may *not* fit well with plans to make instruction and resulting learning effective for the great majority of learners in a class or training program.

Absolute Standards

In many instances, the primary goal of our instructional design is to have as many learners as possible reach a satisfactory level of achievement. Therefore, learning outcomes must be measured against a *specific standard* rather than a relative standard. The specific standard is the criterion specified by the instructional objectives. Criterion-referenced testing includes the measurement of how well each learner attains the required level of comprehension and competence specified for each objective. This degree of achievement is *independent of the performance of other students.*

The terms *competency-based instruction, performance-based instruction,* and *mastery-based instruction* are used interchangeably with *criterion-referenced instruction.* These methods identify a program that provides experiences intended to bring most learners to a satisfactory level of proficiency in learning or performing a task that will be measured by testing. When criteria are set and learners successfully meet them, the concept of *mastery learning* is realized. This goal partly justifies giving increased attention to self-paced learning methods and providing more than one opportunity for a learner to restudy, self-test, and then be retested until the mastery level is attained.

There is concern about the emphasis on mastery learning in some programs. While it is successful when identifiable competencies are required (e.g., in the training of dental technicians or airline pilots), some people fear that use of conventional letter grading (A-B-C-D-F) will lead to "grade inflation" and lower academic standards; in a well-designed and properly executed instructional program, each learner could attain mastery of each topic and receive an A. Students are especially likely to obtain high grades when the learning situation satisfies a combination of the following conditions:

- The learner group has been carefully selected on the basis of ability.
- Each learner is highly motivated to learn.
- Learners have received excellent prerequisite training.
- Instruction has been carefully prepared, pretested, and proven to be effective.

On the other hand, mastery can be accepted as attainment of *minimum* or *essential* knowledge and skills at a reasonable competency level (e.g., an 80% performance standard), which may guarantee a B or C grade (or possibly a P for pass or credit). Then, to reach a higher level, or an A grade, additional accomplishments may be required, such as answering 95%–100% of the posttest questions correctly or achieving optional objectives and engaging in additional activities. If a number of performance levels above the acceptable minimum is set, each learner could be permitted to choose a goal on the basis of his or her capabilities, background, and motivation. This procedure is similar to the contract concept used in some educational programs.

Measurement Issues

In comparing norm-referenced and criterion-referenced testing and grading methods, a final matter should be emphasized. First, in the norm-referenced approach, tests are constructed so that expected learner attainment levels are purposefully spread out to achieve high, average, and low scores. In measurement terms, the key concern is that items *discriminate* (differentiate) among learners. Given this goal, what item difficulty level (proportion of learners answering correctly) would provide maximum discrimination? The answer is 0.50—an item that is answered correctly by half the examinees and missed by half. Note, by comparison, that an item that is answered correctly or missed by 100% of the examinees provides zero discrimination. In most normative instances, we would not want a test to consist exclusively of items having 0.50 difficulty (nor would our students or trainees be very happy about that). Some easier items should be included to increase motivation and morale.

In the criterion-referenced method, test items are included as *relevant* to the required standards. The results clearly indicate what a learner *has learned* and *can do*. Assuming that training has been effective, you would expect and probably want *most* students to demonstrate "mastery." Items with difficulty levels of 0.80 or higher would therefore be desirable in the criterion-referenced situation.

In summary, guiding and assessing learners to help them accomplish their objectives is a normal procedure in criterion-referenced measurement and mastery learning. This orientation fosters cooperation among learners. The norm-referenced approach, on the other hand, emphasizes competition, resulting in differentiation among learners based on achievement levels.

Standards vs. Conventional Measurement

In K–12 contexts, controversy has been generated in recent years regarding the use of norm-referenced vs. criterion-referenced tests. Perhaps you remember taking norm-referenced standardized achievement tests, such as the Iowa Test of Basic Skills, The Stanford Achievement Test, or the California Achievement Test, when you were in school. These tests involved answering multiple-choice questions in language arts, mathematics, and other core subjects, under strictly controlled conditions. In many school districts, school means on the standardized tests are published in the local newspaper and interpreted by the public and often by district and state administrators as indicators of the success of the individual schools. Needless to say, these conditions typically create a "high stakes" testing environment in which teaching to the test, coaching, and sometimes even cheating may occur in the quest to raise scores (Haladyna, Nolen, & Haas, 1991; Taylor, 1994).

The advantage of standardized objective tests is high reliability of measurement. On the other hand, a growing number of educators have questioned the *validity* of the scores for reflecting students' ability to apply the knowledge and skills they have learned (Taylor, 1994). These concerns have given rise to national efforts to develop standards of achievement that focus on demonstrations of higher-level learning (e.g., writing essays, solving problems, participating in a debate) rather than simple recall of knowledge. You may remember from Chapter 4 that a traditional behavioral-type instructional objective might read something like, "Given a familiar topic and 30 minutes time, the student will write a 500-word essay on that topic containing no grammatical errors and fewer than *five* errors of spelling or punctuation." A language arts *content standard* in the same area, however, might read, "The student will write a persuasive essay that shows a clear sense of purpose and audience, and that uses language forms accurately, clearly, and appropriately." Associated *benchmarks* for that standard would then specify what students should know and be able to do at developmentally appropriate levels (e.g., for a ninth grader: "introduces and clearly states a position," "supports main points by relevant and accurate information," "clearly conveys the main points of the opposing argument," etc.).

The standards approach shares some similarities with Gronlund's (1985, 1995) cognitive objectives (see Chapter 5) in the sense of operationally defining a generally stated outcome (the standard) in terms of more specific competencies (the benchmark). The main difference is that objectives tend to be more narrow and unit-specific, whereas standards delineate an entire curriculum, quite possibly for all subjects and all grades in the school system. Associated with content standards are *performance standards*, which specify the criteria for assessing student achievement at different skill levels (e.g., for exiting primary grades, intermediate grades, middle school, or high school). These assessments are criterion-referenced in nature and employ tasks requiring relatively realistic or "authentic" demonstrations of skill and knowledge. An example would be requiring students to test a hypothesis in science by performing a simple experiment. This approach contrasts with *reading about* an experiment and answering multiple-choice questions about it, as on a norm-referenced achievement test. What is the advantage of the performance assessment? Clearly, it is increasing external validity (realism), and orienting instruction toward meaningful learning. The disadvantage, however, is the difficulty of scoring such performances reliably for both everyday feedback and formal grading such as report cards. (We will return to the reliability issue in Chapter 11.)

What does the standards movement mean for instructional designers? Designers working with schools using standards-based curricula will need to link instructional material directly to those standards and benchmarks (as they would with conventional objectives). Although lower-level learning (e.g., memorizing facts and dates) will still be required, greater emphasis than in the past will be placed on teaching such knowledge as a natural part of performing more complex, real-world tasks (e.g., learning history facts by completing a project on the Civil War, learning punctuation through reading and writing). Assessments will also need to be integrated with learning activities such that students demonstrate what they know and can do through portfolios, exhibitions, and projects (see Chapter 11 for more discussion). For classroom teachers, instructional design skills (formal or otherwise) will likewise become increasingly valuable as they attempt to address standards by creating meaningful performance-based tasks to replace traditional seatwork and drill exercises. This trend is already being evidenced in several of the New American School restructuring projects (Stringfield, Ross, & Smith, 1996).

STUDENT SELF-EVALUATION

Successful learning is enhanced when individuals receive feedback on how well they are learning as instruction takes place. This can be accomplished by allowing learners to grade their own short tests at the end of a unit or set of learning activities. The results will indicate to them whether the material has been learned satisfactorily or whether further study is needed.

By completing such self-check tests, learners can individually evaluate progress, recognize difficulties or confusion in understanding, and review material prior to taking the instructor's test covering the same objectives. This procedure can better ensure learner preparation for and success with the unit posttest.

PRETESTING

Up to this point, we have discussed different approaches to evaluation and measurement instrument selection. Our final focus in this chapter is the question of when and how to use pretests as part of the evaluation design.

Suppose you want to begin a strenuous swimming, cycling, or running program. What is advisable to do before starting? Having a physical examination seems necessary to ensure that your body is prepared for rigorous exercise. A similar practice is important in the instructional process. Specifically, *pretesting* is used to assess learners' entry skills for a course or a particular unit of study.

Pretesting serves two important roles in the instructional design process. One role has two functions: (a) to assess the learner's preparation to study the course or topic and (b) to determine which competencies for the course or topic the learner may have already mastered. The second major role is to measure the degree of improvement after instruction is completed.

Testing for Prerequisites

A *prerequisite test* determines whether students have appropriate preparation for starting a course or studying a topic. For example:

- Can junior high school students perform basic arithmetic at a level that qualifies them to start learning algebra?
- Is an apprentice entering a furniture manufacturing training program competent in using such machines as a table saw, a belt sander, or a router?

Refer to the listing of subject content for the topic or the analysis of the task to be taught (Chapter 4). Enumerate the required competencies that a learner should have *before* starting this phase of the program. From the list, develop appropriate methods, such as those on the following list, to gather information about necessary prerequisite knowledge and abilities:

- Paper-and-pencil tests (sometimes standardized tests in fundamental areas like reading, writing, mathematics, chemistry, or physics)
- Observations of performance and rating of competencies exhibited by learners
- A questionnaire to determine learner background, training, and experiences
- Review of learners' previous or related work
- Talks with supervisors or other persons with whom the learner has worked

The results of this prerequisite testing will indicate which learners are fully prepared to start studying the topic, which need some remedial work, and which are not ready and should therefore start at a lower level. Do not assume that grades in previous or related courses necessarily indicate the degree of readiness for a learner to be successful in a program. The objectives of courses taken elsewhere may be quite different from what you interpret them to be by reading the titles or descriptions of those courses. Do your own prerequisite evaluation of each learner's preparation.

To determine learners' previous experience with a topic, you might use a pre-topic questionnaire or even an informal, oral questioning of the class (e.g., "How many of you have ever used an ohmmeter?") instead of a formal test. Have learners reply with a show of hands. For mature learners, a questionnaire, in which each learner indicates his or her level of skill or knowledge for all items to be studied, will go further than the few questions of a pretest.

Testing for Improvement in Performance

A second reason for pretesting is to determine the degree to which learners improve in critical competencies as a result of the instruction. Since the accomplishment of instructional objectives is measured by the evaluation test for each objective, some authorities recommend using the actual evaluation test (or a modified form of it) for both pretesting and final evaluation (the posttest). In this case, the amount of learning is determined from *the gain in scores between pretesting and posttesting.* An illustration of this is shown in Figure 10–3. Note that large gains are indicated on objectives 1, 5, and 7, while only small improvements occurred on objectives 3 and 8.

    If the final examination is too detailed for use as a pretest, select only the most important or representative test items. Do not test only the easiest (often knowledge level) or the most difficult (higher cognitive levels) objectives. Maintain a fair balance.

Benefits of Pretesting

For the more traditional group instruction situation, in which learners move together through all teacher-controlled activities, pretesting may have limited value. The instructor may discover a range of preparation within the group. Not much can be done to provide for the differences among learners other than to recommend some remedial work while the instruction moves ahead as planned. If some learners show on the pretest that they already are competent with some of the content to be treated in the class, they most often still have to sit through the regular instruction. Only infrequently does a concerned instructor adjust assignments to accommodate these learners.

FIGURE 10–3
Using pretests and posttests to determine improvements in performance

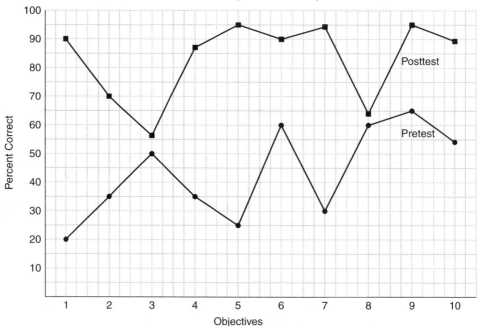

If you plan to individualize or provide for self-paced learning, then pretesting will be important for the following reasons:

- It determines learners' readiness for the program by alerting each of them to what they do and do not know about the topic.
- It indicates to both learners and the instructor the point at which to begin the program or complete remedial (or lower-level) course work before starting the program.
- It may motivate learners to study the topic by arousing their curiosity and interest as they read pretest questions or otherwise experience what they will be learning.
- It informs learners of what will be treated during study of the topic so that they realize what will be required of them.
- It indicates the testing methods the instructor will use in the final examination since there is a close relationship between pretest and posttest.
- It provides baseline data for determining learner growth in learning by comparing scores on pretest and posttest.
- It provides formative evaluation information useful to help the instructor modify parts of the course or program (adding or eliminating objectives and/or activities) so that the program can start at the point of learner readiness.

Whether or Not to Pretest

Given the advantages of pretesting, you may believe that pretests are always desirable. This is not the case. Disadvantages of pretests are that they take time away from instruction, may cue the learner to concentrate on certain things (while neglecting others), and may produce negative feelings. The latter point seems the most critical. When learners have little background in the topics to be taught and therefore are likely to perform at a very low level (e.g., by making random guesses) on the pretest, there is little point in administering a pretest. Without useful performance information, anxiety or frustration may result. In light of these concerns, when you do pretest, be sure that learners understand the purpose. Explain clearly why the pretest is being given and that it in no way counts toward grades.

SUMMARY

1. Evaluation is used to provide information about the success of a course or unit of instruction.
2. One general category of evaluation is formative, which focuses on instructional processes and outcomes during development, tryout, and the progression of the course.
3. Summative evaluation assesses the degree to which instructional objectives have been achieved at the end of the course.

4. Whatever evaluation approach is used, there must be a direct relationship between instructional objectives and assessment measures. Multiple data sources are particularly valuable in providing a more accurate and comprehensive picture of a particular outcome than any single measure could provide.

5. For assessing knowledge, both objective tests (completion, multiple-choice, true/false, matching) and constructed-response tests (short essay, long essay, problem solving) may be used.

6. For assessing skills and behavior, recommended measures are direct testing of performance, analysis of naturally occurring events, ratings and checklists of behavior, and authentic testing.

7. Attitudes are commonly assessed by observing instruction, observing behavior, using rating scales, surveying, and interviewing.

8. A test has a high degree of validity if it measures the behavior or trait specified by the instructional objectives. Test scores have a high degree of reliability if they remain consistent from one testing to the next. To be valid, a test must be reliable.

9. Relative standards of evaluating achievement are reflected in norm-referenced grading in which people are compared with one another, often for selection purposes.

10. Absolute standards are reflected in criterion-referenced grading, in which performance is judged relative to established criteria, regardless of how other learners score.

11. An emerging form of criterion-referenced testing in K–12 schools is standard-based assessment. These tests ask students to demonstrate the application of knowledge and skills by performing authentic, real-world tasks.

12. Student self-testing allows learners to check their own learning level as they progress through a program.

13. Pretesting is used to determine how well prepared a learner is to start an instructional program or a specific unit. Pretests are also useful in providing a baseline performance from which to judge the degree of improvement resulting from the instruction.

FROM HERE TO THERE

You are asked by a school system to evaluate a new health sciences program that they have purchased to teach "healthy habits" to elementary school children. Before you design the evaluation, you first determine what questions the school system is trying to answer. Because the program is "complete" as purchased and implemented (i.e., it cannot be easily modified), summative rather than formative evaluation is desired. The teachers and administrators involved with the program indicate that, aside from issues concerning cost and training requirements, their main interest is with the effects of the program in increasing positive attitudes and knowledge about healthy practices.

To increase the validity of your findings, you decide to use multiple data collection instruments, including a teacher survey and interview, student interview, parent interview, student attitude survey, and a test of student learning of health principles. For the latter two measures (attitudes and learning), you also arrange to assess "control" students who attend similar schools as program students. In constructing the test of learning, you create some criterion-referenced sections to determine the percentage of students who have mastered particular program objectives. One performance-based section asks students to demonstrate treatment for minor cuts, using actual first-aid materials. You also create some norm-referenced sections especially designed to compare program and control students on knowledge and application of key health principles. Your synthesis of results from these multiple data sources will form the basis for conclusions about the effectiveness of the program for achieving the district's objectives in the health education area. A member of the school board, however, asks why the evaluation contains "so many things." What would you say to defend the use of multiple measures? What would you concede to be disadvantages?

REFERENCES

Gronlund, N. E. (1985). *Stating behavioral objectives for classroom instruction*. New York: Macmillan.

Gronlund, N. E. (1995). *How to write and use instructional objectives* (5th ed.). New York: Prentice-Hall.

Haladyna, T. M., Nolen, S. B., & Haas, N. S. (1991). Raising standardized achievement test scores and the origins of test score pollution. *Educational Researcher, 20,* 2–7.

Slavin, R. (1994). *Educational psychology*. Englewood Cliffs, NJ: Prentice-Hall.

Stringfield, S. C., Ross, S. M., & Smith, L. J. (1996). *Bold new plans for school restructuring: The New American Schools Development Corporation designs*. Mahwah, NJ: Erlbaum.

Taylor, C. T. (1994). Assessment for measurement of standards: The peril and promise of large-scale assessment reform. *American Educational Research Journal, 31,* 231–262.

DEVELOPING EVALUATION INSTRUMENTS

"How do instructional objectives dictate the selection of evaluation methods?"

"What type of test should I use to measure comprehension rather than simply memorization?"

"Should multiple-choice items include five alternatives, or is four enough?"

"How can I assess what students like and don't like about the instruction?

"If it is not practical to assess skills in real-life situations, are there any alternative ways of assessing performance?"

"How should portfolios be evaluated?"

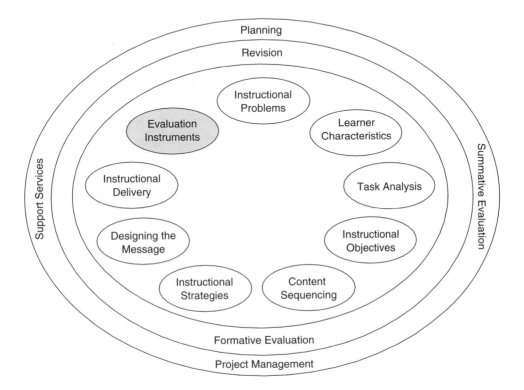

In Chapter 10 we discussed the purposes of evaluation in training and education and major principles relating to designing and conducting evaluations. As the opening questions suggest, we now turn to the more specific topic of constructing instruments to address each evaluation interest. Begin the process by asking questions such as these:

- What measure(s) are likely to provide the most valid assessment of learning outcomes?
- Is using a particular measure complicated or precluded by practical constraints (cost, time, accepted practices)?
- What are appropriate procedures for constructing the selected measures and analyzing results?

Reexamine the first question concerning the types of measures needed. To answer it, classify the learning outcomes according to whether they deal primarily with knowledge, skills and behavior, or attitudes. We will work with this scheme, as we did in Chapter 10, for identifying and discussing alternative measures relating to each category.

TESTING KNOWLEDGE

The acquisition of relevant *knowledge* is central to most instructional programs. Pilots, for example, need to know principles of aeronautics before attempting to fly planes, doctors need to learn medical facts and concepts, and teachers require procedures for classroom management and grading (as well as expertise in the subjects they teach). Given the importance of knowledge in the learning process, assessing it becomes a critical part of instructional evaluations. This area mainly concerns the **cognitive domain** of instructional objectives.

The Relationship Between Evaluation and Instructional Objectives

A direct relationship between instructional objectives and test items must exist. Thus, it is customary to derive test items directly from the objectives. You may recall from Chapter 5 that two recognized approaches to writing objectives are *behavioral* (what the learner must do to master the specified knowledge is precisely stated) and *cognitive* (general outcomes and specific behavior samples are described). The verb component of both of these types of objectives indicates possible forms that test items should take. Here are some examples:

> *To identify or recognize:* Choosing an answer in an objective-type test item (see types in following discussion)
>
> *To list or label:* Writing a word or brief statement
>
> *To state or describe:* Writing or speaking a short or lengthy answer
>
> *To solve or calculate:* Writing or choosing a solution or numerical answer
>
> *To compare or differentiate:* Writing about a relationship or choosing an answer that shows a relationship
>
> *To operate or construct:* Rating the quality of performance or product against criteria
>
> *To formulate or organize:* Writing a plan or choosing an order of items relative to a plan
>
> *To predict or judge:* Writing a description of what is expected to happen, or choosing from alternative decisions

While some variation in interpreting the verb's meaning is inevitable, these examples illustrate the close relationship that is necessary between an instructional objective and a test item. A student should anticipate being tested on *the same type of learning or behavior* indicated by the objective, and the verb in an objective alerts the student to the content that is particularly important to study.

Most cognitive-domain objectives are evaluated by various types of paper-and-pencil tests grouped into two categories: **objective** and **constructed-response**. Some instructional objectives might preferably be measured by one type of test rather than another. You should therefore become familiar with the considerations that can influence your choice. Let's look at the features of each of the commonly used types of tests. (For further help with formulating properly stated test questions, see the references at the end of this chapter.)

Objective Tests

Persons scoring objective test items in the cognitive domain can easily agree on the correct answer; hence the term *objective test* is used. This category includes questions for which the student must recognize and select an answer from two or more alternatives or respond to prepared statements. Typically, no writing, other than marking an answer, is required. Objective-type tests are of three major types: multiple-choice, true/false, and matching.

Multiple-Choice.   Multiple-choice is the most useful and versatile type of objective testing. It consists of a *stem,* which is a question or an incomplete statement, plus the *alternatives,* which consist of a correct answer and several incorrect answers called *distractors.* Typically, it is best to use from three to five alternatives. More than five may stretch the test developer's creativity for devising reasonable options while increasing the reading demands on the student.

Multiple-choice items can be written at all levels of Bloom's taxonomy. Thus, compared to true/false and matching items, they can more easily test higher-order learning, including conceptual reasoning. You will probably find them to be somewhat limited, however, especially compared to essay questions, for testing synthesis and evaluation, the two highest levels in the taxonomy.

Here are examples of multiple-choice questions on the first four levels of the Bloom taxonomy:

1. *Knowledge*
   How does cardiovascular death rank as a killer in the United States?

   a. first
   b. second
   c. fifth
   d. tenth

2. *Comprehension*
   When the temperature of a moving air mass is lower than that of the surface over which it is passing, heat transfer takes place vertically. This principle results in which designation for the air mass?

a. k

b. w

c. A

d. P

3. *Application*

An operator can be expected to drill 6 holes a minute with a drill press. What is the amount of time required to drill 750 holes?

a. 3 hours, 14 minutes

b. 2 hours, 30 minutes

c. 2 hours, 5 minutes

d. 1 hour, 46 minutes

4. *Analysis*

Examine the sample photographic print. What should you do to correct the condition shown?

a. Use a different grade of paper.

b. Expose the paper for a longer time.

c. Develop the paper for a longer time.

d. Use dodging to lighten shadows.

Multiple-choice tests have two advantages: that of measuring a variety of learning levels and that of being easy to grade. They have the disadvantages, however, of testing recognition (choosing an answer) rather than recall (constructing an answer), allowing for guessing, and being fairly difficult to construct.

Some novice developers think that the best multiple-choice item is one that is "tricky" or complex. Actually, the key to writing valid items is to make the item as clear and straightforward as possible. The purpose is to test learning, not reading skill, mind reading, or puzzle solving. Here are some guidelines for writing multiple-choice items, with examples of both poor and good questions (an asterisk denotes the correct answer):

1. *Make the content meaningful relative to the instructional objectives.* Do not test trivial or unimportant facts.

Poor: Skinner developed programmed instruction in _____.

a. 1953

*b. 1954

c. 1955

d. 1956

Better: Skinner developed programmed instruction in the _____.

a. 1930s

b. 1940s

    *c. 1950s
    d. 1970s

2. *Reduce the length of the alternatives by moving as many words as possible to the stem.* The rationale is that additional words in the alternatives have to be read four or five times, in the stem only once.

   Poor: The mean is _____.

  *a. a measure of the average
  b. a measure of the midpoint
  c. a measure of the most popular score
  d. a measure of the dispersion of scores

   Better: The mean is a measure of the _____.

  *a. average
  b. midpoint
  c. most popular score
  d. dispersion of scores

3. *Construct the stem so that it conveys a complete thought.*

   Poor: Objectives are _____.

  *a. used for planning instruction
  b. written in behavioral form only
  c. the last step in the instructional design process
  d. used in the cognitive but not the affective domain

   Better: The main function of instructional objectives is _____.

  *a. planning instruction
  b. comparing teachers
  c. selecting students with exceptional abilities
  d. assigning students to academic programs

4. *Do not make the correct answer stand out as a result of its phrasing or length.*

   Poor: A narrow strip of land bordered on both sides by water is called an _____.

  *a. isthmus
  b. peninsula
  c. bayou
  d. continent

   (*Note:* Do you see why *a* would be the best guess given the phrasing?)

   Better: A narrow strip of land bordered on both sides by water is called a(n) _____. (The same choices as above would then follow.)

Poor: In Bloom's cognitive taxonomy, analysis involves _____.

a. memorizing
b. valuing
c. understanding
*d. breaking down knowledge into parts and showing the relationship between the parts

Better: In Bloom's taxonomy, analysis involves _____.

a. memorizing information verbatim
b. learning to value something
c. understanding the meaning of material
*d. breaking a whole into parts

5. *Avoid overusing **always** and **never** in the distractors.* Students who are good test takers quickly learn never to pick those choices.

6. *Avoid overusing **all of the above** and **none of the above**.* When *all of the above* is used, students can eliminate it simply by knowing that one answer is false. Or they will know to select it if any two answers are true. When *none of the above* is the correct answer, the student leaves the question having recognized what is not true but may still not know the correct answer. For example:

The capital of Tennessee is _____.

a. Birmingham
b. Atlanta
c. Albany
*d. None of the above

Some designers routinely add *all of the above* or *none of the above* when they run out of ideas for good distractors. A better strategy might be to include fewer choices rather than to use these two options indiscriminately.

7. *Questions phrased in a positive direction are generally preferred over those phrased negatively.*

Negative stem: Which of the following is *false?*
Positive stem: Which of the following is *true?*

Negative stems may be good choices in some instances, but use them selectively. One disadvantage of such items is that the correct answer is a noninstance rather than the actual response to be learned (see guideline 6). Also, students may have more difficulty when interpreting negative phrasing. Underline, capitalize, or italicize the *not* to make sure that the student notices it.

8. *Randomly select the position of the correct answer.* This guideline is probably the easiest to follow, but we suspect that many instructors rely instead on making these selections subjectively. The problem is that they may have unintentional biases in favor of certain response positions. Consequently, students may learn, for example, that alternative *a* is a better guess than alternative *d* in Mr. Tessmer's class.

True/False Items. True/false test questions are presented as statements that the learner judges as *correct* or *incorrect*. Only content material that lends itself to "either/or" answers should be written in this format. Consequently, the range of content that can be tested is fairly narrow, often limited to factual information.

True/false tests have the advantages of being fairly easy to write and very easy to grade. Their disadvantages are that they test recognition rather than recall, allow for a high probability (50%) of guessing the correct answer, and limit assessments to lower levels of learning (knowledge and comprehension). Some guidelines for true/false testing are as follows:

1. *Be certain that the statement is entirely true or entirely false.*

   Poor: A good instructional objective will identify a performance standard. (True/False) (*Note:* The correct answer here is technically false. However, the statement is ambiguous. While a performance standard is a feature of some "good" objectives, it is not necessary to make an objective good.)

   Better: A performance standard of an objective should be stated in measurable terms. (True/False) (*Note:* The answer here is clearly *true.*)

2. *Convey only one thought or idea in a true/false statement.*

   Poor: Bloom's cognitive taxonomy of objectives includes six levels of objectives, the lowest being knowledge. (True/False)

   Better: Bloom's cognitive taxonomy includes six levels of objectives. (True/False)
   Knowledge is the lowest-level objective in Bloom's cognitive taxonomy. (True/False)

3. *Unless there are special circumstances, use true/false questions sparingly.*

The 50% guessing probability is a major disadvantage of this type of item. This factor, along with the limited levels of learning that can be assessed, make true/false, in general, less desirable than other testing forms.

Strategies for reducing these weaknesses are (a) requiring learners to write a short explanation of why false answers are incorrect or (b) incorporating third or fourth choices such as *opinion* (as opposed to *fact*); *sometimes, but not always true; cannot be resolved;* and the like (see McBeath, 1992, for additional discussion and examples.) Note that in the first case, we are converting the standard true/false question into a type of short-answer item; in the second case, it is being converted to a three- or four-alternative multiple-choice item. We might therefore consider whether we would have been better off in the first place with using alternatives to true/false testing.

Matching Items. Matching items are a specific form of multiple-choice testing. They require the learner to identify the relationship between a list of entries in one column with a list of responses in a second column. A matching test is highly appropriate when each listing forms a category of related items (e.g., state capitals, chemistry elements, levels of Bloom's taxonomy). It is most suitable for testing ability to discriminate between

- definitions and terms,
- events and dates,
- achievements and people,
- descriptions or applications and principles, and
- functions and parts.

The main advantage of a matching test is that a large amount of material can be condensed to fit in less space on a page than would be required for multiple-choice testing of the same content. By your careful selection of terms, students have substantially fewer chances for guessing correct associations than on multiple-choice and true/false tests. A disadvantage of matching tests is assessing recognition rather than recall and lower levels of learning (knowledge).

Here are examples of matching tests:

A. In column I are descriptions of geographic characteristics of wind belts. For each statement, find the appropriate wind belt in column II. Answers may be used more than once.

Column I	*Column II*
1. Region of high pressure, calm, and light, baffling winds	a. Doldrums
2. The belt of calm air nearest the equator	b. Horse latitudes
3. A wind belt in the northern hemisphere	c. Polar easterlies
4. Most of the United States is found in this belt	d. Prevailing easterlies
	e. Prevailing westerlies

B. Select a lettering device in column II to carry out the task in column I. Answers may be used only once.

Column I	*Column II*
1. Making a thermal transparency quickly	a. Soft lead pencil
2. Preparing a transparency directly on clear acetate	b. Broad-tipped felt pen
3. Quick lettering for a paste-up sheet	c. Fine-tipped felt pen
4. Producing colored lettering for a large poster	d. Mechanical pressure
5. Preparing titles, without equipment, to be photographed as slides	e. Dry transfer
	f. Photocopying
	g. Word-processing software

Following are some guidelines for constructing matching tests:

1. *Limit the number of items to a maximum of six or seven.* It becomes very confusing to try to match a greater amount.
2. *Limit the length of the items to a word, phrase, or brief sentence.* In general, make the items as short as possible.
3. *Provide one or two extra items (distractors) in the second column.* Their inclusion reduces the probability of correct guessing. This also eliminates the situation that may occur in equal-sized lists, where if one match is incorrect a second match must also be incorrect. Note from examples A and B that this "double jeopardy" limitation can also be removed by allowing answers to be used more than one time.

Constructed-Response Tests

The major limitation of objective-type tests is that learners are not required to plan answers and express them in their own words. These shortcomings are overcome by using constructed-response tests. The requirements of such tests may range from a one-word response to an essay of several pages. An important advantage of constructed-response tests is that high-level cognitive objectives can be more appropriately evaluated. The main disadvantage, as will be seen, is obtaining reliable scores.

Short-Answer Items.   Short-answer items require a learner to supply a single word, a few words, or a brief sentence in response to an incomplete statement or a question. The terms *fill in the blank* or *completion* are also used in referring to this type of constructed-response question.

As a category of tests, these items fall between objective types and essay questions. Since the expected answers are specific, scoring can be fairly objective. Another advantage, and a similarity to multiple-choice items, is that they can test a large amount of content within a given time period. A third advantage is that these items test recall rather than recognition.

On the other hand, short-answer items are limited to testing lower-level cognitive objectives, such as the recall of facts (knowledge level), comprehension, or the application of specific information. Also, scoring may not be as straightforward and objective as anticipated. Remember that while one mind (the instructor's) designs test questions, there will be many minds (the learners') to interpret and analyze each question. Here are examples of short-answer test questions:

1. The type of evaluation designed to assess a program as it develops or progresses is called _____ evaluation.
2. Guessing is considered the greatest problem for which type of objective item?
3. List the four types of reliability defined in your text.
4. Define *criterion-referenced testing*.

The most important guideline for writing short-answer items is to word them so that only one answer is correct. Otherwise, scoring will become more subjective, and, when grades are at issue, arguments with students will become more frequent.

> *Poor:* The first president of the United States was _____ _____. (two words)
>
> (*Note:* The desired answer is George Washington, but students may write *from Virginia, a general, very smart,* and other creative expressions.)
>
> *Better:* Give the first and last name of the first president of the United States: _____ _____

Essay Questions. Essay questions are most useful for testing higher levels of cognitive learning. In particular, instructional objectives emphasizing analysis, synthesis, and evaluation can be measured effectively when learners are required to organize and express their thoughts in writing. A "short" essay, which may be restricted to a few paragraphs or a single page, will typically require a highly focused response. A "long" essay will allow the learner more opportunity to express and defend a point of view. The trade-off, of course, is that the more expansion or divergence allowed, the more difficult the grading. (We will return to the grading issue shortly in discussing advantages and limitations of essay tests.) Among the advantages are these:

- They are relatively easy to construct, taking less time than does the design of a comparable objective-type test.
- They require learners to express themselves in writing, a verbal skill that is highly important for students at all levels to develop.
- They are superior to objective tests for assessing higher-order learning, such as application, analysis, synthesis, and evaluation.
- They provide instructors with considerable information about learners' understanding of the content taught.

Disadvantages of essay tests include these:

- Because students will have time to write only a few essays, a limited number of concepts or principles relating to a topic can be tested.
- If the questions asked are not focused, students may stray off the topic or misinterpret the type of response desired. Scoring becomes more difficult and unreliable as a result.
- Because of the subjective nature of grading essay tests, attention by instructors to "style over substance" may result in a learner with good writing skills receiving higher grades than his or her knowledge of the subject warrants. Similarly, a student who is a poor writer will be at a disadvantage.
- Time required for different learners to complete an essay test will vary greatly.
- Much time and care must be taken when grading so as to be as objective as possible and avoid making personal judgments about individual learners.

Here are examples of essay questions:

1. Prepare a hypothetical route weather forecast from your station to a location 500 miles away. Assume that a winter cold front exists at the beginning of the forecast period halfway between the two locations, with squall lines and icing conditions below 12,000 feet MSL. Make reference to the general situation, sky conditions and cloud base, visibility, precipitation, freezing level, winds aloft, and other factors you deem important. (20 points)
2. In your judgment, what will be the most difficult change human society will have to adapt to in the 21st century? Support your position with reference to at least three utopian objectives and their significance for the future. (15 minutes maximum; 2-page limit; 20 points)

Guidelines for constructing essay tests are as follows:

1. *Make the questions as specific and focused as possible.*

   Poor: Describe the role of instructional objectives in education.

   Discuss Bloom's contribution to the evaluation of instruction.

   Better: Describe and differentiate between behavioral (Mager) and cognitive (Gronlund) objectives with regard to their (a) format and (b) relative advantages and disadvantages for specifying instructional intentions.

2. *Inform students of the grading criteria and conditions.* Will spelling count? How important is organization? Are all parts of the essay worth the same number of points? Can a dictionary be used? Do dates of historic events need to be indicated? Unless you specify the criteria, students may perform poorly, simply because they do not know what type of response you expect. Also, keep in mind that certain criteria may be less relevant to *evaluation* needs. It may thus be desirable to derive separate scores for various criteria.

3. *Write or outline a model answer.* Essays are difficult to grade reliably. Incidental qualities such as length, handwriting, vocabulary, and writing style can all influence the overall impression and divert attention from the content. Writing a model answer makes it easier to focus on content, assigning points to key concepts included and grading more objectively and reliably.

4. *Do not give students a choice of essays; have all respond to the same questions.* All essay questions are not created equal. If one student selects a biology question on, say, cell division, while another selects a question on oxidation, they are essentially taking two different tests. Also, when students are given a choice, they can adapt the test to their strengths in the process.

5. *Grade essays "in the blind," that is, without knowing the writers' identities.* As noted already, the subjectivity involved in evaluating essays can reduce reliability. When you grade an essay knowing the identity of the writer, you may be swayed by

an individual's prior performance and attitude. To reduce this effect, have students write their social security number (or some other code) instead of their names on their answer sheets. True, you may identify some individuals by handwriting or other tell-tale signs (purple ink, smudges, etc.), but you'll have enough doubt about most papers to make blind scoring worthwhile.

6. *When multiple essay questions are required, evaluate a given question for* all *students before scoring the next essay.* It is challenging enough to obtain reliable scores while concentrating on one question at a time; jumping around from question to question will complicate the scoring task immensely.

Problem-Solving Questions.   Like essays, problem-solving questions are well suited to evaluating higher-level cognitive outcomes such as application, analysis, and synthesis. Another advantage is that such questions are generally easy to construct. The main disadvantage, as you probably have anticipated, is scoring. In some instances, the problem will have a single correct answer that can be derived in only one way. Scoring those answers is easy. The other extreme is a situation in which there are alternative solution approaches and possible answers. An example would be statistically describing and interpreting a set of test scores. A high class performance (based on the mean) in the eye of one analyst may appear mediocre to another (who focuses on the median or some other property of the results).

Following are some examples of problem-solving questions:

1. One worker can build 5 benches in 1 day. For a particular job, 20 benches are needed in 1 day's time. How many workers need to be assigned to this job? Show all work and circle your final answer.
2. You are given a beaker that contains one of the five chemical solutions used in previous laboratory exercises. Describe a procedure that you would use to positively identify the particular solution and rule out the other alternatives. (Be sure to list each major step in your procedure.)

Here are some guidelines for constructing problem-solving items:

1. *Specify the criteria for evaluation.* For example, indicate whether students should show their work in addition to the final answer.
2. *Award partial credit or give a separate score for using correct procedures when the final answer is incorrect.* On many problems, a careless error may result in a wrong answer, even though the work shown conveys full understanding of the problem.
3. *Construct a model answer for each problem that indicates the amount of credit to be awarded for work at different stages.*

Remember that regardless of which type of test you employ (multiple-choice, essay, problem-solving, etc.), the key concern is that it provides a *valid* measure of performance. In the case of objective tests, validity will mostly depend on the appropriateness of the content tested and the clarity of the items. For constructed-response tests, an additional element becomes the reliability of scoring. The guidelines provided here for the different constructed-response modes should be helpful toward that end.

TESTING SKILLS AND BEHAVIOR

In evaluating skills and behavior, we examine overt actions that can be directly observed. Frequently, the target behavior is some type of performance reflecting how well a trainee or student can carry out a particular task or a group of related tasks. Some examples are:

- Using a power saw to cut boards of different thicknesses
- Doing a dance step for 10 repetitions without error
- Debugging a computer program so that it runs effectively
- Giving a speech that incorporates the "10 speaking skills" taught in a course
- Leading a group to resolve a conflict successfully

The standards of performance are judged according to the requirements of the instructional objectives and should be the same as those covered during instruction. Accordingly, each of the preceding general goals would need to be broken down into more precise descriptions of expected performance. Prior to testing, the learner should have had sufficient opportunities to practice and apply the skills to be able to demonstrate the learning. If so, he or she should be prepared to complete the test successfully.

Preliminary Considerations

When preparing to evaluate performance, look for answers to the following questions:

1. *Will process, product, or both be evaluated?* When a learner performs a task, the confidence, care, and accuracy with which he or she carries out the procedures usually are important. This is a measurement of the process portion of the task, which may include elements such as:

- Following a proper sequence of actions or steps
- Performing detailed manipulations
- Using tools or instruments properly
- Working within a specified time period

Product evaluation focuses primarily on the end result or outcome of the effort. Attention is on the quality and possibly quantity of a product, or on the final action that results from applying the process. The evaluation of most tasks includes both process and product components.

2. *What constraints or limitations should be recognized when planning a performance evaluation?* The conditions under which a task is normally performed should be considered before developing the test. Such elements as the following can help you decide whether to use a realistic or a simulated testing situation:

- Size and complexity of the task
- Cost for materials or services required
- Human safety factors
- Time needed for testing

Other matters that need attention when deciding on the method of testing include:

- The required place for testing
- Necessary or specialized equipment
- Instruments, tools, and supplies needed
- The required involvement of other persons

3. *Will the testing conditions be simulated or realistic?* By considering the various factors indicated in the answer to the previous question, you can be prepared to decide whether the test can be conducted under realistic conditions or, if this is impractical, whether it can be handled in some abbreviated or simulated fashion. The simulation should be as joblike as possible in order to serve as a valid measure of performance.

Today many of those involved in K-12 education are placing increasing emphasis on assessing student *performance* in addition to their recall or recognition of content. *Performance assessments* are frequently confused with *authentic assessments*, even though they do not mean the same thing. Authentic assessment involves the student demonstrating the performance in a real-life context (Meyer, 1993). In your opinion, would going on a field trip, returning to class, and then writing an essay in a one-hour class period be an authentic assessment of writing? Probably not, since the conditions for the writing performance are contrived. A more authentic context would be one where, similar to a journalist given an assignment and a deadline, the students have a day or two in which they can use a variety of resources (e.g., school or community library, Internet, textbooks) to generate the written report.

Whether the testing takes place under realistic or simulated conditions, an evaluator should give consideration to recording the performance on videotape. With this procedure, evaluation of a performance can take place at a later time and may involve the learner in the review. Depending on the evaluation needs and conditions, one or more of the alternative measures described next may be used.

Types of Skill/Behavior Assessments

Direct Testing.   For certain types of performances, it may be feasible to test the student or trainee *directly* to determine level of skill. The primary focus is on *products* (final outcomes), but examining *processes* (actions that lead to the products) will also be of interest in most situations.

Examples

Keyboarding speed and accuracy
Operating equipment
Marksmanship
Assembling parts
Using a hammer
Drawing geometric shapes

Procedure. The first step in developing the test is to review the instructional objectives and details of the task to be evaluated. Then use the following procedure:

1. Review the task analysis (Chapter 4) for the task, and identify the steps or specific procedures of the task that comprise the criteria to be judged. Establish the proficiency level that will be accepted (as indicated by the performance standard component of the objective).
2. Plan how the performance will take place, including its location and the application of the procedure.
3. List the equipment, tools, materials, and printed resources to be made available.
4. Consider any special matters like safety and other persons needed.
5. Write the instructions that direct the actions of the learners during the test.

For example, in evaluating marksmanship skill, a designer might establish the standard of hitting 15 or more out of 20 targets from 50 feet within a 120-second time limit. Trainees perform at a shooting range where they are scheduled at 30-minute intervals, given instructions and the equipment needed, and tested under controlled conditions (e.g., with proper safety precautions and spectators kept away from the vicinity).

Because the scores obtained will be reflective of each individual, it is highly important to establish appropriate conditions of testing to ensure that the scores are valid. For example, it would hardly seem appropriate to assess keyboarding speed in a room with insufficient lighting or on an unfamiliar word processor.

Analysis of Naturally Occurring Results. Certain *skills* or *behavior* may be evaluated as products of activities naturally performed in realistic contexts. By assessing these products, the evaluator obtains a direct measure of the objective in question, without having to develop instruments or collect new data.

Examples

Number of absences from school
Number of traffic citations received this year

Sales volume during the second quarter
Verbal score obtained on the Graduate Record Exam
Courses selected for the spring semester

As with direct testing, the score by itself reflects the target performance (or behavior), which thus makes the validity of that score the key concern. For example, if the measure of interest was sales volume in a given month, an evaluator would want to be sure that nothing unusual happened during that period to change outcomes that would normally occur. Weather, student illness, or special conditions in the business could have unanticipated effects in this regard. Similarly, following their completion of a driver's safety course, students may receive very few traffic citations, but the main reasons for their increased "driving success" may be local sales on radar detectors and the city's cutback on traffic officers. The evaluator, therefore, needs to make sure that the available data are *valid* indicators of performance associated *with the instruction*.

Procedure

1. Based on the instructional objectives for the instruction, identify any relevant results (behaviors or products) that naturally occur as the individual performs his or her job or normal activities.
2. Arrange to obtain the results. (Permission from the student and/or other individuals, such as supervisors or administrators, may be required.)
3. Ensure that the results reflect representative performance/behavior. If conditions seem unusual (e.g., a bad month for sales), increase the time frame to include additional data collection periods.

Ratings of Performance.   In many situations, especially when the *process* component of performance is to be evaluated, it becomes necessary for the instructor or other qualified judge to observe learner actions and rate them in terms of the necessary criteria.

Examples

Speaking ability
Applying colors in a painting
Technical skill in a gymnastics routine
Interpersonal skills
Carpentry ability in building a deck

The ratings are commonly made using one of the following instruments.

Checklists.   A checklist can be used to determine whether sequential steps in a procedure or other actions are successfully performed. The evaluator indicates yes/no or done/not done for each element. A checklist, however, does not allow assessments to be made of *quality* of performance. An example of a checklist is shown in Figure 11–1.

Rating Scales.   With a rating scale, special values can be assigned to each element of a performance. Only behaviors that can be observed and rated reliably should be

FIGURE 11–1

Checklist for task: Dry-mount a picture

Skill	Performed (Yes/No)
1. Plug in press.	_____
2. Set press at 225 degrees.	_____
3. Plug in tacking iron.	_____
4. Set tacking iron on *high*.	_____
5. Wait for press to reach temperature before use.	_____
6. Dry picture in press.	_____
7. Dry cardboard in press.	_____
8. Tack dry mount tissue to back of picture.	_____
9. Trim picture and tissue together.	_____
10. Align picture on cardboard.	_____
11. Tack tissue under picture in two corners.	_____
12. Seal picture to cardboard in press for 10 seconds.	_____
13. Remove and immediately cool mounting under weight.	_____

included in a rating scale. A numerical scale is commonly used. It consists of standards from low to high, such as these:

0	1	2
Unacceptable	Acceptable with corrections	Acceptable

1	2	3	4
Poor	Fair	Good	Excellent

Using descriptive terms is recommended to differentiate and clarify the meaning of the individual rating categories. It would make little sense, for example, to ask an observer to rate a manager's "leadership skills" given only a rating scale of 1 to 10. What would a 10 indicate? How would a 4 differ from a 5? Without clearer definitions, the ratings will be completely arbitrary and unreliable. Depending on the situation and the descriptors used, rating scales may be *norm referenced*, where learners are judged in comparison to each other, or *criterion referenced*, where they are judged relative to the acceptable standards for performance. Here is an example of a norm-referenced descriptive rating scale:

1	2	3	4	5
Unsatisfactory	Below average	Average	Above average	Superior

An important limitation of rating scales can be any personal bias an evaluator may have in preferring one learner over another for any of a number of reasons. Also, careful attention is required to discriminate each level of performance from the others on a scale; thus, most rating scales are limited to three to five levels. Training of evaluators may be necessary to standardize their measurements.

In addition to evaluating the process component of a skill, a rating form should be used to judge the quality (and quantity) of a resulting product. Such factors as these may be included:

- General appearance of product
- Accuracy of product details (shape, dimensions, finish)
- Relationships between components or parts (size, fit, finish, color)
- Quantity of products produced during a time period

Figure 11–2 illustrates a rating scale that includes both process and product evaluations.

Before the rating instrument is used, it should be tried out with a sample of two or three persons from the potential learner group or equivalent. This trial allows checking for (a) the learner's clear understanding of the testing procedure, (b) the effectiveness of each part of the instrument, and (c) the required length of the testing period for each learner. Also, if more than one evaluator will use the scale, the procedure must be standardized so that each person making a judgment grades similar performances equally. That is, *interrater reliability* (consistency) must be established.

Rubrics.   A relatively new evaluation approach involves the use of *rubrics* to judge the quality of performance. In contrast to a conventional rating scale, a rubric is intended to give a more descriptive, holistic characterization of the quality of students' work. Specifically, where multiple ratings items might be used to evaluate isolated skills in a complex task (see Figure 11–2), the rubric represents a general assessment of the overall product. In designing and using a rubric, the concern is less with assigning a number to indicate quality than with selecting a verbal description that clearly com-

FIGURE 11–2
Rating scale for using direct instruction

Procedure	Rating			
	Poor			Excellent
1. Introduces objectives	0	1	2	3
2. Gives overview	0	1	2	3
3. Reviews prerequisites	0	1	2	3
4. Shows enthusiasm	0	1	2	3
5. Uses clear examples/explanations	0	1	2	3
6. Asks appropriate questions	0	1	2	3
7. Keeps students on task	0	1	2	3
8. Provides sufficient independent practice	0	1	2	3
9. Provides review	0	1	2	3
10. Closes lesson effectively	0	1	2	3
11. Summary rating	0	1	2	3

FIGURE 11–3
Rubric used in evaluating writing in grades K and 1

Holistic Evaluation Scale (K and 1)

5   Focused to starter sentence; story structure is recognizable; contains successful attempts in sentence construction (i.e., capitalization, punctuation, etc.)

4   Focused to starter sentence; story structure is recognizable but contains little evidence of sentence mechanics

3   Some words are recognizable; may or may not have mechanics; has connection with starter sentence, but little story development

2   Some words are recognizable; no connection with starter sentence; no mechanics and little story content

1   No recognizable words, mechanics, or story content

Note: Created by Michele Woodward. Used with permission.

municates, based on the performance or product exhibited, what the student knows and is able to do. Thus, rubrics can be highly informative and useful for feedback purposes. On the other hand, the need to develop distinct categories and meaningful verbal descriptions makes them challenging to develop and to score reliably. Figures 11–3 and 11–4 illustrate rubrics used, respectively, in evaluating writing in grades K–1 and at the secondary school level. Note that these types of assessments are much more informative about students' skill levels compared to receiving simply a letter grade or numerical score. To the extent that standards-based education continues to gain acceptance, we can expect to see rubrics becoming increasingly pervasive as an evaluation and feedback tool.

Anecdotal Records. An anecdotal record is an open-ended instrument for evaluating performance in a narrative fashion. An outline-type form containing behaviors to be observed is prepared. In addition to a description of performance, interpretations of what was done along with recommendations for improvement may be included in such a record. The written record should be made while observing the performance, or brief notes should be taken and then expanded on the record form immediately after the evaluation session.

Examples

Observing a student teacher
Attending a presentation given by a student who has completed a public speaking course
Spending a day in an office to evaluate how a manager interacts with her employees

FIGURE 11–4
Rubric used for evaluating writing at the high school level

Score	Content	Organization	Expression	Mechanics
4	Focus is clear and on a limited topic; ideas are developed and supported with concrete details; evidence of consideration of possibilities and complexities of the issue	Strong introduction; transitions between paragraphs help tie information together; strong conclusion	Varied sentence structure; use of vivid language; tone is consistent with text; audience and purpose clearly defined; individual voice present	Use of standard grammar and punctuation; correct spelling
3	Focus may be clear but ideas developed minimally; no consideration for complexity of an issue	An introduction but may not be strong; transitions made between paragraphs; conclusion but may not be strong	Appropriate use of language and diction; tone is consistent with text; audience clearly defined; no individual voice	Same as 4
2	Focus there but predictable; ideas not developed; no complexity	May lack either an introduction or conclusion; few or illogical use of transitions	Simple, clear diction; lacks a sense of voice may use inappropriate tone for audience at times	A few mechanical errors
1	No clear focus; little or no development of ideas	Lacks introduction; series of unrelated paragraphs	May use inappropriate or incorrect language; no sense of audience	Numerous mechanical errors which interfere with reading

Note: Created by Michele Woodward. Used with permission.

Procedure

1. Develop a general set of guidelines to focus your observations according to the objectives of the evaluation. (The guidelines may be modified over time as considered appropriate.)

2. Determine whether the observation will be prearranged or unannounced. The advantage of the prearranged visit is ensuring that the observation can be done at a particular time and that your appearance will be accepted. The advantage of the unannounced visit is observing events as they naturally take place, without special preparation (to impress an observer). Regardless of the orientation used, permission to observe from school or company officials will most likely be required.

3. If you want to use a tape recorder or video camera, be sure to obtain approval from the individual(s) being observed as well as from school or company authorities.

4. Take brief notes during the observation. Expand the notes on a record form as soon after the observation as possible.

5. Make additional observations if needed. The more observations, the more complete and accurate the information obtained. The disadvantage is the time involved and possible disruption caused by the visits.

For example, two months after trainees complete a corporate training course on "group leadership," the evaluator contacts them to identify times when they will be leading a group on the job. A prearranged visit is then coordinated with a given trainee, and permission is obtained to tape-record the session. The evaluator arrives at the meeting early and sits in the back of the room to be unobtrusive. The trainee introduces the evaluator to the group members at the beginning of the meeting and tells them her purposes for being there (and tape-recording the meeting). The evaluator carefully observes the trainee's behavior during the meeting and takes notes, which she later expands. Following the meeting, she decides that the observation produced sufficient information and that a second one with this trainee will not be needed. She decides, however, to observe several other trainees to compare the results.

Descriptive evaluation is time-consuming and often impractical with large numbers of learners. As with rating scales, a degree of subjectivity can easily, and often unknowingly, find its way into an evaluation report. But when carefully prepared, with reference to a number of tasks over a period of time, an evaluator can gather valuable cumulative data on the performance of an individual.

Indirect Checklist/Rating Measures. In some instances, it is not feasible for the evaluator to observe the behavior directly. Sometimes the problem is cost. For example, in a course designed to teach individuals how to make more effective presentations at conferences and meetings, it may prove too expensive for the evaluator to attend the presentations of enough former students to make valid judgments about their performances. Or, it might prove too costly to observe teachers to determine how well they are applying classroom management skills taught in a recent workshop.

In other situations, direct observations are impractical. Common examples are courses designed to help people improve social interactions, interpersonal skills, employee relations, and the like. The difficulty is that, short of following an individual around during the day, the evaluator cannot be present when typical situations requiring such skills arise. And, if the evaluator was present, the situations would probably become unnatural or artificial as a direct result. For example, suppose you and your friend started arguing about whose turn it was to pay for lunch. Would you respond in a "natural" way if an evaluator were there specifically to observe your behavior? Probably not.

If direct observations or tests of behavior are not practical, the next best option might be to seek parallel information from individuals who are present when former students typically demonstrate the criterion skills. One source of data might be reactions from the former students themselves regarding the effectiveness

FIGURE 11–5
Job-based survey

Skills	Degree of Use		
	Not at all	Some	A great deal
Reducing nervousness before presenting	☐	☐	☐
Reducing nervousness while presenting	☐	☐	☐
Improving planning	☐	☐	☐
Improving organization	☐	☐	☐
Improving interruptions	☐	☐	☐
Controlling interruptions	☐	☐	☐
Maintaining proper pacing	☐	☐	☐
Using visual aids	☐	☐	☐
Responding to questions	☐	☐	☐

Note: Copyright 1991 The Dow Chemical Company. Used with permission.

of training for developing certain skills. Figure 11–5 displays items from such a survey. This instrument was administered to former students several months following their completion of a corporate training course on making effective presentations. Individuals were asked to rate the helpfulness of specific course features for improving the quality of presentations that they subsequently made. Instrument development essentially involves identifying, from the course objectives and materials, the criterion performance and the enabling (or component) skills involved. The skills/behaviors are then listed for evaluation by students using a conventional rating scale format.

Another indirect measure would be ratings or checklists submitted by individuals who work or interact with the former students in situations where the target skills are likely to be exhibited. Figure 11–6 illustrates this type of instrument, as employed in the presentation skills evaluation referred to earlier. The instrument was developed by identifying component and criterion skills for the course. The skills were then listed with accompanying five-point rating scales for judging frequency of practice by the student, as observed by the respondent. In the actual evaluation (Morrison & Ross, 1991), respondents were managers, peers, and subordinates who worked with corporate trainees who completed the presentation skills course.

Portfolio Assessments.   Performances frequently culminate, by design, in the creation of tangible products. Examples include paintings, essays, poems, musical compositions, and pottery. The nature of these products change over time as a function of

FIGURE 11–6
Job application survey

Item	Always	Most of the time	Sometimes	Never	Does not apply
1. This individual uses overhead transparencies or other visuals to communicate ideas.	☐	☐	☐	☐	☐
2. This individual uses overhead transparencies to summarize main ideas.	☐	☐	☐	☐	☐
3. It is evident that this individual has spent time preparing and rehearsing the presentation.	☐	☐	☐	☐	☐
4. This individual uses graphs or pictures to emphasize the points he or she wishes to make.	☐	☐	☐	☐	☐
5. This individual begins a talk with a statement of the purpose and expected outcome to focus the audience's attention.	☐	☐	☐	☐	☐
6. This individual emphasizes the main points of the presentation.	☐	☐	☐	☐	☐
7. It is easy to follow the logic in this individual's presentations.	☐	☐	☐	☐	☐
8. This individual uses personal examples or analogies to explain a point.	☐	☐	☐	☐	☐
9. This individual identifies the benefits of implementing the presented idea.	☐	☐	☐	☐	☐
10. This individual arranges the room appropriately (e.g., seating, temperature, overhead projector, etc.) before the participants arrive.	☐	☐	☐	☐	☐
11. The presentations this individual makes have the appropriate level of detail needed for the audience.	☐	☐	☐	☐	☐

Note: Copyright 1991 The Dow Chemical Company. Used with permission.

the student's experience and of the situation. Thus, examining only one sample (e.g., an essay on Thomas Jefferson written in a composition class) may provide a very limited view of the skills acquired from a composition class.

Portfolios represent a form of "authentic testing," a movement today to assess performance in realistic contexts. Tierney, Carter, and Desai (1991) specifically define portfolios as

> systematic collections by both students and teachers. They can serve as the basis to examine effort, improvement, processes, and achievement as well as to meet accountability demands usually achieved by more formal testing procedures. Through reflection on systematic collections of student work, teachers and students can work together to illuminate students' strengths, needs, and progress. (p. 41)

In the same manner, portfolios can also be used to illuminate strengths and needs in the instruction itself.

Procedure

1. Involve students in selecting samples of their work for the portfolio.
2. Update the portfolios over time so that improvements or changes in the quality of the work may be noted.
3. Based on instructional objectives, identify criteria for judging the work. For example, for evaluating a portfolio of writing samples, such criteria might include organization, expression, use of a topic sentence, correct grammar, and spelling.
4. Identify the evaluation mode. Possible modes, which may be used separately or in combination, would include checklists (yes/no), rating scales (e.g., poor, average, superior), and comments (e.g., "shows good effort, but lacks fundamentals").

By examining group results for different criteria at various times of the year, the designer can obtain useful information about how effectively skills are being applied. For example, it may be found that carpentry students' early work evidences very poor routing skills, but later products show high proficiency in this area.

Just as there are different types of objective tests or rating scales, portfolios can take varied forms. Anderson (1994) describes four formats she has used in working with elementary-school children:

- Showcase: Presents the student's "best" work while emphasizing self-assessment, reflection, and ownership.
- Evaluation: Presents representative work to be evaluated on the basis of showing movement toward a specific academic goal.
- Process: Asks students to reflect on work produced over time for the purpose of developing points of view on their long-term learning process and subject synthesis.
- Documentation: Presents work that represents academic accomplishment for presentation to parents, other students, or school administrators.

Portfolios potentially offer clear advantages over objective testing for assessing complex skills. But do they provide *accurate* assessments of student performance? Research on portfolio usage suggests inconsistency across studies regarding this issue (Herman & Winters, 1994). Suppose that you were evaluating a high school student's portfolio in a science class. What factors might compromise the validity of the score you assign? One could be the high subjectivity of judgments being made. A second could be how the student's products (also called "artifacts") were selected (do they represent *best* or *typical* work?). A third might be the extent to which the student did the work independently. A fourth could be the limitations of using fairly restricted scales (see Figures 11–3 and 11–4) to judge quality of performance on complex tasks.

Compared to objective testing, portfolios provide a means of obtaining a richer, more meaningful impression of what students are able to achieve, but perhaps at the risk of some measurement precision. By using each type of test to its best advantage, evaluators/designers can increase the depth and range of information obtained about student learning.

Exhibitions.   For some types of instruction, the culminating products are best displayed in a special type of performance before an audience. These performances, commonly called *exhibitions,* are characterized by being public and requiring many hours of preparation (Woolfolk, 1992).

Examples

Reciting poetry

Playing an instrument

Singing

Acting

Giving a speech

Performing a gymnastics routine

Procedure.   Evaluating exhibitions involves procedures comparable to those used for portfolios, as well as similar advantages and disadvantages compared to objective testing. Typical procedures might include:

1. Identify skill behaviors and criteria based on instructional objectives.
2. Develop instruments such as checklists, rating scales, or some combination to evaluate the performance.
3. Use criterion-referenced measurement by focusing on how well the student has attained the desired level of competence for each skill.
4. Add comments to explain certain ratings, describe noteworthy events, and convey overall impressions of the performance.

ATTITUDES

Just as it is a challenging task to write affective domain objectives, much planning and thought are required to assess individuals' feelings and attitudes toward instruction. Feelings, values, and beliefs are very private matters that cannot be measured directly. Attitudes can be inferred only through a person's words and behaviors.

The problem of evaluating attitudes is further compounded by two factors. First, a response expressed by a learner on an attitudinal survey may be stated so as to be socially acceptable, regardless of the individual's actual feelings. Therefore, true sentiments may not be conveyed. Second, outcomes of the most important objectives in a course may not become evident until some time after the course is completed, which thus makes it impossible to measure an attitude at the end of the study time for a unit or course. We sometimes hear students say something like, "I hated that course and old Dr. Brazle's lectures when I took it, but it really helped me in Algebra II."

In spite of these limitations, there can be benefits from attempting to determine, at the conclusion of a unit or portions of an instructional program, whether it satisfied attitudinal objectives. At the same time, student attitudes provide formative evaluation data regarding how positively different aspects of the course instruction are perceived.

Two Uses of Attitude Assessment

We commonly find two general categories of attitude assessments in formative and summative evaluations: evaluating instruction and evaluating affective outcomes. These approaches are similar in their basic methods and instruments employed (e.g., surveys, interviews, rating scales). What distinguishes them is their focus—the instruction itself or desired affective outcomes of the instruction.

Evaluating the Instruction. In this approach, the interest is in determining how students or trainees react to the instruction they have received—what they like or do not like, and their suggestions for improving it. The *instruction,* not the learner, is the focus. Exemplary evaluation questions are:

- Was the course material well organized?
- Did you have sufficient time to learn the material?
- What suggestions do you have for improving the manual?

Evaluating Affective Outcomes. In the second approach, the learners and their feelings toward certain ideas or behaviors are the focus. Of particular interest may be measuring how much attitude changes as a direct result of the instructional program (a pretest-posttest design). For example, prior to a dental hygiene workshop, only 13% of the enrollees (practicing dentists) agreed that working with gloves is an important hygienic practice. Following the workshop, the agreement rate increased to 87%, which suggests that the workshop was successful in promoting that view. Other examples:

- Nurses' attitudes toward showing empathy to patients
- Employees' feelings about tardiness and absenteeism
- Police officers' attitudes toward using force in stopping crime
- Students' interest in visiting museums
- Home builders' attitudes toward using cypress wood as a siding

As we will see, regardless of whether the focus is on attitudes toward the instruction or attitudes toward behaviors/practices, a variety of data collection methods is available.

Observation/Anecdotal Records

Just as observation is useful for evaluating performance (see pp. 199–205), it can provide a valuable source of information about student attitudes. Observation is often carried out by the instructor while learners are at work in their normal study or activity area. The instrument for recording what is observed can be a simple questionnaire, a rating scale, or an open-ended form on which descriptions and comments are made as in an anecdotal record.

What you focus on during an observation will depend on the evaluation objectives. Normally, there will be interest in how students react to the instruction—what holds their interest, what loses it, and the like. Relevant attitudes will thus be conveyed in observable behaviors such as attentiveness, affect (e.g., smiling, nodding in agreement, laughing), and engagement (taking notes, answering questions, raising hands, etc.). Exemplary items that might be included in an observer rating scale are:

Student Attitude	Low	Some	High
Interest in lesson	1	2	3
Attentiveness to lesson	1	2	3
Actively engaged	1	2	3
Positive affect (smiles, laughter)	1	2	3

Assessment of Behavior

Students may smile frequently and be very enthusiastic about the instruction but not transfer their feelings about what is learned outside of class. Consider, for example, a college-level art appreciation class that is intended to increase students' knowledge and interest in music, art, and theater. Although students might like the class very much, few may increase their attendance at concerts, exhibitions, or plays. Positive attitudes toward instruction do not necessarily transfer to the subject, at least to the extent that behavior is changed.

The most powerful type of instrument for assessing behavioral changes would be direct observation of learner activities. For example, we may find that 60% of Ms. Leyton's Algebra I students elect to take Algebra II, whereas only 10% of Mr. Petza's students make that choice. A clear implication (assuming similar class makeups) is that Ms. Leyton's course is more successful in producing positive attitudes toward algebra. Similarly, it may be found that 40% of the nurses in a particular health care facility voluntarily attend a workshop on CPR methods compared to a 10% rate for nurses in a neighboring facility.

You could probably think of many examples where such direct observation or measurement would be very impractical. After all, we cannot easily follow students around to see what they do after class (e.g., how many visit the local art museum this month). In those cases, the best alternative is to construct a brief survey that asks students to supply this information.

Questionnaire/Survey

Probably the most common means of assessing attitudes is through questionnaires or surveys. Such instruments may include two types of items: (a) open-ended questions to which the learner writes answers, and (b) closed-ended questions with a number of fixed responses from which learners choose the answer that best reflects their opinion. A variation of this latter type consists of a longer list of alternatives from which the learner checks interesting or important choices or rates the alternatives on a numerical scale.

The decision to use open-ended or closed-ended items (or some combination of the two) may depend on the time available to tabulate the replies. The open-ended type provides data that are time consuming to analyze but may be more valuable in conveying learners' feelings and the reasons for them. Closed-ended questions are quicker and more reliable (objective) to process but limit the depth and detail of expression. Examples of open-ended and closed-ended questionnaires are provided at the conclusion of this section.

A *rating scale* is a modification of the questionnaire on which the learner replies to a statement by selecting a point along a scale. The scale may be comprised of two points (*yes/no*), three points (e.g., *yes/no opinion/disagree*), or up to five points (e.g., *very often/quite often/sometimes/hardly ever/never*). A commonly used scale is the five-point Likert-type scale consisting of *strongly agree, agree, undecided, disagree,* and *strongly disagree.* Here are some guidelines for writing questionnaire and survey items:

1. *Limit the number of rating scale points to a maximum of five.* People usually have difficulty making finer discriminations. The younger the age group, the more

restricted the choices should be. For example, in surveying first-grade students about their interest in reading, a simple yes/no scale should probably be used. A comparable survey for sixth-graders might use a three-point scale of *agree, uncertain, disagree.* For high school students, a five-point scale would be an option. The more scale points, the greater the amount of information that will be obtained, but the greater the chances of confusing the respondent.

> *Poor:* Rate the organization of the course on a 10-point scale, where 1 = Very poor and 10 = Very good.
> *Better:* Rate the organization of the course on the following 5-point scale, where 1 = Superior; 2 = Slightly above average; 3 = Average; 4 = Slightly below average; 5 = Inferior.

2. *Use verbal descriptors to define numerical rating points.* Examples are:

Rate the enthusiasm of clerical employees in the automotive division.

Low		Average		High
1	2	3	4	5

Rate the difficulty of the mechanical assembly for you.

Very easy	Somewhat easy	Average	Somewhat difficult	Difficult
1	2	3	4	5

3. *Use rating points that are clearly separable and nonoverlapping.*
   Poor: How often do you play sports?

Never	Occasionally	Sometimes	Often	Frequently
1	2	3	4	5

   Better: How often do you play sports?

Rarely/never	Sometimes	Frequently
1	2	3

Note that even in the last case, the meaning of *sometimes* and *frequently* may be ambiguous to students. Is twice a week "sometimes" or "frequently"? It would therefore be preferable to define these categories objectively, such as rarely (less than once a week), sometimes (once or twice a week), and frequently (more than twice a week).

4. *Use clear and concrete language to express the idea to be rated.*
   Poor: There is adequate equipment in the office.

FIGURE 11–7
Sample questionnaires, rating scales, and interview guide

Questionnaire (Open-ended)

1. What is your general reaction to this topic? Comment specifically on the content treated, the way it was taught, your participation, and any other aspects that you feel are relevant.

2. In your opinion, what was the greatest strength of the teaching approach used for learning the material on this unit?

Questionnaire (Closed-ended)

Select the response on each item that best reflects your reaction.

1. Learner interest

   a. I feel this topic challenged me intellectually.
   b. I found the material interesting but not challenging.
   c. I was not stimulated very often.
   d. I do not feel the topic was worthwhile.

2. Topic organization

   a. I could see how the concepts on this topic were interrelated.
   b. The instructor attempted to cover only the minimum amount of material.
   c. I didn't know where the instructor was heading most of the time.

Rating Scale

1. Did you have any difficulty or trouble operating the equipment?

   ____ No   ____ Yes   Comment:

2. How do you rate the self-study activity as a learning experience?

0	1	2	3	4
Waste of time	Slightly useful	Satisfactory	Good	Excellent

3. How demanding was the format used in the experimental unit compared to that in a conventional unit?

   ____ More demanding   ____ About equal   ____ Less demanding

4. Indicate your feeling about the value of wearing goggles for safety on your job:

1	2	3	4	5
No value				High value

Interview Guide

1. What is your reaction to the value of the unit you have just completed?

2. How would you rate the amount of assistance that the instructor and the assistants provided you outside of the discussion sessions?

   ____ None   ____ Low   ____ Some   ____ Sufficient   ____ Excellent

   Comments:

3. Do you feel the criteria adopted by your instructor for assigning letter grades in this unit were fair to you? If not, why not?

4. What suggestions do you have for improving the activities you completed for this topic?

Better: I have the equipment that I need to do my office work.

Poor: The instructional strategy employed was beneficial.
Better: The teaching method used was helpful to me in learning the material.

5. *Express only a single idea in each item.*
   Poor: I like working with my clients and my coworkers.
   Better: I like working with my clients.
      I like working with my coworkers.

Interview

An interview allows learners to discuss their reactions toward instruction in more detail than can be done on a survey or questionnaire. The questions can be structured or unstructured. A structured interview has the advantage of being more controllable with regard to time and content. An unstructured interview, on the other hand, may provide an opportunity to probe more deeply to clarify learners' responses as well as to follow up on unanticipated responses that may yield new insights. The disadvantage is loss of control and increases in time. It is generally valuable to tape-record interviews, but be sure that the interviewee approves of this. Also, for objectivity, the interviewer should be a person not affiliated with the instructional program.

For further descriptions of the various instruments, including their benefits and limitations, see the references for this chapter.

Examples of questionnaires, rating scales, and an interview guide appear in Figure 11–7.

SUMMARY

1. The selection or development of evaluation instruments begins with a reexamination of the evaluation questions and the types of outcomes they assess: knowledge, skills and behavior, and/or attitudes.
2. Critical to the assessment of cognitive outcomes is the matching of test items to the level of learning specified by objectives.
3. Objective tests, such as multiple-choice, true/false, and matching, have the advantage of being easy to grade. The disadvantage is their restriction to assessing recognition learning and relatively low levels of learning.
4. Short-answer tests have the advantage over multiple-choice tests of assessing recall rather than recognition. Other constructed-response tests, such as short-answer, essay, and problem solving, have the advantage of

assessing higher levels of learning (application, analysis, and synthesis) but the disadvantage of being difficult to grade reliably.

5. Evaluations of performance frequently focus on both process (the behaviors that lead to an outcome) and product (the outcome).

6. Alternative means of assessing skills and behavior are direct testing, analysis of naturally occurring events, ratings of performance, anecdotal records, indirect checklist/rating measures, portfolio assessments, and exhibitions.

7. Attitudes cannot be directly measured but must be inferred on the basis of learners' verbal reports and behaviors. Common means for assessing attitudes are anecdotal records, observation of behavior, questionnaires, and interviews.

FROM HERE TO THERE

You have just completed designing a training unit for basketball referees to be employed by the city park commission. At this point, you want to add an evaluation component both to assess trainee skills and to evaluate the effectiveness of the instruction. Because a main emphasis of the unit is learning the specific rules for league play at different age levels, you first create an objective test featuring 25 multiple-choice questions and 15 short-answer questions (e.g., "At the Bantam Level, how many seconds can an offensive player remain in the key without being called for a violation? _____ "). However, correctly applying rules and using proper protocol are also critical outcomes. For this area, you videotape five scenarios (e.g., "over and back," "technical foul," "traveling," "intentional foul," and "angry parent") to which trainees will be asked to react via open-ended responses ("What would you do here?"). Next, you develop a ratings instrument, using rubrics defining four categories of skill level, to evaluate each trainee during an actual game. Finally, you create a brief open-ended survey to collect feedback from the trainees regarding the effectiveness of the training unit. Would portfolios possibly be useful here as well? What is your reaction to this approach? What is your opinion?

REFERENCES

Anderson, R. S. (1994). Using portfolios in K–2 classrooms. Unpublished manuscript. Memphis, TN: University of Memphis.

Herman, J. L., & Winters, L. (1994). Portfolio research: A slim collection. *Educational Leadership, 52*, 91–98.

McBeath, R. J. (1992). *Instruction and evaluation in higher education: A guidebook for planning and learning.* Englewood Cliffs, NJ: Educational Technology Publications.

Meyer, C. A. (1993). What's the difference between authentic and performance assessment? *Educational Leadership, 51*, 39–40.

Morrison, G. R., & Ross, S. M. (1991, October). *Evaluation report for presentation skills: Final report for Dow Chemical USA.* Memphis, TN: Memphis State University.

Tierney, R. J., Carter, M. A., & Desai, L. E. (1991). *Portfolio assessment in the reading–writing classroom.* Norwood, MA: Christopher-Gordon.

Woolfolk, A. E. (1992). *Educational psychology.* Needham Heights, MA: Allyn & Bacon.

SUPPORT SERVICES AND PLANNING TOOLS

"Are sufficient funds available to purchase the materials we need?"

"Where do we find a room that can be adapted for a learning lab?"

"Do we have the appropriate equipment for learner use in the program we've planned?"

"Is there a way, other than writing on paper, to handle the mechanics of planning?"

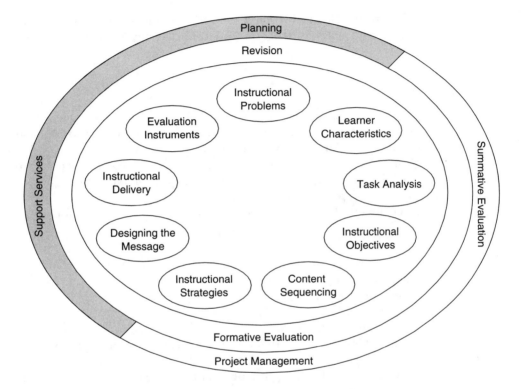

A long with the specification of the instructional strategies and the selection of instructional resources, a number of logistical matters must be considered for supporting the successful delivery of instruction. These include:

- Budgetary matters
- Facilities
- Materials
- Equipment
- Personnel services
- Time frame for completing phases of the planning and development
- Coordination with other activities

Also, a designer must recognize any constraints or limitations within which a new program may have to be developed and implemented. For example:

- Monetary limitations (a budget, or the lack of one!)
- The time when the program must be ready for use (next year, next semester, next month, tomorrow)
- The equipment on hand that should be used ("Last year we purchased video-disc players . . . use them!")
- The size of an available room ("Only 20 computers can be put in that room.")
- The length of the instruction ("We cannot justify 5 days in a classroom.")

BUDGET

All new programs require funds to get started. Any institution or organization interested in supporting innovation in its instructional program must provide money for development, operation, and implementation. For a school or university, the funds can be gleaned from the organization's budget or contracts or grants obtained from outside agencies for instructional development purposes. For a corporation the funds must be allocated as part of a budget or possibly obtained as a "loan" if the group is a profit center. Financial support may be necessary for any or all of the following items:

During Development

- Professional planning time
- Clerical support time
- Construction or renovation of required facilities
- Purchase and installation of equipment
- Design, development, and production of instructional materials, which can include fees for using others' materials (e.g., music and photographs) and production costs
- Development of testing instruments for evaluation of both learning and the program
- Consultative services
- Tryouts, including personnel time and consumable materials
- Time for planning any necessary revisions, materials needed, and preparation
- Time for training instructors and staff for implementation phase
- Administration time for coordination and supervision
- Administrative costs (travel, telephone, overhead)

During Implementation or Program Operation

- Faculty and staff salaries
- Replacement of consumable and damaged materials
- Servicing and maintenance of equipment
- Depreciation of equipment
- Overhead charges for facilities and services
- Updating the program periodically (time and materials)

Chapter 14 includes further discussion of financial matters as part of program cost measures.

FACILITIES

Facilities to carry out an instructional program may require any of the following:

- Room for presentation to groups of average size (20–40), or to large groups (100 or more), requiring chalkboards/whiteboards, media projection, computers, and sound amplification
- Self-paced learning study stations (carrels or open tables) of a suitable size to hold necessary equipment and study materials for learner use
- Small-group meeting rooms with informally arranged furniture for teacher-learner or learner-learner interaction, equipped with chalkboards/whiteboards and provisions for media projection
- A resource center where materials and equipment are gathered, organized, and made available to instructors and learners
- Staff meeting room and workroom

When deciding on facilities for a learning center to serve a self-paced learning program, consider the following five questions:

- How many learners are expected in the program?
- How many hours will the average learner spend in the learning center?
- How many stations or carrels will be required, or how many pieces or sets of equipment will be needed?
- How many hours should the center be open weekly (possibly with supervision)?
- Should the center be open evenings and weekends?

If you can answer any three of these questions, you can calculate the number of hours the center should be open to students. For example:

100 learners
4 hours (the average study time per learner in a week)
10 stations, fully equipped, to be provided
Question: How many hours should the center be open weekly?
$100 \times 4 = 400$ student hours per week
$400 \div 10 = 40$ hours of use per week

Thus, this learning center should be available a minimum of 40 hours per week. This assumes continuous, full use of each station. Add a factor of 10% to 20% to allow flexibility for repeated use by some learners, equipment failure, variations in learner schedules, and other unforeseen needs. So, in this problem, 45 to 48 hours of operation should be provided. If this is too many hours for the staff or budget to support, they might alleviate the problem by increasing the number of stations.

As the need for specific facilities becomes obvious, consider which existing rooms can be used without modification, which ones require minor or major adaptations, and where new construction is essential. Many ideas for adapting present facilities can be obtained by visiting locations that have similar programs in operation. It may also be necessary to consult with qualified experts who know about space needs for various activities, availability of special equipment, electrical requirements, and other technical matters.

MATERIALS

Once you've amassed the resources to support activities, it is necessary to locate and acquire specific commercial items or to prepare materials. Reference librarians or media specialists can assist with catalogs and other sources of available media materials.

If materials are to be prepared, then follow a planning and production sequence for media and multimedia materials based on the instructional design plan. Then, arrange for or carry out the production by preparing graphics, taking pictures, making slides, videotaping, audio recording, editing, programming or authoring, and so forth. If computer-based training materials are to be prepared, the use of a suitable authoring system, or help from programming experts, would be necessary. Once the original material is completed and accepted, make the necessary duplicate copies. (For specific details and guidance in all media planning and production steps, see Kemp & Smellie, 1994.)

Other required materials, including printed items such as information sheets, study guides, worksheets, and workbooks, need to be written and prepared in sufficient copies for the number of learners to be served. If instructors, other than those active on the planning team, will be involved in delivering instruction, then teaching guides may be required.

EQUIPMENT

When you are deciding which materials to use in a program, consider the equipment required for using the materials. Is sufficient equipment already available, or must it be obtained? Although decisions about equipment usually depend on your choice of materials, sometimes the kind of equipment available may influence the type of material you will use. For example, still pictures in the form of slides might be preferred for self-paced learning, but if video players are available, it might be preferable to copy the slide/tape program to videotape or create a computer presentation from the scanned slides.

Here again, expert help may be advisable. Because such a wide variety of equipment is available for both group presentations and individual use, knowing what to choose without having an extensive background and up-to-date experience can be difficult. Find out which kinds of equipment have proved durable and easy to use and cause the least damage to the materials. However, do not leave the final decision on equipment to consultants. The individuals who will be involved in a new program should themselves carefully examine and try out whatever equipment is recommended. Have learners also work with the equipment before you make a final decision.

Sometimes we are impressed with highly sophisticated, complex equipment that apparently can do many things, some of which may not be needed. Less complex and less costly equipment often can serve equally well. The cost of maintenance and the replacement of parts must also be taken into consideration. This is particularly true with respect to interactive computer and video equipment. (Remember that if copyrighted materials will be used, permission is required to duplicate or convert them to another format.) Be practical in requesting what you will need, but be reasonable in terms of available funds, the complexity of the equipment, and the eventual cost of upkeep. (For media equipment sources, see materials published by the International Communications Industries Association.)

PERSONNEL CAPABILITIES

Professional and technical skills in at least 13 different areas are often essential for planning an instructional design, developing the resources, and implementing and testing a program. Very likely some members of a planning team will either possess a number of these skills to some degree or they will be able to acquire them. Persons with special skills can be called upon as needed. The responsibilities of the various members of a planning team are described in the following sections.

Instructor or Manager

The instructor or manager knows the characteristics of the learners for whom the instruction is to be designed. He or she must be well informed of the instructional problem. When the new program is being carried out, the instructor or instructor team has the major responsibility for its success.

Subject-Matter Expert

The subject-matter expert (SME) (a role often filled by the instructor or instructor team) must be competent in the subject. Such a person suggests content topics, recommends the sequence for presenting them, and selects activities based on the course objectives. This expert must be able to check the accuracy of the subject content and the treatment of content in instructional materials chosen or produced for the program. He or she must be well aware of the relationship of this subject to other subjects in the curriculum or training program. The role requires a person who has a fresh, broad, and imaginative view of the subject and its applications. Further attention is given to this role in Chapter 13.

Instructional Designer

The person who holds the assignment of instructional designer has a background in instructional technology and educational psychology. This person must be experienced with the instructional design process and know about instructional strategies and instructional resources. He or she must be able to guide the planning process, work with all personnel, and coordinate the program with administrators. The designer must supervise the scheduled completion of materials, assist in evaluating the tryouts, and help put the program into operation.

Some educators believe instructional designers should be competent in the subject area in which they work. Others feel the designer should have experience in teaching but not necessarily in the content area being planned. Without being involved in the teaching role or in the subject of the course, the designer may guide the planning and view the objectives, content, methods, resources, and procedures of evaluation in a fresh, unbiased way. (Chapter 13 gives further attention to the role of the instructional designer.)

Evaluation Specialist

The role of the evaluator is to assist the professional staff in developing testing instruments to pretest learners' previous learning levels; measure cognitive, psychomotor, and performance accomplishments as the instructional program proceeds; and test achievement at the end of course units. The evaluator will assist in formative testing during program tryouts and in applying the findings for improving the program. He or she may be asked to develop attitudinal and rating scales and to design summative evaluation measures to determine the effectiveness and efficiency of the program. It is strongly recommended that the evaluator be someone who has no connection to the program so the analysis and resulting recommendations will be as objective as possible.

Project Manager

The program manager, a role often filled by the instructional designer, supplies administrative leadership and usually arranges schedules, personnel assignments, equipment, and budget allocations and requests facilities as the program moves from planning into development and implementation. This person should coordinate all components of a project to reach successful implementation. (See Chapter 14 for further details on project and instructional development agency management.) The project manager should also be responsible for managing the "politics" associated with introducing any new program in an organization, including obtaining permissions or clearances, being alert to human conflicts, and supporting staff actions.

Media Producer

The media producer plans, supervises, or carries out the production of all instructional materials made locally, including print, graphic, photographic, audio, and video forms. The media producer also supervises the adaptation of facilities needed in connection with the use of the media and must be able to instruct teachers and learners how to use the materials and equipment.

Computer Specialist

If computer technology for computer-based instruction and interactive multimedia applications will be used, then services of a computer specialist are necessary. This individual will be proficient in the use of an authoring system, digital video, and graphic packages. This individual might be a programmer or computer specialist.

Librarian

The librarian must have a broad knowledge of what may be available in order to suggest commercial print and nonprint materials for teaching/learning activities. The librarian is responsible for locating needed materials as well as for providing the services for using them during implementation of the program.

Media Technician

The media technician's job is to prepare instructional materials, package items needed for the program, and install as well as maintain equipment.

Aides

Aides (sometimes called tutors, proctors, or facilitators) assist teachers and others on the staff with semi-instructional and housekeeping tasks. These duties may include preparing simple materials, supervising laboratory and learner-group activities, handling and distributing materials and equipment, providing remedial or special assistance to learners, and administering and grading tests. Aides may be graduate students in the subject field, undergraduates or former trainees who have previously completed the new program, or paid or volunteer assistants.

Secretary

The secretary's duty is to handle all office and clerical work, including typing; maintaining correspondence; filing; ordering materials; preparing reports; duplicating and labeling materials; and assisting the instructional designer, instructor, and administrator.

Learners

Increasingly, former students are participating in activities that affect them. Many learners are intellectually mature and articulate. Their reactions and suggestions to proposed instructional plans can be beneficial. Select two or three learners who have already studied the subject, and ask them to participate in review sessions. They can react to activities and evaluate unit materials.

The Planning Team

The initial planning team should be small, consisting of perhaps one or more SMEs, an instructional designer, and an evaluation expert. A team of two individuals may possess all the necessary skills. Persons with other abilities should be brought into the program as their services are required.

TIME AND SCHEDULES

Next to personnel, the allocation of time is the most difficult category of support service to deal with during the development of any new program. Finding time to work on the many aspects of a project may be formidable. Often the idea of a new program will not be accepted by the administration until some preliminary planning has been completed and a detailed proposal presented. The time for this preliminary work may have to be borrowed from time that would have been spent on other activities. A real dedication is often required to complete the initial planning.

When a design project is approved, time is required for professional planning, for staff and clerical assistance in locating and preparing materials, for support services to adapt facilities and install equipment, and for numerous other tasks. After the planning is completed, schedules must be set for trying out the program. During the same period, time must be scheduled for staff orientation and training, as necessary. Finally, work schedules must be drawn up for instructors, aides, and learners in order to put the instructional program into operation.

In a self-paced learning program, learners must be encouraged to assume responsibilities for completing their assignments within a given time period. In scheduling learner time, be alert to the tendency that some will procrastinate on their responsibilities. Therefore, set deadlines for learners to complete work and take tests.

COORDINATING WITH OTHER ACTIVITIES

Too often, a new instructional program in an institution or organization is treated as if it occupies a special world of its own. It may be given preference over regular classes in using facilities, and its participants may seem to have special privileges that other teachers and learners know little about and may resent. Coordinating and communicating with others in the building or in the organization can develop understanding and thus maintain good feelings. Therefore, it is a good plan to explain a new program to all members of a department or organization and to keep them advised of progress. Inform them of any activities that may interest them professionally or that may have some influence on them or on their learners.

PROJECT MANAGEMENT TOOLS

As you work on the various elements that comprise the instructional design plan, you will recognize that a close, sequential relationship must be built among them. Specifying one element can affect the treatment of other ones. For example, the insight gained when writing test items may clarify the intent of an instructional objective. In this creative process of planning, therefore, changing, deleting, reordering, and adding items will be necessary.

It may be your usual practice to put thoughts, plans, and procedures on paper. However, a sheet of paper is a very limiting medium for use in instructional planning. Lists on paper are static, making changes or additions difficult.

Cards

A more flexible procedure is to make entries on three-by-five-inch index cards. Write a single item—an objective, an element of content, an activity, an evaluation item, and so forth—on each card. Consider using different-colored cards for the various planning elements. Write large, with a fine-tipped felt pen, so that words can be easily seen when the cards are displayed. You can then tape these cards to a wall or tack them to a board.

With this method, it is easy to shift, add, remove, and rewrite items until you find the best sequence. A number of members of the planning team can observe the program as it develops. When completed and accepted, the plan can be copied as a similar layout on paper for continuing reference.

Post-It® Note Pads

Instead of using cards, write on sheets from three-by-five-inch Post-It® Note Pads. The adhesive strip on the back edge of each sheet will hold securely to almost any surface—wall, chalkboard/whiteboard, cardboard sheet. As with cards, Post-Its® are available in many different colors.

Projected Computer Displays

As planning information is generated, you can use a word processor to record your ideas. A video screen, however, is too small and is not suitable for viewing by more than one or two persons. An alternative is to use a video or LCD projector to display the document(s) on the screen to the group. Changes, additions, and corrections can be made instantly, discussed, and then, with an attached printer, paper copies can be printed and provided to the participants immediately.

Project Management Software

The last option for planning your project is to use project management software. These packages will help you identify each task and the personnel resources, and time frame needed for the task. You can then generate a variety of reports in formats ranging from tables to flow charts to PERT charts. You will need to weigh the benefit of entering and maintaining the information with software against the size and scope of your project. For smaller projects, a database and spreadsheet may be more than adequate for project management needs.

SUMMARY

1. Seven categories of services are necessary to support instructional planning: budget, facilities, materials, equipment, personnel, time schedules, and coordination with other activities.
2. Budgetary requirements include financial support for project development and implementation.
3. Facilities should be available for classroom presentations, small-group activities, and self-paced learning.
4. Materials and equipment requirements depend on resources specified in the design plan.
5. Personnel capabilities include 13 categories of responsibilities.
6. Allocating time and maintaining a schedule for completing phases in planning, materials preparation, program tryout, and implementation need consideration.
7. Coordination with other organizational activities contributes to project success.
8. There are both visual and intellectual benefits for using a planning board to display cards on planning details as an instructional design project is developed.
9. Project management software is often useful for large or long-term projects that have a significant management and budgetary component.

FROM HERE TO THERE

Your consulting group is preparing a proposal for a local bank with 23 branches to train the tellers in the correct procedures to follow during a bank robbery. The training you have proposed will use a multimedia format with students attending the three-hour training session at one of the remote training sites. Your client, however, wants two solutions. First, you have 30 days to prepare "some type of training" they can deliver. Second, they will give you up to six months to produce a 30-minute "live" introduction to be delivered by one of the bank's training staff, a 30- to

45-minute multimedia simulation, and a manual. You have access to several bank employees, including tellers who have been robbed, the head of bank security, and the instructor who used to teach the course. You must prepare a budget and timeline by noon tomorrow. What are your requirements?

REFERENCES

Kemp, J. E., & Smellie, D. C. (1994). *Planning, producing, and using instructional technologies.* New York: HarperCollins.

THE ROLE OF THE INSTRUCTIONAL DESIGNER

"How do I distinguish between the subject-matter expert and client?"

"What responsibilities does the instructor or client share in the design process?"

"How does an instructional designer work with media personnel and other support staff?"

"What are the instructional designer's responsibilities for administering or managing a project?"

The instructional designer is typically the individual solely responsible for implementing and following a systematic design process. This chapter will focus on the role of the instructional designer as a designer, that is, the individual who has the primary responsibility for designing and developing the instruction. The designer's role as a project manager is addressed in the next chapter. At times, the roles may appear to conflict with one another, but mostly they will complement each other.

The Role of the Designer

The instructional designer has the primary responsibility of ensuring that the instruction is designed, developed, and produced in a systematic manner that will consistently produce efficient and effective learning. This task is accomplished by carefully following an instructional design model. A distinction is needed between rigidly following a model and applying a model to an instructional problem. No model is so carefully planned and flexible that it can account for all conditions. Following a model in a rigid fashion will result in a misallocation of resources and lost time fulfilling the "needs" of the model rather than solving the instructional problem. The design model should serve as a *guide* for designing the instruction. Those steps that are not relevant to the particular problem are skipped, so that the effort can be concentrated on the parts of the model that are most applicable.

With each project the designer must decide how much design is required. This decision is influenced by the time frame for addressing the problem, the nature of the delivery, and the resources available. The following sections describe each of these decision factors.

Time Frame

First, consider the issue of the time frame. Some problems require immediate attention either because of the number of the individuals affected or the critical nature of the problem. For example, suppose a company or university installs a new telephone system and all phones are switched at midnight Monday. Thus, everyone reporting to work on Tuesday has an immediate need to know how to use the telephone system. After Tuesday, the need is gone except for the need to train new employees. Thus, the training is short term; the problem exists only for a day. A designer needs to determine whether this need is best addressed by a major instructional design project that could take a month or more to complete, or whether the designer should spend a few hours with a subject-matter expert (SME) preparing a group presentation or a job aid.

An instructional problem with a longer time frame might be a technical training issue, such as determining whether an acid treatment will improve the production of an oil well. This need is one that will probably apply to all new engineers in a particular area for many years. Since the training is repetitive (e.g., offered for each new employee), the need would justify a carefully designed unit of instruction if there is a sufficient audience. Similarly, you might decide to create a unit of instruction for students who serve as office assistants to teach them how to correctly answer the phone and take messages. Again, this is a need that will apply to new student workers each year until either the school's name changes or the phone system is changed.

The designer's role is likely to vary between two extremes. First, the designer can serve as a consultant to an SME for a short time period to help the SME organize and sequence the content. The actual design and delivery is left to the expertise of the instructor/SME. Second, the designer can assume a more active leadership role and carefully design a project following a model. Compared to the role as a consultant, the designer is more likely to assume a leadership role and direct the full development of a self-paced or mediated unit of instruction. The designer's role then becomes central to the project as he or she is responsible for the content analysis, objectives, instructional strategies, test items, formative evaluation, and, possibly, the actual writing of the materials.

Nature of Delivery

In Chapter 9 we described several strategies for delivering instruction to large groups, small groups, and individuals. The role of the designer is often influenced by the type of delivery method selected. Let's examine two examples.

An instructor approaches a designer for help in structuring a new course that involves lectures. The designer's role could take one of three possibilities. First, the designer could assume a *proactive* design and leadership role. In a proactive role the designer serves as a leader and uses a model to guide the design of the project. Second, the designer and SME could agree on a cooperative relationship in which they share the responsibility for design. In this role, the SME or instructor often assumes responsibility for defining the problem and for doing the task analysis. The designer then works with the SME or instructor to design the strategies for each individual lecture. Third, the designer's role is one of a consultant who is a sounding board and a resource for the SME's ideas. When designing a lecture-based course, the SME is likely to maintain a more dominant role in the design of the instruction, since he or she will ultimately deliver the information.

A second example involves the development of a computer-based instruction unit that is delivered as individualized instruction. When the delivery method is individualized, the designer is more likely to assume a proactive role in design and leadership. The SME, then, will tend to be the consultant to the project. This shift in roles may be due to the shift from the classroom, where the SME typically has control, to an individualized environment that may utilize a form of technology to deliver the instruction.

A third example is a teacher who serves as an instructional designer with a team of other grade-level teachers on a development project. The designer/teacher has two options. One is to assume the role of an instructional designer and lead the group through the design process. Assuming such a role would require an agreement amongst the other teachers to follow the process. Second, the designer/teacher can serve as both an SME and a design consultant.

Resources Available

The final factor that can influence the role of the designer is the resources available for the project. The primary resources—personnel, time, and money—can influence the designer's role on a continuum from consultant to proactive designer and leader. A lack of design staff personnel, short time lines, or a lack of funds may require the designer to accept a role as a consultant as opposed to a proactive designer. Working under such constraints, the designer may need to question the acceptance of the consulting role on the basis of the amount of impact the designer can or will have on the project. The decision, however, must also consider organizational and political factors.

PREPARING FOR THE INITIAL MEETING

Prepare for the first meeting by familiarizing yourself with background information about the project through reading the proposal, a report, or a memo that may serve as the basis for the project. Also talk informally with persons who may have information relative to the need for the project. Then, at the first meeting, get to know the client and other members of the planning group who will work with you on the project. Since first impressions are very important, establish rapport by giving attention to:

- Learning the names of those who are in attendance
- Meeting in a suitable, informal environment
- Avoiding disturbances (telephone calls) and other distractions
- Employing personal behavior techniques that are commonly used in counseling (low-key, pleasant attitude, positive body language, active listening, careful questioning, etc.)
- Exploring the purposes for the project (encourage the client to describe the situation, needs, expectations, and desired outcomes)
- Finding out who, besides those present, will need to review and possibly approve the output as work is performed
- Defining constraints, including time, personnel, space, and budget limitations
- Agreeing on responsibilities, methodology to be followed, and initial tasks to be performed by each person, then setting a schedule for completion of project phases and times for meetings

THE CLIENT AND THE SUBJECT-MATTER EXPERT

Each design project has a client and an SME; however, these individuals are not always easily identifiable. The following section describes the participants of a design project in a business organization, higher education, and a company that develops materials for other companies.

Business Training Environment

In this business environment, all the participants are usually employed by the same company; however, they may be separated geographically in different offices, buildings, states, or countries (Morrison, 1988). The client is typically the individual who "owns" the problem. The client/owner is usually a manager or supervisor of the target audience (the individuals with the problem). Transfer of real or paper money does not always identify the client. Another manager, a vice president, or even the training manager might "pay" for the instructional product. A client's primary responsibility in this environment is to provide access to the target population and to identify qualified SMEs.

The role of the SME is that of a consultant who often is not an employee of the training or instructional design group. The SME usually has some association with the target population (e.g., he or she worked at that level and was promoted) but is seldom the client. The primary responsibility of the SME is to provide accurate information during the task analysis and verify the accuracy of the products. This separation of roles between the SME and client allows the designer to contract with the client for the work and to assume the role of a proactive designer and leader.

Higher Education Environment

The client in the higher education environment is usually the professor who approaches the instructional designer for assistance (Tessmer, 1988). Since the professor both owns the problem and is the SME, the professor typically maintains the leadership role. The structure of the higher education environment and the organizational environment is often responsible for placing the instructional designer into a consulting role rather than a proactive designer role.

The SME is responsible for the accuracy of the content. If the designer assumes the role of a consultant, the client/SME may see the designer in a service role and limit requests to assistance with media production. On projects requiring the development and use of technologies such as interactive video, the client/SME may request that the designer take a more proactive role.

The role of the designer is often influenced by the function of the instructional group. If the department or group is perceived as providing a service to faculty members (e.g., preparing overhead transparencies), the designer's role may be seen as simply offering a service of suggesting and producing media.

Developing Training for Third Parties

The final illustration is a business that develops instructional materials for other companies under a contract. There may actually be several clients (Foshay, 1988). First, the individual who signed the contract is one client, but he or she may not be involved in the project further until the final product is delivered. A second client includes the individuals in the contracting company who will judge the technical accuracy of the instructional materials. Finally, the third client is the instructional designer's manager who may manage the contract. The designer has the responsibility for addressing the needs of each client and resolving conflicts between their needs. Correctly identifying all of the clients is essential for a project of this nature.

When doing contract work, the SME can be an employee of the contracting organization, an employee of the designer's organization, or an independent consultant hired for the duration of the project. If the SME is an employee of either organization, the designer may face problems negotiating for the SME's time. If the SME, however, is hired specifically for the project, then access to the SME is seldom a problem.

Typically, in contract work the designer has the responsibility of assuming a proactive role for instructional design. This role is usually facilitated by the nature of the relationship between the clients and SME. Sometimes, the designer must also fulfill the role of the project manager. While the project manager role can enhance the role of a proactive designer, the burden of administrative responsibilities can reduce the time a designer can spend on the design role. A designer fulfilling both roles will need to maintain a balance between the two roles.

PREPARING FOR THE JOB

There are three additional skills designers need that are not often explicitly taught in graduate programs.

Time Management

When working as an instructional designer, planning your time and setting priorities is an extremely important skill because you will typically have more than one project in progress at a time. A designer must know how to establish priorities and budget time. A new instructional designer may find that a course or book in time management is helpful. There are several planners (e.g., Daytimer™, Franklin Planner™, and ClarisOrganizer™) that provide useful tools for planning your time and setting priorities. In addition, a planner or calendar is useful for tracking the amount of time associated with a particular task. This information is then summarized at the end of a project and used for billing and/or planning and pricing future projects.

Computer Skills

Computer literacy is a requirement for an instructional designer in most any environment today. Proficiency with a word processor can increase your productivity and reduce your reliance on a typing pool. With practice and experience, you should develop your proficiency to the level of being able to compose your documents at the keyboard. Development and turnaround time for materials can be considerably reduced, which results in increased productivity.

Developing a working knowledge of database, spreadsheet, presentation, and project planning applications can assist you with the project management responsibilities. Databases are useful for tracking the personnel associated with the project, the status of individual components (e.g., under development, in review, etc.), and planning and budgeting the total project. Spreadsheets are useful for calculating and managing budgets; presentation software is useful for preparing reports for management and clients; and project management software is useful for planning and managing the time lines for a project.

Group Process Skills

As a designer, you will lead several groups during the life of a project. For example, at the beginning you will need to lead a planning meeting to discuss the goals and direction of the project. Having the necessary skills to organize and lead a meeting are essential for the success of the project. A designer should know how to plan a meeting, prepare an agenda, keep the group on track, lead discussions, and resolve conflicts.

WORKING WITH SUPPORT PERSONNEL

Many instructional design projects result in the development of instructional units that may include a range of activities and the use of numerous media materials. The services of various support personnel are often required for preparing materials, locating commercial items, making materials available to learners, selecting and installing equipment, adapting facilities, or filling other needs. The instructional designer is responsible for involving the necessary support personnel and coordinating the preparatory work.

As the design of the project progresses, involve staff members at appropriate times. For example, inform production staff (graphic artist, photographer, video producer, audio recording specialist, computer programmer) about materials they will need to prepare, how they relate within the instructional plan, and the date required for completion. Always allow adequate time for the production and revision of the needed media materials.

WORKING WITH AN EVALUATOR

The size and scope of the formative evaluation and testing (see chapters 10, 11, and 15) determine the need for an evaluator. Projects requiring extensive formative evaluation often require an independent evaluator. Similarly, a designer may wish to include an evaluator in the project if extensive test items, specialized test items, or certification tests are required.

If the services of an evaluator are required, typically it is the designer's responsibility to bring this person into planning meetings at suitable times. The evaluator is responsible for developing tests and other measurement instruments. Sometimes an "outside" evaluator (someone who is not part of the program) is employed to measure the outcomes of a program when it is fully implemented (summative evaluation). To be as objective as possible, such a person should have had no previous contact with the project and may need a limited orientation to the program.

For projects requiring extensive formative evaluation, the evaluator will need access to other SMEs to review the materials for accuracy and members of the target population for field testing. Projects of this size typically include the evaluator during the early stages of the design process so that review and evaluation can begin with the completion of the instructional objectives.

WORKING WITH THE SUBJECT-MATTER EXPERT

The instructional designer and the SME are the two most critical roles in an instructional design project. The relationship between the two roles varies from complementary and collaborative to adversarial. Disagreements are often centered on content issues, with the SME desiring to include content that the designer perceives as "fluff" or unrelated to the achievement of the objectives. The following section provides eight guidelines for working with SMEs (Morrison, 1987).

1. *Recognize that the SME's main priority is to produce income for the organization, not to develop instructional materials.* A professor's major role in a university is to teach assigned classes, provide a service, and conduct research. An SME's role in business is to perform the assigned tasks that contribute to the profits of the company. Thus, the SME may see instructional design as intrusion into his or her work time and productivity. Keeping this perception in mind, you as the designer need to prepare adequately for each meeting with the SME. You should determine the goals for the meeting, prepare for the meeting by checking your understanding of the instructional problem, and gather the necessary materials.

2. *Build a rapport and gain the SME's confidence.* For many SMEs, this project may be their first encounter with the instructional design process. Because of the nature of the design process (e.g., task analysis), the SME will be placed in an unfamiliar role in which his or her knowledge and expertise are revealed and often questioned. You as the designer must develop a rapport with the SME and gain the SME's confidence for a successful project. Your background and that of the SME are usually quite diverse, so a common ground of interest (e.g., sailing, woodworking, sports, family, etc.) is often needed to establish rapport. Confidence is often built by involving the SME in the design process and recognizing the SME's contributions.

3. *Avoid confusing the SME with instructional design jargon.* Find some common words to use when you need to explain the design process or specific steps. For example, when explaining formative evaluation, simply describe it as a process to test the materials to see whether they work as expected rather than as "a systematic assessment process to ascertain the functionality of separate instructional components."

4. *Do not coerce the SME to follow an ID methodology directly.* An SME is not likely to understand the instructional design process; he or she may even resist following the steps. As a designer, you should attempt to be as flexible as possible to accommodate the SME. For example, if the SME does not want to write objectives, ask him or her to write a single test item that would measure the learning. You can then translate the test item into an objective.

5. *Avoid us–them conflicts with the SME.* As a designer, you may find a situation in which a client or another stakeholder (i.e., someone with an interest in the project) wants to influence an aspect of the project (e.g., include specific content). Consider having the client or stakeholder attend a meeting with the project team to explain his or her position. Using this approach can keep you from having to explain and defend the stakeholder's interest, thus reducing the chances of placing you in the middle of an us–them conflict if the members of the project team disagree.

6. *Develop a sense of material ownership in the SME.* An instructional design project is successful only if it is adopted and used by the target audience. A project can be successfully "sold" if the SME feels a sense of ownership in the program and promotes it to his or her superiors, peers, and subordinates. A sense of ownership can be developed in not only the primary SME but in those individuals involved in the initial planning and review processes by encouraging their input and then incorporating the input. For example, you might ask an important individual to provide an example page from a report for use as an illustration.

7. *Recognize that motherhood, apple pie, the flag, and the SME's favorite ideas are sacred cows.* All of us have ideas of what content is needed in a course. These ideas, however, often conflict with the instructional design process that tries to limit the content to only the information needed to achieve the objectives. It is highly probable that you will encounter a situation in which the SME *insists* that certain content be included in a particular project. Attempting to slay this sacred cow is a risky proposition. For example, you might approach the client or a manager for help, only to result in a higher form of blessing on the cow. Allow the SME to slay a sacred cow to maintain rapport and avoid a conflict with the SME, even though this process takes time and some manipulation. Often, the SME will recognize that the content does not fit with the unit and suggest that it be deleted. Another tactic is to mention that you are approaching the maximum page count (or time limit for film or video) and something must be deleted. Hopefully, the SME will delete the unnecessary section.

8. *Approach evaluations and reviews diplomatically.* Evaluating and determining the action needed to deal with reviewers' comments is often a difficult task, especially for the SME. Most SMEs are not accustomed to having their work reviewed and critiqued by their peers in the manner required by formative evaluation. You need to protect the SME's ego and filter the comments. For example, some reviewers may make comments that directly question the SME's competence. Your responsibility is to determine why the comment was made and then translate it for the SME. Providing the SME with a series of critical rather than constructive comments could damage the working relationship and endanger the success of the project.

SUMMARY

1. The role of the instructional designer varies between consultant and proactive designer and leader. This role is affected by the time frame of

the problem, the form of instructional delivery, and the resources available. Economic and time constraints will also influence the amount of instructional design a designer can contribute to a project.

2. Each project will involve a client who owns the problem, an SME who provides accurate content, and an instructional designer who is responsible for the design of the instruction. At the beginning of each project, a designer needs to identify the various roles, the number of clients, and other stakeholders so that each of their needs is addressed. Failure to identify these individuals and their needs can result in problems both with project development and implementation.

3. Finally, the designer must establish a good working relationship with SMEs. Three aspects of instructional design—identifying the clients, providing leadership, and building rapport—are essential for the success of the project. A successful designer is a good listener and flexible in his or her approach to instructional design.

FROM HERE TO THERE

Your work with a leading copy machines manufacturer has led you to identify a major problem with the way field service technicians repair "broken" copiers. It seems that their approach is more one of replacing each part until the copier works rather than using the built-in diagnostics to identify the actual problem. You have sold management on your idea of creating a new troubleshooting course that will focus on identifying the faulty part. To help you with the project, the warranty and service manager has assigned one of his top design engineers as your subject-matter expert. Although this individual is a few years younger than you, she has the respect of many in the company as one of the most knowledgeable and capable people in her area.

During your second meeting, you, your SME, and a service technician are visiting a customer's location that has three broken copiers. You are amazed with how your SME is able to lead the service technician through the troubleshooting process. In an instant you know that this project will be easy due to your SME's knowledge. On the way back to the office, you ask the SME some additional questions to complete the first draft of your task analysis. She asks what you are doing and why the notes. After you explain, she says that she sees no reason for you to do this project as she and the other engineers in her department are more than capable of developing this training without your help, and they can do a better job than you. It is obvious that she has no desire to work with you on this project. Since you and management are highly committed to this project, what do you do?

REFERENCES

Foshay, R. (1988). I don't know is on third. *Performance and Instruction, 27*, 8–9.

Morrison, G. R. (1987). Nonviolent instructional development. *Performance and Instruction, 24*, 25–27.

Morrison, G. R. (1988). Who's on first. *Performance and Instruction, 27*, 5–6.

Tessmer, M. (1988). What's on second. *Performance and Instruction, 27*, 6–8.

MANAGING INSTRUCTIONAL DEVELOPMENT SERVICES

"Where is the instructional design department located within the structure of an organization?"

"What personnel are necessary to complete instructional design projects?"

"Are special facilities required to support the instructional design efforts?"

"How are instructional design departments financed?"

"What policies need attention as guidelines for instructional design activities?"

"How can I evaluate the benefits of the instructional design departments to the organization?"

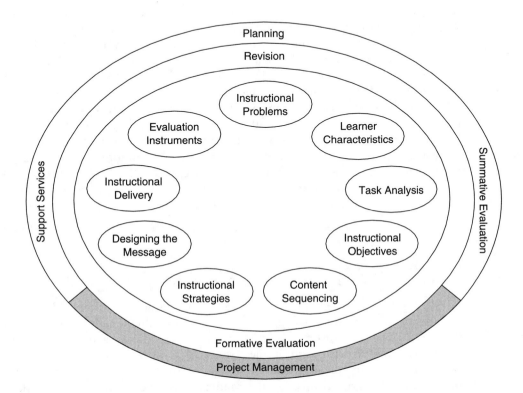

I f instructional design activities in an organization are to require more than only casual or single-project attention, then a plan for supporting and managing the department is needed. The structure of an instructional design department or service requires a statement of (a) purpose, (b) the service provided, (c) placement of the program within the organization, (c) staffing and facility requirements, (d) budget required to accomplish the objectives, and (e) operational policies. The manager is also responsible for the continual evaluation to determine the benefits of the effort.

PURPOSES AND SERVICES

The application of instructional design is based on the assumption that productivity and learning are improved through the application of a systematic planning process.

It follows that a person who is skilled in applying an instructional design procedure can work with subject-matter experts (SMEs) to design effective instruction. To continue to function as a department, the decision makers in the organization must realize the benefits of the instructional design process.

The department's purpose is partially determined by the function it serves. For example, most instructional design or training groups have a primary mission in the organization. In education most departments provide a service to faculty members and departments. In business a design department also offers a service, but the nature of the service can vary. In some organizations, the department provides a service to others based on needs or requests. Such departments are classified as **cost centers**. Other organizations see the department as a **profit center** as the services or courses are sold both inside and outside the company to generate income. Although the purpose of both departments is to improve productivity by improving both instruction and learning, the mission can influence which projects are selected. The department that is viewed as a profit center will most likely take a more entrepreneurial attitude when selecting projects. A department seen as a cost center can use a variety of criteria for selecting projects.

PLACEMENT WITHIN THE ORGANIZATION

Within a school or college program, instructional design departments benefit from administrative placement as close as possible to the chief academic officer (often the curriculum director or academic vice president). Services are readily available to any academic area through simple requests.

The trend in business in recent years is to decentralize the training and instructional design groups. Some organizations place the instructional design department or staff in the personnel or human relations department (HRD). The mission of this group is often to provide management, secretarial, and new employee training. Instructional design groups providing support for technical training are often placed in the department they are supporting. For example, in an airline company there may be one instructional design group associated with the ground operations department and another associated with flight training. In a manufacturing company the design group may reside in the customer service department or field services department, depending on the clientele served. Similarly, a separate design group might work only on technical training for the sales staff.

In all situations there is a direct working relationship among instructional design, reproduction, and media departments. If a separate testing or evaluation office exists, it should have close ties with instructional design. All these departments should report to the same administrator so that project activities can easily involve each department in a cooperative fashion.

STAFFING

The staffing of the department should match the needs of the organization. In some organizations the manager and secretary may manage the department and perform the required instructional design services. In larger organizations, a distinction is often made between organizational management and project management. Organizational management might include a broader scope of all training functions (e.g., design and delivery) requiring one or more managers, an administrative assistant, one or more secretaries, and a registrar to register and track employees enrolling in courses. The instructional design staff might include a manager, a secretary or clerk typist, and instructional designers. If the mission includes both the design and delivery of instruction, the department might also include instructors and/or SMEs (see Figure 14–1).

Subject-matter experts are usually not permanently assigned to an instructional design group. Since each project requires its own SME, such individuals are drawn from appropriate teaching or operational departments in an organization or institution. The assignment, then, is usually temporary, which can range from full-time to only a small percentage of the SME's time during the life of the project.

The roles of the project manager (often the designer) and the organizational department manager vary from organization to organization. The responsibilities of the project manager often include the following:

- Communicating the purposes of the project to all personnel involved
- Assigning tasks and responsibilities
- Setting schedules and ensuring that deadlines are met for completion of all components
- Arranging for resources as needed (e.g., media, production, evaluation)
- Approving and checking budgetary expenses
- Making certain that ongoing evaluations take place at specified approval points, including completion of instructional design components, resource design, resource completion, formative evaluation, and project completion

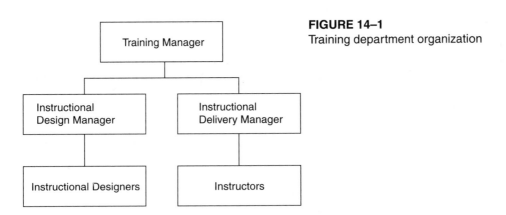

FIGURE 14–1
Training department organization

- Reporting status of project periodically
- Reporting when program is ready for use
- Reporting program results after implementation

The organizational management functions performed by the group's manager include the following items:

- Normal administrative functions, such as assigning personnel to projects and managing organizational budgets
- Informing superiors of progress of projects and related activities
- Preparing reports
- Anticipating problems and resolving conflicts
- Participating in long-term planning and allocation of resources
- Participating in identifying areas of need

CONTRACTS OUTSIDE THE ORGANIZATION

Occasionally, a need arises when some or all of the instructional design effort is contracted with outside consultants or vendors. Several situations could prompt such a need:

- Resources (e.g., time, money, or personnel) are not available to complete the project.
- Current staff lack the necessary skills required for the project (e.g., producing a videodisc, duplicating a videotape for foreign distribution, translating materials to a foreign language).
- A consultant is needed to fill a particular instructional design role—assessing needs, advising on instructional procedures, or evaluating learning of a completed project.

FACILITIES

Facilities should include offices for the staff and one or more conference-type planning rooms. A conference room should project an informal, congenial atmosphere, with a table for seating at least six people. One wall should contain a large planning board for the planning sessions. Provisions are also needed for a projection screen to review materials.

BUDGETARY SUPPORT

The method of funding and selecting instructional design projects differs between educational institutions and businesses.

Education

There are three ways to provide financial support for instructional design activities in an educational environment. First, money is budgeted for the departments from the institution or organization. Allocations are made to fund personnel time and designate costs for projects that are commissioned, selected through a competition, or requested. Second, an academic department or a division uses its funds to contract for a specific project. Third, funding from outside the institution is obtained as a grant specifically to support a project. This latter method usually requires the submission of a written proposal that is evaluated according to certain criteria, often in competition with other proposals.

Business

The budget for an instructional design group in business is usually influenced by its mission (e.g., cost center or profit center). There are four general types of funding. First, the department is given a *fixed budget* either to complete a specific number of projects or to remain operational during the year. Projects can be selected based on need, number of individuals impacted, cost, or other benefits.

Second, the group can work on a *direct charge-back* system where other departments contract for the work and pay for the instructional design effort out of their budget. A marketing economy is used to select the projects, although management may provide additional funding for critical needs.

Third, there is an *indirect charge-back* in which the costs of the instructional design department are included in the general overhead costs. Projects are often selected on a similar basis as a department working on a fixed budget.

Fourth, a department with a mission to produce a profit may approach management as any other department and request funds in the terms of a *loan* to develop a project. Management views the instructional project as another product that the company can produce for profit, even though the customers are often members of the same company. With this type of funding approach, projects with the greatest potential to return a profit are most likely to receive funding.

Funding is used in part to pay for the personnel assigned to the project. This funding may include time spent by the instructional designer, the SME, the evaluator, and the support staff. Also, costs are covered for such expenses as those incurred for developing or purchasing materials and equipment, adapting facilities, or meeting overhead charges and other requirements. (See Chapter 12 for further information about program cost factors.)

PROPOSAL PREPARATION

For some projects, a client or funding agency may request a proposal or bid. Such a request is often referred to as a request for proposals, or RFP. Some agencies (e.g., the National Science Foundation) provide a number of forms and specific instructions on how to prepare and submit the proposal. Internal proposals or proposals prepared for corporate clients may not specify a structure. Regardless of the client, a proposal should include the details of the project.

A proposal should include seven parts. First is the *statement of purpose*. This section should describe the need or problem the project will address and a statement of goals.

Second is the *plan* of work. This section might include a brief description of the instructional design process that will be used. The reader is probably unfamiliar with instructional design process and the terminology, so the section should be written in terms a layperson can understand.

The third section specifies *milestones* or major accomplishments of the project. Typical milestones might include the completion of the needs assessment, completion of the design, final version of print units, rough edits of videotapes, and completion of the field test. Again, the design model can help identify the milestones.

The fourth part of the proposal is the *budget,* which details all the costs associated with the project. One approach to doing a budget is for the designer to complete a task analysis for each of the milestones to identify the tasks associated with each. Then, the designer must determine the personnel, travel, and other costs associated with each task.

The fifth part consists of a *time line* describing the work on each milestone. The sixth section is a listing of all the *deliverables* for the project, which could include planning documents, evaluation results, and finished products. Each deliverable is usually associated with one or more milestones. The final section describes the *project personnel,* perhaps a brief biographical sketch of individuals or a vita or résumé.

When writing a proposal, the designer should always keep the readers' perspective in focus and write the proposal for the reader, not for other instructional designers. Many agencies place a page limit on the proposal (e.g., 25 pages of narrative). A good proposal is concise and addresses the purpose. An unnecessarily long proposal may bring negative results. The following checklist will help you assess your own proposal:

1. Does the project title describe the purpose and nature of the project?
2. Are the goals or major objectives of the project clearly defined?
3. Is the procedure to develop the materials clearly defined?
4. Are personnel, resources, facilities, and departments required for the project identified?
5. Does the budget clearly describe the costs of personnel, materials, travel, resources design and production, reproduction of print and nonprint materials, evaluation departments, and other departments? These estimates should be based on the work effort required to complete the project.
6. Are the time frame, including completion, evaluation and reporting points, and other requirements for carrying out the project included?
7. Are the approval and sign-off points by the client identified?
8. Are the actual products, including instructional and learning resources, stated?

9. Is any subcontract work identified and explained?
10. Is the payment schedule described? (Payments are often requested at the completion of planning steps, design of materials, final preparation of materials, formative testing, or final completion.)
11. Are the qualifications of primary project personnel described?
12. Are other important matters (how to proceed with the project; other personnel, resources, or departments you might call on for use, etc.) included in the proposal?

OPERATING POLICIES

While the details for initiating and managing an instructional design project receive attention in chapters 12 and 13, some general policies need identification as part of management functions.

Sometimes provision for incentives or rewards is advisable or even necessary for the instructors or SMEs who participate in an instructional design project. In a business organization, such inducements may not be of serious concern because employees are rarely free to reject a directive for participating in a project. With success of the project, they may receive a promotion or a raise in salary. A manager may present a simple plaque or commemorative to recognize cooperative individuals and foster future projects.

In an academic institution, participation is much more voluntary. Therefore, it is advisable to recognize, encourage, and reward participation in acceptable ways. These may include:

- Release time to participate in the project as opposed to required overtime for the work
- Extra monetary payment for time devoted to the project (during vacation or summer, or as extra compensation)
- Recognition of success in project work through acclaim by colleagues
- Opportunities to report on project procedures and results through presentations at meetings and acceptance of articles written for professional journals
- Opportunities to follow up with additional projects or other desirable activities
- Recognition of work as support for tenure and/or promotion in professional rank

ROYALTY PAYMENTS FOR PROGRAMS OR MATERIALS

Another area for management decision-making relates to the ownership of materials and programs developed during a project. In a commercial organization, program resources usually remain the company's property. They may even be marketed to other organizations for use in their training programs. Each institution and corporation has a policy on including the names of individuals who developed the materials. Many corporations do not allow the authors and/or instructional designers to include their names in the finished product, while others encourage the inclusion.

An academic institution may establish a policy that allows the institution to hold title to all program components of a project it funds. On the other hand, a different policy may allow an agreement to be made between the institution and faculty members to share royalties on the sale of materials. Also, a faculty member can utilize experience gained in developing instructional materials for a project and redesign them completely outside of the institution. The instructor can then contract with a publisher, or other distributor, to handle sales.

If an institution receives money for the sale of materials resulting from instructional design projects, such funds could justifiably be returned to the instructional design office to support further projects. This income could prove to be a sizable amount of money.

Legal Liabilities in Training

Consider the following situations:

"I was not told these chemicals could hurt me."
"I did not know that operation of this equipment was dangerous."
"I was not shown how to protect myself while carrying out this procedure."
"I did not understand what was explained about safe practices during training."
"It became stressful when I was not able to do the job properly."

Each of the above situations could lead to a legal claim that training was inadequate. The individuals designing the training or the instructor might be held liable for not developing or delivering competent training. Therefore, anyone involved in instructional design work should be aware of regulations and statutes that can affect instructional requirements.

Program Design

It is important to become familiar with legislative enactments, judicial precedents, and local administrative regulations that can impact education or training. For example, some major federal statutes to examine include:

- Occupational Safety and Health Act (OSHA)
- Equal Employment Opportunity Commission (EEOC)
- Americans with Disability Act (ADA)
- Environmental Resources Act (ERA)
- Toxic Substance Control Act (TSCA)

In addition, other governmental agencies regulate work in different environments.

While some statutory provisions may specify topics or actions that require attention in training, planning and implementation methods for others are left to local decision makers. You can ensure compliance by consulting with appropriate SMEs and the legal department and by keeping records of all evaluations that require students to demonstrate achievement of the objectives.

Contracts

A project director is required to draw up a proper legal contract when hiring a sub-contractor to perform a task. You should check with your organization's legal department and personnel department for specific guidelines and policies before you make the initial contact with any contractor. Any contract or letter of agreement should be either initiated or approved by the legal department.

PROJECT REPORTING ON SERVICES

Any new endeavor like an instructional design group must be accountable for proving its value within an institution or organization. Therefore, careful and detailed records should be kept on planning, progress, personnel time required, and costs incurred. Reports should indicate not only the number of courses developed, number of students served, and related statistical data but also benefits of the department to the organization. Recall the statement near the beginning of this chapter about the importance of the decision makers' understanding the value of the department. The reporting process can aid the understanding and justification of the group.

Reported benefits should specify the contributions that successful projects make to increasing the organizational effectiveness, efficiency, and productivity, as well as the resulting cost benefits. (See Chapter 15 for how these outcomes are determined.)

Keeping people in the institution or organization informed about instructional design activities, progress, and successes is often essential for continued support and requested increases in personnel and funding for projects. You may find that weekly, bi-weekly, monthly, or quarterly status reports are helpful for keeping others informed. Projects funded by agencies such as the NSF often prepare newsletters or Web pages to inform others of their progress.

In addition to separate reports on individual projects and annual reports of all yearly activities, consider a cumulative report for a longer period, perhaps five years. This report can illustrate the ongoing, overall benefits to an organization that supports strong instructional design departments.

Progress reports on an instructional design project can take two approaches. One approach is to detail the completion of each step in the instructional design process. A second, more desirable approach is to follow a product-based reporting process. Rather than reporting the completion of each step, develop a report for each milestone in the instructional design process. For example, a project might submit the first report (product) when the problem is identified or the goals are established. The report would describe the problems and/or goals. The second product might be a listing of the objectives developed after the task analysis. A third product is the design plan, which describes the instructional strategies and delivery plans. A fourth product is the results of the formative evaluation and field test. The last report would include the final product. It might summarize the accomplishments of the milestones and critique the instructional design and project management processes, with recommendations for future projects. A product-reporting approach gives managers or administrators solid evidence of the project's progress.

SUMMARY

1. The first step in establishing an instructional development service within an organization is to recognize that systematic planning can make an important contribution to education or training.
2. The service should be directly responsible to either the chief academic officer or the director of training.
3. There are practical reasons why design services outside the organization might be utilized.
4. Staffing considerations should cover both administration and management of the services and management of projects with facilities and budgetary support provided.
5. Establish a format and procedure for preparing proposals to be considered for outside support.
6. Decide on operating policies for managing projects and recognizing professional work with royalty payments.
7. Be alert to legal liabilities and responsibilities relating to instructional program design and implementation.
8. Keep persons within the organization informed by reporting progress and results in writing.

FROM HERE TO THERE

You have just received a consulting contract to evaluate a company's training organization. They have 13 different training groups (all in one city) that address the needs of different divisions in the company. Some of the groups have access to advanced technologies while others rely completely on overhead transparencies and lectures. The quality and cost of the products also vary between groups. Funding for each training group varies with some using direct chargeback, others funded by division overhead, and three groups charge for their services.

Your client is interested in improving the design, development, and delivery of training in the corporation. What factors would you address in your report, and what recommendations would you make based on the above information?

Using Evaluation to Enhance Programs: Conducting Formative and Summative Evaluations

"At what stage of instructional development does formative evaluation begin?"

"How can formative evaluation results be used to improve instruction?"

"Can subject-matter experts be helpful for conducting formative evaluations?"

"How can an instructional designer provide evidence that systematic instructional planning does pay off?"

"What is the actual cost of an instructional program?"

"How can a training program be valuable if it doesn't directly produce income for the company?"

"How do I disseminate results of formative or summative evaluations?"

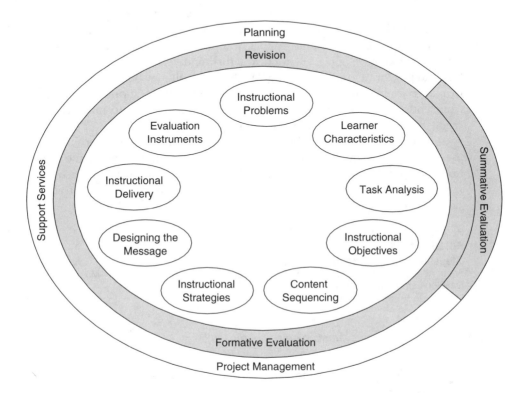

In Chapter 10, we differentiate between the two broad categories of evaluation—formative and summative—used by instructional designers. Now that you have a better understanding of the functions of evaluation as well as instrument construction, we will turn to the procedures for conducting each type of evaluation.

A Basic Model for Formative Evaluation

Formative evaluations are used to provide feedback to designers for making course improvements. These evaluations take place as instruction is "forming," and thus they precede the development of the final version of the instructional unit or course. As is true for the design of instructional material, formative evaluations must be carefully planned to be effective. To help structure the evaluation planning, Gooler (1980) suggests the eight-step approach summarized in Figure 15–1. Each of the steps is examined next.

Purposes

The first step in conducting the evaluation is to determine its purposes: Are they to improve the materials, determine time requirements, or satisfy administrative requirements of the corporation or institution? Perhaps the most important question is whether an evaluation is really needed. Suppose, for example, that you are asked to evaluate a computer-based instruction (CBI) unit for a course on basic electricity. After questioning the course administrators, you discover that the unit cannot be changed without the software being rewritten. You further determine that there are no available funds to pay for new programming. While there still may be good reasons for doing a formative evaluation, you certainly seem justified in questioning its purpose at the front end. That is, if the evaluation results cannot be used to make changes, is this really the best time for an evaluation to be performed?

The purposes of the evaluation are usually defined through consultation between the evaluator and the *stakeholders* of the course or program. As the name implies, stakeholders are individuals who have a "stake" or vested interest in the instruction. They might include company or school administrators, course vendors, training professionals, and/or teachers or trainers.

FIGURE 15–1

Steps in planning formative evaluations
Note: Adapted from D. D. Gooler (1980), "Formative Evaluation Strategies for Major Instructional Development Projects," *Journal of Instructional Development, 3,* 7–11.

•Purpose

  Why is the evaluation being conducted?

•Audience

  Who are the target recipients of the evaluation results?

•Issues

  What are the major questions/objectives of the evaluation?

•Resources

  What resources will be needed to conduct the evaluation?

•Evidence

  What type of data or information will be needed to answer the evaluation questions?

•Data-gathering Techniques

  What methods are needed to collect the evidence needed?

•Analysis

  How will the evidence collected be analyzed?

•Reporting

  How, to whom, and when will the results of the evaluation be reported?

Audience

An additional part of the initial planning is to determine the intended audience(s) for the evaluation results. Will they be administrators, teachers, course developers, or a combination of several groups? Depending on who the primary audience is, different types of information will probably be collected and reported. Clearly, teachers will be better able to use evaluation results dealing with the delivery of instructional material than results on the readability of the workbook; the workbook author, however, would have the opposite need. The key target audience(s) will usually be identified in the initial discussions with key stakeholders.

Issues

As is the case for designing instruction, specifying *objectives* provides the foundation for the evaluation process. Now that you know the overall purposes of the evaluation (step 1) and the primary audience (step 2), what specific questions need to be answered? Is there an interest in student attitudes, learning gains, or the quality of certain materials? Once defined, the evaluation objectives will determine what information sources (data-collection instruments) and analyses are needed to answer the questions of interest. Evaluation objectives may be written as questions or statements. Examples using the question structure are:

- After receiving the instruction, can students correctly enter the data into the spreadsheet?
- Which exercises in the recycling unit do students find *most* understandable and *least* understandable?
- Did students perceive the diagrams to be helpful?
- On average, how long does each practice unit take to complete?
- Do subject-matter experts regard the instructional material accurate and well designed?

If a statement format is preferred, the first two examples might be rewritten as follows:

- To determine students' accuracy, following the instruction, in entering the data into the spreadsheet
- To identify the exercises in the recycling unit that students find *most* understandable and *least* understandable

Resources

Given the evaluation objectives (step 3), what resources are needed to address each? In the previous example objective 1 implies the need for students to be tested, the need for computers and spreadsheets for the students to use during testing, and the need for keyboarding test(s) for measuring the degree of change from pre- to postinstruction. Objective 2 will also involve gathering data from students, but this time using a survey or interview to determine the exercises they most and least prefer. The resources needed therefore differ from objective to objective. Common types of resources include

- Students (or trainees)
- Subject-matter experts (SMEs)
- Instructors
- Data-collection and analysis instruments
- Copies of materials
- Physical facilities and equipment

Evidence

In conjunction with identifying resources, careful consideration must be given to the types of evidence that will be acceptable for addressing the evaluation objectives. For objective 1 in our example, we will obviously want to obtain keyboarding scores, but will scores from, say, five students on one test suffice, or will additional students and/or multiple testings be required? For objective 2, thought must be given to the type of student reporting (in reacting to the exercises) that will be most valid and informative. We might be skeptical, for example, about the validity of impressions conveyed in an interview immediately following a difficult final exam. In deciding what will constitute acceptable evidence, the evaluator and the stakeholders may want to consider these points:

- Sample size
- Objectivity of the information sources
- Realism of the testing context
- Degree of control in the testing context
- Need for formal statistical reporting
- Reliability/validity of SME reviews

Data-Gathering Techniques

This step involves making final decisions about the instrumentation and data-collection methods to be employed. Two key, and often opposing, factors need to be weighed: *precise measurement* versus *feasible* or *practical measurement.* For example, in planning a formative evaluation of a carpentry training program, the designer initially elects to rate actual projects that students complete on the job. But, once the practical problems of identifying and validly assessing actual projects are considered, it is decided instead to employ a controlled assessment, specifically, a cabinet door of a specified design and size completed at the training site. Similarly, in order to reduce time and cost, planned interviews with 30 students may be reduced to include only 10 students. Or perhaps the designer may substitute an interview for a survey when he or she considers that the former will provide opportunities to probe for more in-depth explanations.

The data-gathering techniques available as options are the ones we discussed in the two previous chapters. They include performance tests, written tests, observations, ratings, surveys, interviews, portfolios, and exhibitions. At this stage, the designer should consider the advantages and limitations of each type for addressing the evaluation objectives as well as the resources necessary for each. In Chapter 10 we recommended the use of multiple measures to increase validity (through the "triangulation" of findings across measures) and the provision of as much relevant information as feasible. Current cognitive and constructivist paradigms have increased awareness of obtaining data regarding learning *processes* as well as products (Ross & Morrison, 1995). By knowing about processes—how instructional material is used—designers are in a better position to interpret products (outcomes) and thereby, improve the material.

Analysis

Once the data are collected, the next step is analyzing the results. If the term *analysis* conjures up thoughts of complex statistics and formulas, reflect again on the main purpose of *formative* evaluation. It is to provide usable information for designers to improve instruction. Although the need for complex analyses should not be ruled out, the questions of interest are often best addressed by straightforward and fairly simple *descriptive* analyses. These types of analyses generally tell us how students performed or reacted on a particular lesson. Typical analysis procedures would include:

- Frequency distributions
- Frequency graphs or histograms
- Descriptive statistics, such as percentages, means, and medians

Figure 15–2 shows a frequency distribution and descriptive statistics for a class on a unit achievement test (maximum score = 100%). Note that the "bars" on the graph represent the number (frequency) of scores obtained within 10-point intervals (20–29, 30–39, etc.) in which scores were obtained. From the distribution, it is clear that performances were quite spread out (range = 75) and also somewhat low for many students (mean = 68.1). While it is possible that these are desirable performances for this unit (i.e., it may be very difficult material), chances are that the designer will not be satisfied and will conclude that the instruction needs to be revised.

In many cases, an introductory-level knowledge of statistics will suffice for completing the data analysis. If more complex analyses are required, the designer can always seek assistance from a statistical consultant.

Reporting

The evaluation effort will generally be of little value unless the results are disseminated to individuals involved in the instructional unit or course (e.g., instructors,

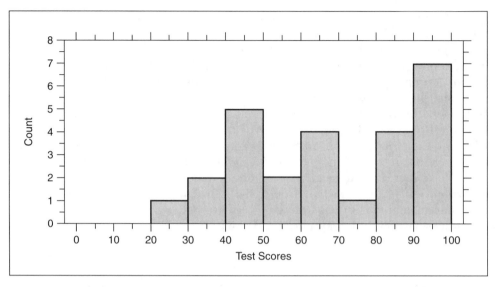

Mean:	Std. Dev.:	Std. Error:
68.077	22.765	4.465

Minimum:	Maximum:	Range:
23	98	75

FIGURE 15–2
Histogram of test scores

administrators, or designers). The most common means is the evaluation report. There is no single standard reporting format; in fact, the best strategy is to adapt the report to the primary target audience with regard to content and style of writing. A "typical" report, however, is likely to include most or all of the following sections:

    I. Executive summary (abstract)
   II. Purposes of evaluation
      A. Evaluation objectives
      B. Description of target course/unit
  III. Methodology
      A. Participants
      B. Instruments
  IV. Results
      A. Analyses
      B. Findings
   V. Conclusions and recommendations

A second common dissemination mode is oral reporting. Depending on the context, such reports may be formal presentations, group meetings, or one-to-one discussions.

Keep in mind that, whatever the form of reporting, the overall goal of formative evaluation is to recommend and make changes (as suggested by the results) to *improve instruction*. Formative evaluation results are unique to the particular project and thus will have limited generalizability to projects outside the same educational context or curriculum.

TYPES OF FORMATIVE EVALUATION

As just described, the initial planning clarifies the purpose(s) of the evaluation and the target audience for results. These decisions then dictate the evaluation approach that is most appropriate for the particular project. According to Flagg (1990), the most commonly used evaluation approaches can be classified into four categories: connoisseur-based, decision-oriented, objectives-based, and public-relations-inspired studies.

Connoisseur-Based Studies

A connoisseur-based study employs SMEs and other appropriate consultants (e.g., media and design experts) to examine the instruction and give opinions regarding its accuracy and effectiveness. An important part of the expert's report is any recommendations for revising the instruction where improvements are needed. Expert review can be useful at all stages of the design process, from initial drafts of instructional material to the completed versions.

In using expert review, the experts are assumed to be competent and interested in the evaluation task. An important task for the designer is to determine the number and types of experts needed, the particular individuals who will fill these slots, and the best time(s) in the evaluation process to involve each.

Expert review can provide valuable information for refining instruction. However, an important limitation of connoisseur-based studies is that so much depends on the biases and experiences of the selected experts. Remember, experts in a subject area are not necessarily knowledgeable about instruction and learning. Therefore, it is *not* advisable to blindly follow a recommendation that you question, without seeking other opinions or data sources. In educational research, this type of verification process is called *triangulation*, the procedure of cross-validating a finding by using multiple information sources.

Consider this example: After reviewing a CBI lesson, a media expert suggests that children will not know which keys to press in selecting different branching options. A field test of the program reveals, however, that this problem does not occur—the children actually make very few errors. Implication: Keep the expert's concern in mind, but do not make changes in the screen design without further evidence.

Decision-Oriented Studies

Decision-oriented studies are designed to provide information related to particular questions about the instruction. Example concerns might include:

- Does the lesson require too much time to complete?
- Is the amount of practice examples adequate?
- Are prerequisite math skills required?
- Should a student study guide be developed?

Given these questions, the evaluator then designs specific measures and procedures to address each.

Decision-making evaluations are naturally most valuable when program changes are still feasible and economical. Good communication between the evaluator and the program stakeholders is essential to define the relevant questions around which the decision making will be based. The limitation of decision-making studies is that their results are usually *descriptive,* not *prescriptive.* That is, they tell us how the instruction is working, but not what to do to make it better.

Objectives-Based Studies

A third category of formative evaluation approaches involves investigating how well the instructional program is achieving its objectives. The basic methodology will therefore resemble that employed in a summative evaluation (discussed later) by assessing the amount of progress students have realized from completing the instruction. A summative evaluation, however, uses such information to judge the *worth* of the program. Formative evaluation uses it as a basis for improving the instruction where outcomes fall short of goals.

Objective-based studies frequently employ pretest-posttest designs that measure the amount of gain on measures of achievement and attitude. Their main limitation is the same one noted earlier for decision-making studies: the findings by themselves provide limited direction for making improvements.

Public-Relations-Inspired Studies

By making evaluation results known to targeted individuals, public-relations-inspired studies are used to solicit financial support or backing for a project. An example comes from one of the authors' recent experiences in trying to obtain funding from a private foundation to support an elementary-school reading program. By conducting a formative evaluation of a pilot version of the program, he was able to present preliminary data that convinced the foundation representatives of the program's potential. The result was a foundation grant to expand both the program and the evaluation the next year.

These four categories should be viewed as complementary rather than exclusive. Most studies will employ combinations of two or more of these orientations, depending on the evaluation objectives. For example, in evaluating a new mathematics program for at-risk children, the designers might (a) employ experts to review the instructional materials (category 1), (b) administer surveys and use observation techniques to answer questions about the implementation (category 2), (c) administer achievement pretests and posttests to assess the level of reading improvement demonstrated by student participants (category 3), and (d) publicize the latter results to obtain additional funding for the program (category 4).

STAGES OF FORMATIVE EVALUATION

At this point, we have presented general approaches and a specific procedural model (Figure 15–1) for conducting formative evaluations. A remaining question may be how formative evaluation methods might vary at different stages of the design process. Dick and Carey (1991) address this issue in their three-stage model (see Table 15–1).

The first stage, occurring toward the beginning of the process and usually repeated several times, consists of one-to-one trials or developmental testing (Thiagarjan, Semmel, & Semmel, 1974) in which the designer "tries out" the instruction with individual learners (Brenneman, 1989). The goal is to obtain descriptive information pertaining to the clarity, impact, and feasibility of initial versions of the instruction.

The second stage consists of small-group trials in which a more developed version of the instruction is used with a group of between 8 and 25 individuals. Through observational, attitudinal, and performance data, the evaluator attempts to identify strengths and weaknesses in the instruction before it is put into a "final" form.

The third stage is the field trial, which examines the use of the instruction with a full-sized learner group under realistic conditions. Based on the results from various outcome measures, the instructor would make final revisions and deliver the completed instruction to actual classes. But at this point, the need for evaluation will not be over. Summative evaluation is then required to determine whether the instructional program is achieving its goals.

TABLE 15–1

Stages of formative evaluation

Stage	Instruction Phase	Purpose	Learners	Main Measures
One-to-one trials	Development	Try-out impressions	Individuals	Observation, survey, interview
Small-group trials	Preliminary/ draft version	Identify strengths/ weaknesses	Small group (8–20)	Observation, attitudes, performance
Field trials	Completed	Assess actual	Regular class	Performance, attitudes

SUMMATIVE EVALUATION: DETERMINING PROGRAM OUTCOMES

Too often an instructional designer or an instructor may intuitively be convinced that what is being accomplished is worthwhile and successful. It is often assumed by persons in education and training that the merits of a program are obvious to other persons in the institution or organization. Unfortunately, rarely is either of these conclusions true.

A summative evaluation permits a designer or instructor to reach unbiased, objective answers to questions such as those listed earlier and then to decide whether the program is achieving the goals it was originally intended to reach. With this evidence, his or her intuition can be supported or rejected, and he or she has the facts for correctly informing others about the program results.

The following important issues can be examined through summative evaluation procedures:

- Effectiveness of learner or trainee learning
- Efficiency of learner or trainee learning
- Cost of program development and continuing expenses in relation to effectiveness and efficiency
- Attitudes and reactions to the program by learners, faculty, and staff
- Long-term benefits of the instructional program

In this section, we will examine methods for gathering data that can lead to a conclusion for each of the five issues stated earlier. Attention to these matters may be essential in proving the value of a new instructional program and then ensuring its continued support.

A summative evaluation of a course or program is more than a one-time activity. Immediately after *each* course or training program is concluded, the instructor should utilize some or all of the assessment methods to be described. By accumulating summative data, continuing positive trends in a program can be tracked over time, or deficiencies can be noted as they show up, with possible corrections being made immediately.

Evaluation versus Research

One way of measuring the value of a new program is to compare the results obtained with those of a conventionally conducted course in the same subject. Most often this comparison cannot be made fairly because the two courses were planned to achieve entirely different objectives. It is very likely that there are no stated, measurable objectives for the conventional course that can be used as a basis for the comparison. Also, the subject matter treated in the two programs may be significantly different, with the content of the conventional course often being limited to a lower cognitive domain level than that of the new program.

In some situations, evaluation is performed by using a formal research framework. This means that a carefully designed comparison study is based on control and experimental groups or classes. One or more hypotheses are stated as anticipated outcomes. Then, after instruction takes place, statistical methods are employed to gather data and report the evidence collected about learning outcomes. Conclusions are drawn that support or reject the initial hypotheses.

Such a methodology is usually more appropriate in basic or applied research studies that permit control over extraneous variables and allow for the establishment of reasonably equivalent experimental and control groups. Most instructional design projects are not planned to result in broadly applicable theories. Their purpose is to find out how well the needs that have been identified can be met. Growth in learner knowledge or skill activity, as measured by the difference between pretest and posttest results or by observing behavior before and after instruction, provides evidence of learning that can be directly attributable to the instructional program.

Sometimes the success in learning can be shown only in following up on-the-job work being done by individuals after instruction. For example, after completing a safety course, if accidents involving employees working with equipment are appreciably reduced (say, by more than 30%), then the training can be considered to be successful. Or, if company operating expenses decrease and revenues increase from the pretraining to the posttraining periods, then one could infer that direct benefits are due to the results of training. On the other hand, when results do not meet goals, the evaluation evidence would indicate the shortcomings. Steps can then be taken to improve the program before its next use.

Thus, for evaluating instructional design projects, it is not necessary or even appropriate to perform formal research involving control/experimental groups and a detailed statistical analysis. All that must be done is to gather evidence relative to accomplishments or change from preinstruction to postinstruction for as many of the five components listed above (effectiveness, efficiency, costs, etc.) as are considered important for that course, then to interpret the information to reach conclusions about the success or failure of the instructional program.

A special note: For some of the procedures considered here, it is advisable (or even essential) to start collecting data from the time the program is *initially planned*. By doing this, you will have the necessary information to determine costs, time, and other facts pertinent to the evaluation.

PROGRAM EFFECTIVENESS

Effectiveness answers the question "To what degree did students accomplish the learning objectives prescribed for each unit of the course?" Measurement of effectiveness can be ascertained from test scores, ratings of projects and performance, and records of observations of learners' behavior.

An analysis of scores can be prepared by hand or using a computer statistical package. The data may show the change from pretest to posttest results. Then a summary may be presented in tabular form, as shown in Figure 15–3. The figure illustrates that the group, comprised of six learners, accomplished 90% of the objectives. This figure is calculated by totalling the number of objectives satisfied (represented by the X marks in c). Divide by 6, the number of learners; 4.5 is the average number of objectives accomplished per learner; 4.5 is 90% of the objectives. This result can be interpreted as a measure of the effectiveness of the instructional design plan for this group of learners. The percentage may be considered as an *effectiveness index* representing the percentage of learners reaching a preset level of mastery (satisfying each objective) and the average percentage of objectives satisfied by all learners.

If *all* learners accomplished *all* objectives, the effectiveness of the program would be excellent. If 90% of the learners accomplish 90% of the objectives, could you report that the program has been effective? To answer this question, the

FIGURE 15–3
A sample analysis of test questions measuring cognitive objectives

a. Unit Objectives	Test Questions
A	2, 4, 11
B	1, 7
C	3, 5, 12
D	8, 10
E	5, 9

b. Learner	Correct Answers to Questions											
	1	2	3	4	5	6	7	8	9	10	11	12
AJ	x	x	x	x		x	x	x	x	x	x	
SF	x	x	x	x	x	x		x				
TY	x	x	x	x	x	x	x	x	x	x	x	
LM	x	x	x	x	x	x	x	x	x	x	x	
RW	x	x	x	x	x	x	x	x	x	x	x	
WB	x		x	x	x	x			x	x		x

c. Learner	Objectives Satisfied				
	A	B	C	D	E
AJ	x	x	x	x	
SF		x	x	x	x
TY	x	x	x	x	x
LM	x	x	x	x	x
RW	x	x	x	x	x
WB		x	x	x	x

instructor, along with the administrator or training director, must have previously decided the level at which to accept the program as effective. In a systematically planned academic course, attainment of the 80% level by at least 80% of the learners in a class could be acceptable as a highly effective program. In a vocational or skill area, 90–90 (90% of the trainees accomplishing 90% of the objectives) might be the accepted success level. Similar courses (e.g., in biology or electronics assembly) can be compared with respect to effectiveness indices and conclusions drawn for judging program effectiveness.

Realistically, it is very likely that because of individual differences among learners and a designer's inability to design ideal learning experiences, no one can hope to reach the absolute standard of mastery or competency—100%—in all instructional situations. (Some training programs for which life and safety are critical—medical areas or airline pilot training, for instance—may require the 100% level of mastery learning.)

Then another question must be asked. Assume that your own performance standard requires all learners to accomplish 85% of the objectives but that as a group they actually satisfy 82% of them. What time, effort, and expense are required to redesign the weak areas of your program in order to raise the learning level to 85%? Is the effort to reach the 85% level worth the cost? There may be circumstances that would make this achievement almost prohibitive. You may have to settle for a somewhat lower level of accomplishment until someone can design a revision of the program that will enable reaching the desired level of performance with reasonable effort and cost.

When evaluating the effectiveness of an instructional program, a designer must recognize that there may be intangible outcomes (often expressed as affective objectives) and long-term consequences that would become apparent only after the program is concluded and learners are at work. Both of these matters are given attention in the following sections as part of other summative evaluation components. Here, the evaluation of effectiveness is limited to those learning objectives that can be immediately measured.

Summative Evaluation Methods

The basic procedures for determining program effectiveness in summative evaluations are similar to those described earlier for formative evaluations (see Figure 15–1). Specifically, the major steps are:

1. Specifying program objectives
2. Determining the evaluation design for each objective
   a. Pretest–posttest with one group
   b. One-group descriptive
   c. Experimental-control group
   d. Analysis of costs, resources, implementation

3. Developing data-collection instruments and procedures for each objective
   a. Surveys
   b. Interviews
   c. Observations
   d. Achievement tests
4. Carrying out the evaluation
   a. Scheduling the data collection
   b. Collecting the data
5. Analyzing the results from each instrument
6. Interpreting the results
7. Disseminating the results and conclusions
   a. Evaluation report
   b. Group meetings
   c. Individual discussions

Data-Collection Instruments. As with formative evaluations, data collection will address one or more of the three domains of skills/behavior, cognitive, and affective. The main difference in summative evaluation will be judging a "completed" rather than developing program.

For assessing *skills,* key information sources (as in formative evaluations) are:

- Direct testing
- Analysis of naturally occurring events
- Direct/indirect observations
- Portfolios
- Exhibitions

For assessing *cognition,* measurement options will include objective tests (multiple-choice, true/false, matching) and constructed-response tests (short-answer, essay, and problem-solving).

Assessments of *affective* outcomes entail gathering reactions from both learners and the instructional staff as they look back on the program just completed. Three categories of reactions may be given attention:

- *Opinions:* judgments about the level of acceptance of course content, instructional methods, assistance from and relations with instructor and staff, study or work time required, grading procedure, and so forth
- *Interest:* responses to the value of topics treated, learning activities preferred, and motivation for further study or work in the subject area
- *Attitude:* reactions to the total program in terms of degree of its being pleasurable, worthwhile, and useful

Examples of types of questions for gathering subjective reactions are shown in Figure 15–4.

FIGURE 15–4
Types of questions for gathering subjective responses

Checklist

Check each word that tells how you feel about the group projects and oral presentations used in this course.

_____ Interesting	_____ Informative	_____ Difficult
_____ Dull	_____ Practical	_____ Important
_____ Exciting	_____ Worthless	_____ Stimulating
_____ Boring	_____ Useful	_____ Unpleasant

Rating Scale

Compared to a typical lecture class, how useful was the format used in this experimental class for _learning the course material?_ (Check one response.)

_____ Better   _____ About the same   _____ Not as good

Now that you have completed the course, rate your feelings about history as a subject. (Circle the number that best reflects your reaction.)

Dislike very much	Dislike somewhat	Neutral	Like somewhat	Like very much
1	2	3	4	5

Ranking

Please rank these topics as treated in the management course. Consider their value to you and your job. (Start with number 1 as the topic having the _highest_ value.)

_____ Planning	_____ Organization and management
_____ Self-assessment	_____ Development
_____ Stress	_____ Personnel management
_____ Labor relations	_____ Performance appraisal
_____ Effective presentations	_____ Internal affairs management
_____ Budgeting	_____ Media relations
_____ State-of-the-art technology	

Open-Ended Questions

What is your general reaction to this course: the objectives treated, the way it was conducted, your participation, its overall value to you, and so on?

PROGRAM EFFICIENCY

In evaluating efficiency, three aspects of a program require attention:

- Time required for learners to achieve unit objectives
- Number of instructors and support staff members required for instruction and the time they devote to the program
- Use of facilities assigned to the program

Learner Time Required

Educational programs are designed typically in terms of available time periods—semesters, quarters, or other fixed time intervals (week, weekend, etc.). It is only when some flexibility is permitted that efficiency can be measured. If a conventional training program can be reduced from a period of possibly 6 to 5 weeks, with the same or increased effectiveness in learning, the program can be considered to be *efficient*.

Efficiency can be used for measuring outcomes primarily of programs that give major emphasis to individualized or self-paced learning activities. From the learner's standpoint, the time required to satisfy unit or program objectives would be a measure of efficiency. Mathematically, this measurement is the ratio of the number of objectives a learner achieves compared to the time the learner takes to achieve them. Learners can be asked to keep records of time (a time log) spent studying a unit or set of objectives. Or, in a more subjective fashion, an instructor can observe and make notations to indicate the number of learners at work in a study area during time periods.

For example, Mary satisfies seven objectives in 4.2 hours of study and work. By dividing the number of objectives Mary achieves by the amount of time it takes her to accomplish them, we find that her efficiency index is 1.7 (7/4.2). Bill achieves the seven objectives in 5.4 hours. His efficiency index is therefore 1.3. Thus, *the higher the index, the more efficient the learning*. Such an index can be calculated for each unit, then averaged for each learner to give an efficiency index for the course.

Keep in mind that many instructional programs will not yield such easily attainable and concrete measures of mastery over time. Also, efficiency indices may not be comparable across different units of instruction due to the nature of the material taught and the characteristics of the students. But where feasible the efficiency index can provide highly useful quantitative information for evaluating allocations of time and resources.

Faculty and Staff Required

The number of faculty and staff positions required for instruction, supervision, or support of an instructional program also relates to efficiency. The question is "How many learners are being served by the staff?" If a course requires a half-time faculty position plus the equivalent of one full-time position in assistants and technicians to serve 48 learners, then the faculty:learner ratio would be 1:32 (1.5:48). If the institution-wide ratio of faculty-to-student load is 1:20, then this higher ratio indicates a more efficient use of faculty and staff personnel. Greater *efficiency*, however, may not necessarily mean greater *effectiveness*.

The ratio of 1:32 may be reported on paper, but the actual working time of faculty and staff in the program can give another indication of efficiency. Let's assume that the instructor and support staff indicated earlier (1.5 positions) are spending 60 hours a week on the program (preparation, teaching, consulting with learners, evaluating performance, marking tests, providing resources, etc.). If normal time devoted to a course is 45 hours per week for a staff of similar size, then the procedures may need some revision.

Use of Facilities

Another factor of efficiency is the time that learning facilities—classrooms, learning labs, and so forth—are available during a day, a week, or other period of time. If a facility is used 12 hours a day, this may be considered an efficient use of space. By obtaining these data as a program is expanded, the need to increase use or to provide for additional training space can be evaluated.

A second component of efficient space utilization is the number of learners using the facility during a time period. When 110 learners are being served in a 15-station microcomputer lab on a weekly basis, this may be seen as an efficient use of space. Keep records so that the time learners and staff spend in the program and facility can be calculated and objectively related to this factor of efficiency.

Program Costs

Historically, a major concern in educational programs is the cost of instruction. Expense categories, such as personnel, equipment, and supplies, are established to aid the administration in controlling and reporting about programs. Standard bases that are frequently used for allocating funds in educational budgets are average daily attendance (ADA) in public schools, full-time equivalent (FTE, the number of students equated for taking a full course load) in higher education, the number of faculty assigned in terms of FTE, and student credit hours or student/faculty contact hours. These bases for allocating funds are mainly accounting methods. They provide little information about the real costs of a single program.

Although a school or college is not the same as a business operation, for both we can identify specific factors affecting costs that can be controlled. The education and training literature contains numerous explanations and reports on how program costs can be derived. Formulas that consider many of the variables that affect costs are presented in detail and their complexities are interpreted. Such terms as *cost-effectiveness, cost-efficiency,* and *cost benefits* are frequently used. Our concern here is simply to answer the question "What does it cost to develop and operate a specific program for the number of learners served?" Once we have this essential information, we are able to relate costs to effectiveness, efficiency, and resulting benefits; thus we are able to judge the acceptability of program costs.

Any new course or a program being revised requires attention to the two major categories of costs: **developmental** and **operational costs.**

Developmental Costs

As an instructional project is being planned and developed, some or all of the following costs, sometimes called *start-up costs,* may be incurred:

- Planning time: percentage of salary for time spent by each member of the planning team on the project, or number of hours spent by each member, multiplied by his or her hourly or monthly salary rate, and fees for consultants
- Staff time: percentage of salary for time spent by each member engaged in planning, producing, and gathering materials, or the number of hours spent by each person, multiplied by his or her hourly salary rate
- Supplies and materials for preparing print, media, and other materials
- Outside services for producing or purchasing materials
- Construction or renovation of facilities
- Equipment purchased for instructional uses
- Expenses for installing equipment
- Testing, redesign, and final reproduction of resources in sufficient quantity for operational uses (includes personnel time and costs of materials and services)
- Orientation and training of personnel who will conduct instruction
- Indirect costs: personnel benefits such as retirement and insurance, related to time and salary charged to the project (this information is typically available from the personnel department)
- Overhead: utilities, furniture, room and building costs or depreciation allowance, proportion of other institutional services charged to the project (this information is usually available from the business manager or the controller of the organization)
- Miscellaneous (office supplies, telephone, travel)

Here is an example of the *developmental costs* for a general education college-level course involving two instructors. It includes large-group presentations, student self-directed learning with slide-based CD-ROM and study guide, and small discussion sessions.

Planning Time

2 instructors, 0.50, 1 semester	$25,000
Instructional designer, 0.25 time, 1 semester	7,500
Video producer, 40 hours	1,000
Graduate assistants, 150 hours	1,500
Secretary, 40 hours	600
	$35,600

Development Time

2 instructors, 0.25 time, 1 semester	$12,500
Instructional designer, 0.25 time, 1 semester	3,750
Video producer, 200 hours	5,000

Video engineer, 100 hours	2,500
Graphic artist, 80 hours	1,600
Secretary, 200 hours	3,000
	$28,350

Materials and Supplies

Video supplies	$500
Transparency supplies	150
Master CD-ROM and copies for use	2,000
Master study guide	100
Office supplies	200
	$2,950

Equipment

20 CD-ROM players and monitors	$14,000
20 barcode readers	2,000
	$16,000

Renovating Facility

Constructing 20 learning stations	$2,000
Electrical power	500
	$2,500

Formative Evaluation and Revisions	$3,000

Indirect Costs

Staff benefits	$21,000

Overhead

Planning and production facilities	$4,000
Total Development Costs	$113,400

Operational Costs

When the project is fully implemented and instruction is taking place, the recurring operational costs include the following:

- Administrative salaries (based on percentage of time devoted to project)
- Faculty salaries for time spent in the program (contact hours with groups and individual learners, planning activities, evaluating program, revising activities and materials, personnel benefits)
- Learner or trainee costs (applicable in business-oriented training programs: salary, travel lodging, income for company reduced while trainee not on job, or replacement cost of a person substituting for a trainee job)
- Salaries for assistants, maintenance technicians, and others

- Rental charges for classroom or other facilities
- Replacement of consumable and damaged materials
- Repair and maintenance of equipment
- Depreciation of equipment
- Overhead (utilities, facilities, furnishings, custodial services)
- Evaluating and updating materials (time and materials)

Here is an example of the *operational costs* for the college-level course developed earlier, over a one-semester term:

Salaries

2 instructors, 0.25 time	$13,500
Benefits	4,000
Graduate students, 1,200 hours	12,000
	$29,500
Replacements and Repairs	$5,000
Overhead	2,500
Total Operating Costs	$37,000

Instructional Cost Index

We cannot attempt to judge whether the costs of an instructional program are acceptable by looking solely at the gross amount expended. If it costs a company $1,000 to manufacture pencils, this sum must be related to the number of pencils made. Then the price per pencil has meaning and can be compared with the price per unit manufactured by other companies. In an instructional program, costs should be related to the number of learners served in the program.

With data available on developmental and operational costs, we can calculate the cost per learner for a program. This is the important "bottom line" amount that allows for comparison of costs between programs leading to the acceptance of expense levels. Cost per learner or trainee may be labeled an **instructional cost index**. It is determined by the following procedure:

1. Spread the developmental costs over a series of time periods (e.g., 10 training sessions or 5 semesters). This would be the anticipated life of the program before it should require major revisions or cease to be useful. This procedure is known as *amortizing* the cost.
2. Add together the above prorated amount of the developmental costs (one-sixth for three years) and the operational costs for one use period (a complete training class or an academic semester).
3. Determine the average number of learners known or anticipated to be in the program with each use. Divide the total in step 2 by this number. The result is the cost per learner, or the instructional cost index.

An example of an instructional cost index calculated from previous developmental and operational costs follows:

Total operational costs	$37,000
Portion of developmental cost ($113,400/6)	18,900
Total cost per semester	$55,900
Number of learners in program: 340	
Instructional cost index ($55,900/340)	$164.41

(This is the total cost for each learner over one semester.)

If this program continues beyond five semesters (at which time all developmental costs will have been amortized) and the number of learners remains the same, the instructional cost index will then drop to $108.82 ($37,000/340). During this period, limited funds are included for minor updates and revision of materials. At the end of five semesters, a reexamination of the program for this course may be advisable. The course then may be continued as is, or new developmental costs—hopefully lower than the original ones—would be required. These would affect the ongoing instructional cost index.

The index number itself has little meaning. Calculations could be made in the same way for traditional program costs in a comparable training or subject area. As previously stated, it is difficult (and usually unfair) to make a comparison between a new program with carefully structured objectives and a traditional program based on generalized objectives. It would seem more appropriate to compare two skill-type training programs, two math classes, or a biology and chemistry course if each one has been systematically planned and implemented. Once an instructional cost index has been calculated, the instructor or designer should ask these questions:

- Is the program *cost-effective?* This is a subjective decision, but useful information can be obtained by relating the instructional cost index to the level of learning outcomes (e.g., 90% of the learners accomplish 84% of the objectives). If a satisfactory learning level is reached and the instructional cost index seems to be within reason, the program would be considered cost-effective.
- Is the program *cost-efficient?* Relate the instructional cost index to efficiency factors (time required by learners to complete activities, staff time required for instruction and support, level of facilities use). If the efficiency index seems acceptable, with a reasonable instructional cost index the program would be cost-efficient.
- Are the costs justified in terms of resulting benefits (*cost/benefit analysis*)? Relate the instructional cost index to the benefits that a company or other organization derives from personnel who complete the training program. (See the following section for details and discussion of potential benefits resulting from training.) If the benefits are high and costs acceptable, then the question can be answered in a positive way.

If the outcomes of a program prove to be acceptable but the instructional cost index remains higher than desired, certain steps might be taken to lower the operational cost portion of the index, as follows:

1. Consider the feasibility of including more learners in the program (as in a distance learning course using television). Perhaps more individuals can be served without reduced quality of instruction.
2. Decide whether assistants might replace instructors for certain activities *without lowering the effectiveness of the program.* This would reduce the higher cost of instructor time.
3. Plan to relieve instructors of some learner contact time by developing additional self-paced learning activities for learners.
4. As a last resort, reduce the training time or lower some of the required performance standards. Shorter instructional time would reduce instructor time and thus costs.

An alternative cost index measure is to calculate the index in terms of *total contact hours.* Thus, a week-long course for 20 people has 800 (40 hours × 20 people) total contact hours.

EVALUATION OF FOLLOW-UP BENEFITS

Instructional programs are most often offered for three general reasons:

- To "educate" individuals so that they may participate as informed, cultured, and productive citizens in society
- To prepare individuals for a gainful vocation
- To improve or upgrade competencies of individuals in a specific task or in certain aspects of a job

For each of these reasons, determining the success of an instructional program requires attention to important outcomes beyond the results of written and performance tests given at the end of a unit or a course. Often the accomplishment of major goals or terminal objectives stated for a program can be assessed only sometime *after* instruction is concluded.

This can be a complex phase of summative evaluation for a number of reasons. After a course is completed, the learners or trainees move to other courses or work at different locations. Observations of them at work or communication with them may require an extra effort. Some important outcomes are in the affective domain. These may be difficult to identify and measure. Responses for evaluation may be needed from other persons (colleagues, supervisors, and others) who may not be understanding or cooperative. Regardless of these obstacles, attempts should be made to follow up on learners after an instructional program has ended. Evidence of follow-up benefits could be the most important summative results to measure.

Educational Programs

Traditionally, the general, long-term benefits of educational programs are measured through statewide and national standardized tests given to students in public schools; college students take undergraduate and graduate admission examinations; and regional or national opinion surveys are conducted at various times. Such tests measure broad, fairly general objectives. The limitation is that those general objectives may be too broad to provide useful information on how well a particular course accomplished its *specific* instructional objectives. Concerns may also arise about the circumstances under which students prepare for or complete the standardized tests (Haladyna, Nolan, & Haas, 1991).

The long-term outcomes of the objectives of specific courses have been examined only casually. Within the framework of the goals and terminal objectives of a program, the following categories of outcomes can be studied concerning learners:

- Capabilities in basic skills (reading, writing, verbal expression, mathematics), as required in following courses
- Knowledge and competencies in a subject as bases for study in subsequent courses
- Proficiencies to carry out job tasks and responsibilities in occupational employment
- Fulfillment of roles as good citizens (law abiding, participating in democratic process, etc.)

As indicated at the beginning of this section, data concerning these outcomes are not easy to obtain. The following methods are commonly used to gather information:

- *Completing questionnaires:* Ask former students, present instructors, or employers to respond to a questionnaire designed to indicate learners' present proficiencies as related to competencies derived from the course or program being evaluated (see Figure 10–2).
- *Conducting interviews:* Meet with former learners, present instructors, or employers to inquire about the present proficiencies of learners as related to competencies from the courses or programs being evaluated.
- *Making observations:* Observe learners in new learning or performance situations and judge their capabilities as a follow-up of competencies acquired in the course being evaluated.
- *Examining records:* Check grades and anecdotal records of former students in school files to ascertain how they are now performing in their classes as based on competencies gained in the course being evaluated. (*Note:* Because of privacy laws, this procedure may require permission from the former students before records can be made available.)

Training Programs

A training program within a business concern, an industrial company, a health agency, or other organization usually has clearly defined outcomes to be accomplished. These planned results may have initially been identified when a needs assessment (Chapter 2) was first made. The consequent benefits are expected to result in improved job performance and often can be translated into dollar savings or increased income for the company.

Three areas may need attention in posttraining evaluation, which is discussed next.

Appropriateness of the Training. Although the program was developed according to identified needs, changes in on-the-job operating procedures and the equipment used could necessitate different job performance from what was taught. Determine whether modifications are required before training is conducted the next time.

Competencies of Employees. It is one thing to pass written tests and perform satisfactorily in the controlled environment of a classroom or laboratory but potentially another to be successful in transferring the learning to a job situation. Determine how well the former trainees now perform the job or tasks they were trained to do.

Benefits to the Organization. The advantages need to be measured in terms of the payoff to the organization as well as to the individual. Some of the criteria that indicate that a training program has been beneficial to the organization are:

- Increased safety through reduced number of accidents
- Increased service abilities, including both work quality and performance speed
- Improved quality of products being produced
- Increased rate of work or production
- Reduced problems with equipment due to malfunctions and breakdowns
- Increased sales of products and greater services, or more income being generated (referred to as "return on training investment")

With respect to affective-type outcomes, the following may be some of the expected results:

- Less employee tardiness and absenteeism
- Less employee turnover on jobs
- Greater job satisfaction
- Higher level of motivation and willingness to assume responsibilities
- Increased respect for the organization

The same methods for gathering information for educational programs would apply to measuring the follow-up benefits of a training program: questionnaires, interviews, observations, and examining records. In terms of actual performance levels, if careful records are kept, comparisons can be made between pretraining and posttraining competencies. A key method of follow-up evaluation can be related to reduction in expenses or greater revenue generated for the company. This approach requires a comparison of pretraining cost factors with the costs and income data determined at a reasonable time after training is completed. This evidence can be one of the best measures to relate training benefits to the "bottom line" with which a company is most concerned. Keep in mind, though, that not all training courses will have a direct, *measurable* impact on the bottom line (e.g., courses in interpersonal relations, public speaking, and the like).

REPORTING RESULTS OF SUMMATIVE EVALUATION

The final step that needs to be taken is to prepare a report of the summative evaluation results for others to read and examine. Careful attention should be given to this activity. Future support for the program, as well as the assistance required for additional instructional design projects, can be influenced by the manner in which a summative evaluation is reported.

First, the designer must decide for whom the report is to be prepared—administrators/training manager, instructors, another supporting agency, or whoever. By considering those persons who are to receive the report, emphasis or special attention may have to be given to certain phases of the summative evaluation. Explaining how and where funds have been spent may be of primary interest, or evidence of follow-up benefits may be of more value than are the efficiencies or effectiveness of instruction.

Second, he or she must decide on the format of the report. Should it be on paper for individual reading, or will it be presented to a group with the support of slides or overhead transparencies? In either case, plan to report results attractively. Not everyone would be as highly interested or as well informed about the project as the designer has been over a period of time. Here are some suggestions:

- Give the report an interesting title.
- Summarize highlights so the key outcomes can be grasped quickly. Do this by setting them off on a page with white space or boxing each statement.
- Describe supporting data in visual ways with graphs rather than as detailed tables; use artwork as appropriate.
- If slides or transparencies will be prepared, limit the information on film to only the key points. Prepare printed materials that correlate with the visuals and contain the details of information for the audience to retain.
- End by making appropriate recommendations for continuing, extending, modifying, or terminating the program.
- Where feasible, adapt the style and content of the report to the main target audiences. Different stakeholder groups will have different backgrounds, interests, and expectancies for what the report will convey.
- The reporting format outlined on page 258 for formative evaluations will generally be appropriate as well for summative evaluations.

SUMMARY

1. Formative and summative evaluations serve the complementary purposes of assessing *developing* and *completed* instructional programs, respectively.

2. A basic model for planning formative evaluations involves addressing eight areas: purposes, audience, issues, resources, evidence, data-gathering techniques, analyses, and reporting.

3. Common formative evaluation approaches can be classified as (a) connoisseur based, in which expert opinions are sought; (b) decision-oriented, in which information related to particular questions is gathered; (c) objectives-based, in which assessments are made of the degree to which particular objectives are obtained; and (d) public-relations-inspired, in which financial support or backing for a project is solicited based on the evaluation findings.

4. Three major stages of formative evaluation consist of one-to-one trials, small-group trials, and field trials. Each successive stage focuses on a more developed version of the instructional program, using larger samples of students.

5. Summative evaluations, unlike experimental research, are designed to provide information about specific instructional programs. They are not used to test general theories and thus do not require rigorous research methods or control groups.

6. Program effectiveness is determined by analyzing test scores, rating projects and performance, and observing learner behavior.

7. Summative evaluations involve similar planning procedures and methodologies as formative evaluations. The emphasis in summative studies, however, is on the full, completed program rather than on preliminary versions of the program.

8. A useful outcome measure for summative evaluations is program efficiency, computed as a ratio of number of objectives achieved to time taken to achieve them.

9. Program costs are evaluated by determining both developmental costs (the expense of designing the program) and operational costs (the expense of offering the program). The instructional cost index is the total cost per learner or trainee.

10. Follow-up evaluations should be conducted after the student leaves the program. In the case of educational programs, the important outcomes are basic skills, knowledge, competencies, and performance in occupational settings. For training programs, important outcomes include appropriateness of the training, competencies of employees, and benefits to the organization.

11. The evaluation report should be carefully prepared and attractive in its appearance. Adaptation of content to stakeholder backgrounds and interests is highly important.

FROM HERE TO THERE

You receive a contract from a software firm to evaluate a series of computer-based instructional units for teaching high school geometry. The units are still in draft stage, with the expectation that they can be revised based on the results of the evaluation. Using the eight-step model (Figure 15–1), you determine the purposes of the evaluation, conduct an analysis of audience, identify issues (questions and objectives), determine available resources, identify the evidence that will be needed, specify and implement data-gathering techniques, conduct the data analysis, and write and present reports of the findings. To address the main interests of the stakeholders (the software developers), you decide to employ small-group trials in which students work through the materials, give "think-aloud" reactions and other feedback, and take unit achievement tests. You also use two subject matter experts (SMEs), three high school geometry teachers, and one CBI design expert to give impressions of the accuracy and quality of the content and user interface. Based on qualitative and quantitative analyses of the multiple data sources, you prepare a report detailing results and making specific recommendations for improving various parts of the units. One of the managers in the software firm criticizes your evaluation for "failing to prove whether or not the units actually increase learning." She further wants to know why you didn't use a control group. How would you respond to the manager's concern?

REFERENCES

Brenneman, J. (1989). When you can't use a crowd: Single subject testing. *Performance and Instruction, 28,* 22–25.

Dick, W., & Carey, L. (1991). *The systematic design of instruction* (2nd ed.). New York, NY: HarperCollins Publishers, Inc.

Flagg, B. N. (Ed.) (1990). *Formative evaluation for educational technologies.* Hillsdale, NJ: Erlbaum.

Gooler, D. D. (1980). Formative evaluation strategies for major instructional development projects. *Journal of Instructional Development, 3,* 7–11.

Haladyna, T. M., Nolan, S. B., & Haas, N. S. (1991). Raising standardized achievement test scores and the analysis of test score pollution. *Educational Researcher, 20,* 2–7.

Ross, S. M., & Morrison, G. R. (1995). Evaluation as a tool for research and development. In R. D. Tennyson & A. Barron (Eds.). *Automating instructional design: Computer-based development and delivery tools* (pp. 491–522). Berlin: Springer-Verlag.

Thiagarjan, S., Semmel, D., & Semmel, M. (1974). *Instructional development for training teachers of exceptional children: A sourcebook.* Bloomington, IN: Center for Innovation in Teaching the Handicapped.

Sample Instructional Design Plan

Problem Statement

A need was identified for information on how to build a picket fence around the perimeter of one's property.

Goal Analysis

General Aim

To demonstrate the ability to properly construct a cost-effective picket fence around a residential property

Specific Goals

To complete the initial planning process
To determine the placement of the posts
To determine the placement of the rails
To determine the placement of the pickets
To build a gate
To install the gate
To identify the materials used in fence construction
To correctly use the tools
To determine the materials needed for the construction

Refinement of Goals

The learner will determine the type and height of the proposed fence.
The learner will acquire necessary building permits.
The learner will prepare a sketched plan.

The learner will obtain the necessary materials.

The learner will install the posts.

The learner will install the rails.

The learner will install the pickets.

The learner will build and install the gate.

The learner will identify the correct tools and materials needed to build the fence.

Rank Goals

Each of the goals listed describe the actions necessary to construct a picket fence. Although no goal is more important than another, the steps needed for the task must be performed in sequence. An introduction describing the appropriate materials needed for the process will precede the other goals.

The learner will identify the correct tools and materials needed to build the fence.

The learner will determine the type and height of the proposed fence.

The learner will prepare a sketched plan.

The learner will acquire the necessary building permits.

The learner will obtain the necessary materials.

The learner will install the posts.

The learner will install the rails.

The learner will install the pickets.

The learner will build and install the gate.

Final Refinement of Goals

The panel of experts decided that the learner would need to have a basic knowledge of the tools required for the project. Thus, the first goal was revised.

Additional research revealed that building permits were not needed for building a fence, which resulted in deleting the goal related to building permits.

The panel suggested that building a gate may prove to be difficult for the novice and decided to give the gate-related goal the lowest ranking. A second unit was planned for gate construction.

Final Ranking of Goals

The learner will identify the materials needed to build the fence.

The learner will determine the type and height of the proposed fence.

The learner will prepare a sketched plan.

The learner will obtain the necessary materials.

The learner will install the posts.

The learner will install the rails.

The learner will install the pickets.

Learner Characteristics

The typical learner will have
basic math skills,
reading ability at the eighth-grade level,
vision corrected to 20/20, and
no physical difficulties.

Prerequisites:

The learner can define basic construction terms.

The learner can demonstrate novice-level skill in measuring, cutting, and nailing boards.

The learner can demonstrate how to use a level, tape measure, circular hand saw, and a posthole digger.

The learner can prepare premixed cement upon following manufacturer's instructions.

Content Analysis

Introduction
Restrictions of the fence itself

Fence is to be cost-effective for the average middle-class family or individual.
The picket style is utilized versus another fence style.
The fence is to be built around residential property.

Restrictions of the "example" fence

The fence height is 6 feet.
The fence is built on-site; therefore, no fence sections are used.
The fence is built on 8-foot centered posts with 6-inch pickets.
The fence will follow the contour of the land.

Initial Planning Process
Determining the type and height of proposed fence

Look at examples in construction books or magazines.
Examine existing fences in the neighborhood for compatibility.
Consult local architects and neighbors for advice.

Producing a sketch on graph paper
Determining exact area:

Determine the location of the lot boundary.
Mark the boundary with a wood stake.
Proceed to measure the layout of the fence site with a tape measure.
Record the initial measurements in inches.

Making a sketch:

On graph paper, draw the dimensions of the fence.

Mark post locations using desired spacing. For fences constructed of wood, posts are 8-feet centered. The measurement is from the center of one post to the center of the next post.

Mark desired gate location. Typically, the gate's width is 4 feet. One post is placed on each end of the gate.

Determining Materials

Based on measurements on sketch, determine the number of rails required:

Count number of posts on sketch.

Multiply number of posts by 2 for exact number of rails needed.

Based on measurements on sketch, determine the number of pickets required.

Six-inch pickets are used in the example fence.

Use the following equation:

Number of feet of fence × 2 = number of needed pickets

Add 10% for waste due to split or warped pickets.

Add two posts for each gate.

Purchasing Materials

Buy at home center or lumberyard.

Examine sale ads.

Compare prices and quality.

Use wood that is chemically treated through pressure to resist rot and decay, if possible.

Hand select wood, if possible, to detect splits, holes, or other defects. Reject any pieces with defects.

Purchase two extra rails to account for warped boards or additional needs.

Obtain the following materials:

Cement: 80-lb. bags (one bag per 2 posts)
Pickets: $1'' \times 6'' \times 6'$
Posts: $4'' \times 4'' \times 8'$
Rails: $2'' \times 4'' \times 8'$
16-penny coated nails (~ 10 lbs.)
6-penny coated nails (~ 10 lbs.)
1×2 boards—3
Roll of string

Marking Post Location

Locating posts

Run a string line around the perimeter of the fence site.

Place a stake at the beginning of the proposed fence site, driving a 6-penny coated nail in the top of the stake. Wood stakes can be made from $1'' \times 2''$ boards cut at 12-inch lengths.

Place a stake at the next corner of the proposed fence site, driving a 6-penny coated nail in the top of the stake.

Using a roll of string, run string between the nails and secure with a knot.

Continue these steps until the string line is around the perimeter of the fence.

Using the proposed fence sketch, mark the first post location with a wood stake.

Measure 8 feet from the center of the first post to the center of the next.

Drive a stake.

Continue marking posts until the last post is marked.

If distance is less than 8 feet from the center of the previous post, allow the last post to be placed at the end of the string line.

If distance is more than 8 feet from the center of the previous post, add an extra post (the last one will be at the end of the string line) or decide to use longer rails between those last 2 posts.

Place stakes at each side of the planned gates.

Installation of Posts

Dig post hole with a posthole digger 18 inches to 24 inches deep.

Set post in hole and ensure it is plumb using a level.

Mix one bag of cement according to manufacturer's instructions. One bag will be sufficient for 2 posts.

Add cement into hole.

Check plumb of posts and the distance between centers of posts for accuracy.

Place 0.25 gallon of cement above ground level at post and taper outward for proper water drainage.

Repeat steps. If possible, allow 1 week to dry to ensure proper stability of posts before placement of rails.

Location of Rails

Position the first rail.

The top of the upper rail should be 57 inches from the ground.

The top of the lower rail should be 15 inches from the ground.

Nail the rails to the posts using 16-penny coated nails; be sure that they are level.

Rails extend from center of one post to center of next post.

Repeat steps using the preceding rail to level the next rail until all are placed.

Placement of Picket Process

Place a picket flat on the ground between the first two posts.

Set first picket on top of the picket on the ground and even with outside end of post.

The pickets should be 0.5 inch off the ground.

The contour of the land should be followed.

Using a 4-foot level, place level against length of the picket and adjust picket until level.

Set the first picket using 6-penny coated nails with 2 nails per rail.

Lightly drive two 16-penny coated nails in the rails at the side of the picket (one per rail) to provide spacing between pickets.

Add pickets according to these steps, removing the nails used for spacing each time, until reaching the length of the picket on the ground (6 feet).

Ensure the upright pickets are still plumb.

Move the picket on the ground 6 more feet.

Add additional pickets until all are placed. For corners, it might be necessary to split pickets to fit them into corners.

Objectives and Classifications

Note: The first, third, fourth, and fifth objectives are written as Mager-style behavioral objectives. The second objective is written as a cognitive objective.

The learner will state the nominal width of a picket.

Fact–Recall

The learner will prepare a plan for the fence.

Determines the number of posts needed for the fence
Determines the number of pickets needed
Determines the number of rails needed
Selects a style of fence that is appropriate for the location
Determines the nails needed to build the fence

Procedure–Application

Given a 4 × 4 fence post, premix cement, and proper tools, the learner will demonstrate how to install a fence post in the correct location that is plumb and secured with the proper amount of cement.

Procedure–Application

Given two rails, two properly set fence posts, appropriate tools and nails, the learner will demonstrate how to correctly attach the rails at the proper height and so that they are level.

Procedure–Application

Given two posts with rails attached, 24 pickets, tools, and nails, the learner will correctly demonstrate how to attach the pickets so they are evenly spaced, plumb, and follow the contour of the land.

Sequencing

The unit will be sequenced according to temporal relations that occur in the real world. The content will be sequenced as follows:

1. Introduction
2. Initial planning process
3. Installation of post process
4. Installation of railing process
5. Installation of picket process

Preinstructional Strategy

An overview was selected for the preinstructional strategy. The overview was selected because it prepares the learner for the learning task.

Overview

Welcome to the world of fence construction! In this instructional unit, you will learn the process of constructing a cost-effective picket fence around a residential property. Since you are familiar with basic construction terms and skills, these areas will not be addressed in the unit. Instead, we will begin with a brief introduction concerning the nature of the fence and then start the construction process. Get your hammer ready—you are about to begin an exciting new adventure in carpentry!

Instructional Strategy

Objective 1

The learner will state the nominal width of a picket.

Fact–Recall

Initial presentation: Provide the learner with a section of three pickets and ruler. Ask learner to measure the width of each picket and record the size.

Generative strategy: Prompt student to rehearse stating that a picket is 6 inches wide (rehearsal strategy).

Objective 2

The learner will prepare a plan for the fence.

Procedure–Application

Initial presentation: Present sequence for planning fence through either a series of still pictures and verbal narrative or a videotape presentation.

Generative strategy: Prompt student to develop to prepare an outline of the steps for planning the fence (organizational strategy).

Objective 3

Given a 4 × 4 fence post, premix cement, and proper tools, the learner will demonstrate how to install a fence post in the correct location that is plumb and secured with the proper amount of cement.

Procedure–Application

Initial presentation: Present sequence for installing the fence post through either a series of still pictures and written or verbal narrative or a videotape presentation.

Generative Strategy: Prompt student to develop an outline of the steps for installing the fence (organizational strategy).

(*Note:* The last two procedure-application objectives would follow a strategy similar to the one for objective 3.)

Test Items

Objective: The learner will state the nominal width of a picket.
Test item: How wide is a picket?

Objective: The learner will prepare a plan for the fence.
Test item: Using the attached map of a residential property, sketch a plan for a fence around the property line that indicates the location of the posts and a gate. Determine the number of posts, rails, pickets, and bags of cement that are needed.

Objective: Given a 4 × 4 fence post, premix cement, and proper tools, the learner will demonstrate how to install a fence post in the correct location that is plumb and secured with the proper amount of cement.
Test item: Install a corner fence post.
Evaluation checklist for instructor:

☐ Mixes one bag of cement according to manufacturer's instructions
☐ Digs post hole with a posthole digger 18 to 24 inches deep
☐ Sets post in hole
☐ Adds cement into hole
☐ Checks plumb with level
☐ Places 0.25 gallon of cement above ground level at post
☐ Tapers outward for proper water drainage

Formative Evaluation

Connoisseur-Based Review: A subject-matter expert (SME) will be asked to evaluate a rough draft of the unit.

Developmental Testing: Two individuals will be asked to work through an early draft of the unit. They will be observed and interviewed regarding their experiences and responses.

Field Trial: A group of 5 to 6 individuals will be asked to work through the final draft of the unit. They will be interviewed regarding their experiences and response and given a knowledge test based on the instructional objectives.

Affective domain   That area of learning devoted to developing attitudes, values, or appreciations

Andragogy   Field of adult learning

Application   Performance requiring the learner to use or apply the information

Behaviorism   Learning theory in which subject content is divided into a series of small steps; the learner participates actively, receives feedback on effort, and is guided to success

CD   See *Compact disk.*

CD-ROM   Computer-controlled compact disk containing quantity of verbal and pictorial information

Client   Person for whom instruction is being planned and who may serve as subject specialist when working with the instructional designer

Cognitive domain   That area of learning devoted to acquiring information, knowledge and intellectual abilities relative to a subject or topic

Cognitive learning style   Unique way an individual receives and processes information as classified on a number of scales

Cognitive strategies   Highest level of cognitive learning, typified by problem solving

Compact disk   High-quality music and other sound recording on a 4.75-inch disk that is read by a laser beam

Competency-based instruction   Providing and evaluating instruction against a specific standard as indicated by the learning objectives for the topic or task

Computer-based instruction (CBI)   Software program that displays information and instructions on a video screen, requiring learner participation and choices

Concept   Name or expression given to a class of facts, objects, or events, all of which have common features

Constructed-response test   Consisting of questions requiring the learner to supply a short answer, write an essay, or solve a problem; allows for evaluation of higher-level cognitive objectives but is difficult to solve reliably

Constructivism   An approach to instructional design based on the assumption that learners generate knowledge structures in their own mind

Cost center   Service provided within an organization for instructional development service with costs carried by the department

Criterion-referenced instruction   See *Competency-based instruction.*

Culturally diverse learners   Students from various ethnic cultures

Curriculum   List of courses and content framework for a subject

Developmental costs   All personnel, resources, and services costs required to plan and develop an instructional program

Domains of learning   Cognitive, psychomotor, and affective categories

Effectiveness   Measuring the degree to which learners accomplish objectives for each unit or a total course

Efficiency   Measuring the amount of learner time, personnel services, and facilities use required to carry out an instructional program, and then deciding whether these amounts are acceptable or excessive

Enabling objective   Subobjective that leads to accomplishing a terminal objective; also called *supporting objective*

Evaluator   Person responsible for assisting the instructor in designing tests to measure student learning, conduct formative and summative evaluation, and analyze results

Expert system   Computer software program using artificial intelligence to carry out processes that imitate human thinking and decision making, here applicable for instructional design planning

Fact   A statement associating one item to another

Feedback   Providing the learner with answers to exercises and other information relative to progress in learning

Flowchart   Visual description of the sequence necessary for performing a task, including decision points and alternate paths

Formative evaluation   Testing a new instructional program with a sampling of learners during the development phase, and using the results to improve the program front-end analysis

Goal statement   Broad statement describing what should take place in an instructional course or training program

Individualized learning   Allowing learners to learn by providing each one with objectives and activities appropriate to his or her own characteristics, preparation, needs, and interests

Instructional cost index   Mathematical calculation of the cost per learner or trainee to accomplish objectives for a topic or course, taking into account a portion of the developmental cost and implementation costs

Instructional design   Systematic planning of instruction in which attention is given to nine related elements

Instructional designer   Person responsible for carrying out and coordinating the systematic design procedure

Instructional development   Managing the planning, development, and implementation procedure for instruction or training

Instructional objective   Statement describing what the learner is specifically required to learn or accomplish relative to a topic or task

Instructional systems   Another expression for the instructional design concept

Instructional technology   Resources (machines and materials) used for instruction; process of systematic instructional planning

Intellectual skills   Organizing and structuring facts for learning to form concepts, principles, rules, attitudes, and interactions

Interactive technologies   Media forms that require frequent active participation by the student as learning takes place

Interpersonal skills   Spoken and nonverbal (e.g., body language) interaction between two or more individuals

Learner characteristics   Factors relating to personal and social traits of individuals and learner groups that need consideration during planning learning

Learning   A relatively permanent change in behavior that may or may not be the result of instruction

Learning styles   Various methods of learning that are preferred by individuals or that may be more effective with different individuals

Learning systems design   Another expression for the instructional design concept

Mastery-based instruction   See *Competency-based instruction.*

Mastery learning   Indicating whether a learner successfully accomplishes the necessary level of learning for required objectives

Module   A self-instructional package treating a single topic or unit of a course

Multimedia   Computer program controlling display of verbal information along with still- and motion-picture sequences in various formats

Needs assessment or analysis   Procedure of gathering information before deciding whether there is a substantive need for instruction or training

Nonconventional learners   Individuals that have characteristics differing from those of typical learners or employees, including ethnic minorities, persons with disabilities, and adults

Norm-referenced testing   Evaluating the results of instruction in a relative fashion by comparing test scores of each learner with those of other learners in the class

Objective test   Consisting of questions for which a learner must select an answer from two or more alternatives and persons scoring the test can easily agree on the correct answer

Operational costs   All costs of personnel resources and services incurred as an instructional program is being implemented

Organization management   Management of an instructional development service that broadly includes all design and delivery functions

Performance-based instruction   See *Competency-based instruction.*

Performance technology   Another expression for the instructional design concept

Posttest   Final examination given at the end of a course or training program (differs from pretest)

Prerequisite test   Portion of a pretest that measures content or skill preparation a learner has for starting the course or unit

Presentation teaching method   Technique used to disseminate information

Pretest   Test administered prior to the start of instruction to determine the level of the learner's knowledge and the necessary preparation relative to a topic or task

Principle   Expression of a relationship between concepts

Procedural analysis   Used to identify the steps required to complete a task or series of steps

Procedure   Sequence of steps one follows to achieve a goal

Profit center   Service provided within and outside an organization for instructional design services with costs charged to the client or sponsor

Project management Responsibilities for all functions that relate to the conduct of an instructional design project

Psychomotor domain That area of learning devoted to becoming proficient in performing a physical action involving muscles of the body

Reinforcement learning Receiving feedback on success in learning, thus being encouraged to continue learning

Reliability Ability of a test to produce consistent results when used with comparable learners

Request for proposal (RFP) Paper form with instructions to be completed when submitting a bid or proposal for a project to be funded

Self-paced learning environment Learning environment that allows the learner to satisfy required learning activities by accomplishing the objectives at his or her own speed or convenience

Subject-matter expert (SME) Person qualified to provide content and resources information relating to topics and tasks for which instruction is being designed

Summative evaluation Measuring how well the major outcomes of a course or program are attained at the conclusion of instruction (posttest) or thereafter on the job

Support services Matters such as budget, facilities, equipment, and materials that require attention for the successful preparation and implementation of a new instructional program

Supporting objective See *Enabling objective.*

Systems approach An overall plan to problem solving that gives attention to all essential elements

Task analysis A collection of procedures for analyzing the information needed to achieve the objectives. See *Topic analysis* and *Procedural analysis.*

Terminal objective Statement of a major outcome for a topic or a task unit or major subject content divisions specified within a course or instructional program

Topic analysis A procedure for identifying and describing the topics related to a goal or need

Validity Direct relationship between test questions and the learning objectives

I N D E X